SENTIME

MODERNISM

SENTIMENTAL
MODERNISM

WOMEN WRITERS
AND THE
REVOLUTION
OF THE WORD

Suzanne Clark

INDIANA UNIVERSITY PRESS

BLOOMINGTON & INDIANAPOLIS

The paper used in this publication meets the minimum requirements of American National Standard for Information Sciences—Permanence of Paper for Printed Library Materials, ANSI Z39.48-1984.

♾ ™

Manufactured in the United States of America

Library of Congress Cataloging-in-Publication Data

Clark, Suzanne.
Sentimental modernism : women writers and the revolution of the word / Suzanne Clark.
p.   cm.
Includes bibliographical references and index.
ISBN 0-253-31374-0 (alk. paper). — ISBN 0-253-20640-5 (pbk. : alk. paper)
1. Modernism (Literature)   2. Sentimentalism in literature.
3. Literature, Modern—Women authors—History and criticism.
4. Literature, Modern—20th century—History and criticism.
5. Women in literature.   I. Title.
PN56.M54C55   1991
809'.89287—dc20   90-47556

1 2 3 4 5 95 94 93 92 91

For Robert and Catherine

C O N T E N T S

Acknowledgments   ix

INTRODUCTION   The Unwarranted Discourse
Estranging the Sentimental   1

PART ONE   THE MATRIX OF MODERNISM

CHAPTER ONE   The Sentimental and the Modern
A Common History   19

CHAPTER TWO   Anarchy as a Literary Figure,
Anarchy as a Female Form
Emma Goldman   42

CHAPTER THREE   *Jouissance* and the Sentimental Daughter
Edna St. Vincent Millay   67

PART TWO   WOMEN AND MODERNISM

CHAPTER FOUR   Medusa and Melancholy
The Fatal Allure of Beauty in Louise Bogan's Poetry   99

CHAPTER FIVE   Revolution, the Woman, and the Word
Kay Boyle   127

PART THREE   WOMEN AFTER MODERNISM

CHAPTER SIX   The Woman in Nature and
the Subject of Nonfiction
Annie Dillard   155

CHAPTER SEVEN   The Sentimental and the Critical
Maternal Irony, Alice Walker, and a
Feminist Conclusion   182

Notes   203

Index   223

A C K N O W L E D G M E N T S

This project was supported by grants from the National Endowment for the Humanities Summer Fellowship Program, the Oregon State University Humanities Center Fellowships, and the University of Oregon Center for the Study of Women and Society. Early versions of parts of the manuscript appeared in "The Unwarranted Discourse: Sentimental Community, Modernist Women, and the Case of Millay," *Genre* 20.2 (Summer 1987); "Jouissance and the Sentimental Daughter: Edna St. Vincent Millay," *North Dakota Quarterly* (Spring 1986); "Annie Dillard: The Woman in Nature and the Subject of Nonfiction," *Literary Nonfiction: Theory, Criticism, Pedagogy*, ed. Chris Anderson (Carbondale and Edwardsville: Southern Illinois University Press, 1989); "Kay Boyle: Revolution, the Woman and the Word," *Twentieth Century Literature* (Fall 1988). I am especially grateful to John Gallman of Indiana University Press for his interest and encouragement.

My work owes a great deal to Nancy Armstrong, whose intellectual example has been as important as her professional and personal warmth. I am indebted to her and to Jane Gallop and Jane Tompkins as well for reading parts of the manuscript and for their support at crucial moments. Teresa de Lauretis enabled me to first present my ideas about the sentimental at the Feminist Theory Conference in Milwaukee in 1985. Julia Kristeva set aside time for an interview and graciously responded to questions. Colleagues and friends at Oregon State University helped me at every stage and provided much-valued companions for discussions, literary and recreational. I especially want to thank Lisa Ede, Sandra Spanier, Chris Anderson, and Robert Wess for their advocacy and their helpful reading of drafts. Jon Lewis, Kerry Ahearn, and Betty Campbell were responsive, benevolent critics. The Center for the Study of Women and Society at the University of Oregon provided an intellectual home for feminist conversation; Nancy Armstrong and Cheris Kramarae both welcomed me there. Linda Kintz informed, interested, questioned, and encouraged me in our dialogues about feminism and critical theory and read a draft with much-appreciated care. I am especially fortunate in my enduring friends Kathleen Hulley and Sheryl O'Donnell, who were part of this project from the beginning. Elizabeth Anne Norris gave me intelligent assistance preparing the manuscript. Lois Gage, Anne Wilson, Anterra, and Diane Slywczuk provided the best printing, typing, mailing, copying, and organizational support for faculty research (and all else) that I have ever encountered.

My family has been partly responsible for my wondering if sentimentality could be all bad. My sisters, Laurie Guttormsen and Ginny Nelson, are practitioners of healthy sympathy. My children, Robert Gillespie and Catherine Clark, to whom this book is dedicated, have earned the notice not only by their long years of supporting Mom's work but also by their astonishing originality. Finally, my parents, whose encouragement remains important to me, were also the first influences on my thought: my father, Robert D. Clark, who read Millay aloud to me, and my mother, Opal R. Clark, who told her own stories.

SENTIMENTAL
MODERNISM

The Unwarranted Discourse
Estranging the Sentimental

NARRATIVE IS NOT MERE ANEC-
DOTE, BUT THE PROJECTION OF
A METAMORPHOSIS OF REALITY.

*—THE REVOLUTION OF
THE WORD*[1]

Discredited by modern opinion,
love's sentimentality must be assumed by the amorous subject as a
powerful transgression which leaves
him alone and exposed: by a reversal
of values, then, it is this sentimentality which today constitutes love's obscenity.

—ROLAND BARTHES,
A LOVER'S DISCOURSE[2]

The sentimental is what Roland
Barthes calls an "unwarranted discourse." Modernism inaugurated a
reversal of values which emphasized
erotic desire, not love; anarchic rupture and innovation rather than the
conventional appeals of sentimental
language. Modernism reversed the
increasing influence of women's writing, discrediting the literary past and
especially that sentimental history.
Women themselves participated in
this unwarranting. When Louise Bogan writes about what modernist poetry achieved, she begins: "Formal
poetry in America in the year 1900
seemed benighted in every sense: it
was imitative, sentimental, and 'genteel.' "[3]

In the United States, this reversal against the sentimental helped to
establish beleaguered avant-garde intellectuals as a discourse community,
defined by its adversarial relationship to domestic culture. Multiple issues
of class and gender, of power and desire, were contained in this opposition
to the sentimental. The richness and complexity of the sentimental were
disguised in the process. So was the powerful operation of domestic fiction
that Nancy Armstrong has taught us to see.[4] Barthes makes visible the

modernist move, relocating the lover's discourse outside the discourse of history, not in the body of a woman but in the body of a text, in figure. This isolates the figurative body of the amorous subject from realistic discourses and denies the intertextuality of discourses. At the same time, modernism intervenes here. The sense of obscenity—and the critical warrant—belongs to "modern opinion," not to the sentimental. At issue is whether the intellectual avant-garde promotes dissidence or the law.[5]

The sense of transgression evoked by the sentimental is indeed powerful. In spite of severing the lover from narration, Barthes elicited a mixed response from critics, who feared the return of bourgeois sentiment. Was Barthes in his later work, including *A Lover's Discourse*, abandoning the avant-garde and restoring the cultural dominion of the feminized middle class? Or was he restoring a sense of the pleasure of the text?[6]

The sentimental as a form, a set of tropes, and a rhetorical stance is profoundly intertwined with the historical conflicts of middle-class culture. The apparent coherence of the term betrays its overdetermined meaning. Women, of course, have a privileged (or fatal) relationship with the sentimental. From the point of view of literary modernism, sentimentality was both a past to be outgrown and a present tendency to be despised. The gendered character of this condemnation seemed natural: women writers were entangled in sensibility, were romantic and sentimental by nature, and so even the best might not altogether escape this romantic indulgence in emotion and sublimity. Or so it might seem to a criticism anxious to make distinctions.

Modernist criticism located women's writing within the obscenity of the sentimental. Yet of course women were modernists. They were writers (Stein, Millay, H. D., Moore, Bogan, Glaspell, Ridge, Hurston, Wylie, Boyle, Barnes), editors (Goldman, Monroe, Anderson, Heap, Beach, Moore, Crosby), and critics (Goldman, Lowell, Bogan, Riding). Women were also important in the ongoing definition of a bohemian, radical, expatriate, artistic,and intellectual community.[7] However, the developing new criticism did not promote female reputations. In the United States, the marginal existence of intellectuals perhaps made the scapegoating especially intense. The sentimental acts as a pivotal ground in a battle over literary and moral value, over the fundamental social warrants constructing discursive agreements. If it calls up literary history, it also calls up the repressed involvement of literature with power—literature as a rhetorical instrument, literature used in the interests of economy and politics, literature as locus of pleasure and transgression.

Episodes of love, like eruptions of the imaginary, appear in the modern, rational conversation, the discourse of our times, as something to be gotten over, grown out of, unwarranted. As Michel Foucault has argued, it is sex, not love, which has been put into discourses connected to freedom, subversion, and the critical, producing increasingly powerful intensities.[8] The appeal to feeling has become both stronger and more suspect, more and more distant from the rational, at the same time that it is rationalized. The modernist revolution heightened this problem. Internationally one manifesto after another, from Marinetti's declaration of Futurism in 1912 ("The imagination without bondage!") to Eugene Jolas's "Revolution of the Word" in 1929 ("THE PLAIN READER BE DAMNED"), sought to invent a new language and to liberate poetry from the banal.[9] However, as the debate over modernism, postmodernism, and the avant-garde suggests, it is not clear whether this was a revolution involving social consequences or separating the aesthetic decisively from the politics of popular culture.[10] The modernist revolution turned away from ordinary language and everyday life. This disconnection from social consequence, from history, has everything to do with the gendering of intellectuality, as I will argue. A crisis emerges from the rejection of the narratives that have explained and legitimated feeling.

As I am going to show, the crisis began with modernist exclusions and continues with postmodern fragmentation.[11] Neither feminists nor the intellectual avant-garde have worked out a position in this postmodern crisis. The reversal of values has extended to make all commitment seem sentimental. The legacy of modernism is to make the debate over the sentimental central to a converging list of critical questions, drawing feminists, Marxists, cultural critics, rhetoricians, and psychoanalytic critics into the struggle. At stake is the question of a critical rhetoric and the effective agency of a critical subject. With Marxism in theoretical disarray, what progressive subject might be credible, what utopian narrative? If narrative itself is suspect, and the desire for narrative is itself sentimental, what kind of subject or ethos may function with authority? What kind of relationship to the audience—what pathos—may be seen as legitimate?

The case against the sentimental has been articulated by Ann Douglas in *The Feminization of American Culture*. Taking femininity to be a debilitating gendering imposed by culture, she argues that women thus feminized were responsible for the domination of the sentimental. They had an adverse effect on American ideology in the nineteenth century, softening the tough rationality of Puritan argument and creating a genteel form of theology which worked by an indirect rhetoric of influence. According to Douglas, this sentimental rhetoric prepared the way for a twentieth-century mass culture dominated by consumerism and emotional appeals, a mass culture which critical reason ought to fear. The scene of little Eva's death in Harriet Beecher Stowe's *Uncle Tom's Cabin* produces "our narcissism and our nostalgia," "Christianity beginning to function as camp" (2). The sentimental undermines the serious. From such a perspective, not only sentimental novels, and not only women's traditions, but the whole of twentieth-century mass culture seems neither interesting nor subversive but rather diseased. The sentimental does not look like the source of transgression, resistance, or progressive cultural change. This point of view, I will argue, is fundamental to American modernism, to its innovations as well as to its reactionary moments. The persistence of antisentimentalism suggests that it cannot easily be argued away.

The other side of the debate challenges the modernist aesthetic and its dismissal of the sentimental. Feminists have joined cultural critics in extending the study of texts to all discourses, not just the literary, placing literature within a rhetorical situation which opens onto culture and social life.[12] Jane Tompkins has brought the issue for feminism into sharp focus and shown the relevance of feminist revisions; literature works on society, and yet modernism defined literature to exclude discussions of its cultural work. In *Sensational Designs*, she argues for the importance of the nineteenth-century sentimental tradition not only for feminism but to challenge the modernist definition of literature. Her book "sees literary texts not as works of art embodying enduring themes in complex forms, but as attempts to redefine the social order."[13] Furthermore, Tompkins reminds us, the sentimentality in Stowe's *Uncle Tom's Cabin* was not ineffective; to the contrary, the novel exercised enormous power over cultural history. Tompkins draws a widely shared conclusion. In defense of the sentimental, then, not only the interests of American feminists but all the postmodern changes in the scope of critical interests ought to justify a return to the popular texts. But I do not believe we can rest here.

A sense of victory against antisentimentalism runs the danger of missing the point. I want to argue that we should restore the sentimental *within* modernism, and the sense of great struggle over subjectivity that the resulting contradictions precipitated. We—theorists, feminists—should become conscious about the rhetorical appeals of the avant-garde to social power. I am writing this book to show how women writers are the key to our understanding of this history. Their importance to us comes precisely because, although they were intellectuals and revolutionaries, women have had to confront and work through the turn against the sentimental. They have had to see the struggle over the subject from the beginning. When women joined the anarchic revolt against convention, they gladly challenged the old traditions of gender as well as the old forms of poetry. Postmodern theory extends this revolution of modernism in its critique of individual identity and the bourgeois subject, and feminists continue to be central to this challenge. But modernism also gendered mass culture, identifying woman with the mass and regarding its productions as "kitsch," as "camp," and, like advertising, as objects of critical disdain.[14] Modernism developed its antisentimentality into a contemptuous treatment of women, who had to struggle both internally and externally with that contempt.

In this book I will write about the forms that revolt and that struggle have taken for several important women: Emma Goldman, Edna St. Vincent Millay, Louise Bogan, Kay Boyle, Annie Dillard, and Alice Walker. Instead of writing about women's modernism as if the facts and the subject were not active promoters of their own interpretation, I am reading women writers whose essays, poems, novels, and criticism have shaped modernist and postmodernist history and whose ongoing attachment and/or debt to the strong sentimental past and to sensibility itself reveals a contradiction *within* modernism, challenging our understanding of it, and indeed of our own work.

Modernism practiced a politics of style, but it denied that style had a politics. Affirming the importance of cultural studies does not address the larger issue signaled by Douglas's scornful tone. The reversal of values did not do away with gendering but rather used it to define the intellectual. A gendered logic still functions to organize culture according to hierarchies of reason, making powerful critical distinctions. Even though the sentimental appears everywhere in postmodern discourses, its presence signals to many the advent of "anything goes." It remains without warrant. The United States is the chief site of this postmodern abandon. Nevertheless, a rationalized order tries to subject the order of emotional connections— sympathy—to its domination and obstructs the formation of social movements by its regulation of emotional appeals. Thus rationality legislates identity, and the transferential processes of identification. The either/or formula of antisentimentalism cannot easily be reversed by the postmodern both/and, since not only logic but the organization of social movements is at issue. The identity of subjects is at stake—in particular, the subject of feminism.

In spite of feminist and postmodernist efforts, the position against the sentimental still operates almost like an unconscious in critical writing. Perhaps the status of the intellectual avant-garde itself is at stake. This has partly to do with reason's long historical battle against emotional appeals, of which I will speak in a few pages. But more specifically, it has to do with the politics of literature in mass culture and the ideological unconscious embedded in style. Literature includes discourses defining identity, experience, and desire that overlap and are in competition with religious, patriotic, and advertising rhetoric, and the subversions of MTV and graffiti. The modernist new critics used aesthetic antisentimentality to make distinctions, to establish a position of authority against mass culture. Mass culture was a feminized enemy they saw as powerful and dangerous.

The modernist revulsion against sentimentality was not really so reasonable as its invective against emotion would imply. The sentimental is at issue because no discourse can escape appealing to the emotions of its audience, and yet modernist criticism pretended to do so. No discourse can escape some relationship with its readers' narcissism or its readers' nostalgia; no criticism can be so objective that it avoids calling up the issues of ideology and subjectivity in its appeal to its audience. No text can escape issues of transference. Yet modernist criticism attempted to export all this out of its domain, to maintain the poem as an aesthetic object. In order to avoid admitting the rhetorical situation of literature, which engages it inevitably in culture, history, and desire, American modernist literary criticism endorsed a formalism which avoided ideology by calling women ideological, and rejected their sensible attachments to the everyday.

Lest we think that the modernist separation of literature from the kitchen was politically innocuous, at worst resisting the influence of a mass culture that was all too powerful outside the domain of literature, consider what else was lost, along with the sentimental. The modernist exclusion of everything but the forms of high art acted like a machine for cultural loss of memory. Consider the forgetfulness about Emma Goldman's presence in the modernist community. Her extensive—and rhetorically interesting—writing does not come into consideration as material for a course on modernist literature, on the assumption which has come to prevail that the revolution of poetic language had nothing to do with a revolution in human society, that anarchic poetics could be separated from the advocacy of anarchy, or indeed from any attempt to influence an audience.

Did the revolution of the word have anything to do with cultural change?[15] Many modernist writers hoped that it would—from Eugene O'Neill and Susan Glaspell in the Provincetown Players to Josephine Herbst and those who moved left in the thirties, including Edmund Wilson and the group around the *Partisan Review*. Hart Crane not only ruptured poetic syntax in *The Bridge*, he also hoped to produce a utopian "new word" which would inflect a progressive alternative to pessimism.

Modernist criticism has suppressed this conflict within modernism by suppressing the women and the question of politics. The revolution of the word opened up a challenge to representation, a crisis which would lead from Baudelaire via Mallarmé and Nietzsche to poststructuralism. This revolution of the word would challenge standard conventions of language, including the way gendering appears to be natural rather than an effect of discursive practices. The modernist reversal includes both the unwarranting of the sentimental *and* the chance for cultural change. The bad news for women is intimately bound up with the good news.

What traps modernism within a problematic of gender is not only the scapegoating of women's writing but also its own sentimentality. Modernism transferred the lover's discourse from an interior of persons to the interior of a text—a poem that became a "new word" by this inflection of absence. The crisis of representation which began in the nineteenth century had everything to do with the crisis in representing woman, or the object of desire.[16] The adoration of the angel in the house became the adoration of images, or texts. The posture of idolatry suggests the resemblance: modernism rejected the sentimental, because modernism *was* sentimental. Modernism was still caught in a gendered dialectic which enclosed literature, making the text the object of a naturalized critical gaze.

When modernist discourse makes the sentimental—not the erotic—obscene, it makes its own genealogy unconscious. Separating the sentimental from the erotic is analogous to separating cultural reproduction from economic production. The appearance in the eighteenth century of a Clarissa, whose sensibility made her desirable, marked a new definition of value articulated primarily by fiction, value which is no longer external, a matter of aristocratic display, but *internal*, a matter of the heart, and of qualities of *mind*.[17] This revolution in value appeared before the American and French revolutions, but it provided a new coding for both the radical and the bourgeois arguments which are going on to this day. The sentimental woman replaced not only the aristocratic family but also other images of difference—the popular, the vernacular, the carnivalesque. The degradation of sentimental writing, made to represent the emotional fakery of women's pleadings, has covered over the transgressive content of the sentimental, its connection to a sexual body, and its connection to the representations of consciousness. This unwarranting has resisted the powers of reproduction (of bodies, of codes, of stories) to restore difference and give authority to transgression. By its reversal against the sentimental past, modernism denied its own reproduction of the internal, the debates of heart and mind—of individual consciousness—that had been valued by domestic fiction and reappear as the self-consciousness of, say, Prufrock.

The text replaces the woman, and the history of domestic writing that produced her. The maternal metaphor operates as more than a figure of speech within modernism, as the recurring madonna image suggests.[18] The poem seems to exist uneasily as the feminine unconscious of male writers such as Stevens, and a cultural bad conscience.[19] Paul Valéry in 1917 wrote "La Jeune Parque" as an "autobiography in the form," with its speaker the emblematic melancholy girl. The moral and erotic passions thrown out by the machinery of culture reappear in the claustrophobic but safe enclosure of the text, inaugurating a cultural depression.

This embodiment of a feminine or feminized speaker in the text complicates the idea that a text might produce a new space for the woman within language. Stevens and Valéry depended upon the ironic relationship of the poem to its male writer—a subject not under question. In a sense, modernism invented an *écriture féminine*, a feminine writing which would rupture male conventions. But it did not make possible the appearance of a feminine subject within language. The unmentionable rhetorical situation with its ironic subtexts defined literature in a way that silenced women as women.

Modernism for women represents, in other words, a doubleness as well as a double bind: not only the unwarranting of feminine authority but a rupture of conventional womanhood that promises freedom. Women such as Emma Goldman or Edna St. Vincent Millay or Louise Bogan or Kay Boyle or even Annie Dillard have been happy to seize the moment to escape from the confining categories of gender. Modernist women worked to change gendered identity within writing; we should not risk missing the extent to which *women* were the modernist revolutionaries.

Like women's writing and feminist criticism, modernism is both caught in and stabilized by a system of gendered binaries: male/female, serious/ sentimental, critical/popular. Upsetting the system—as women do—introduces an instability and reveals the contradictions. As we acknowledge the contributions of women, we see that modernism was both revolutionary and reactionary; the sentimental was both banal and transgressive. A despised history of emotion and sympathy signaled by the "sentimental" was not only external but also internal to the revolution of literary modernism.

Reframing the modernist narrative may help to change the way we think of literary influence, and so the way we think about literature. Modernist writers—male and female, Ernest Hemingway and Kay Boyle—did not operate only within an Oedipal relationship to a literary past, asserting themselves against an established male authority. From another perspective, they also recalled with disgust and longing, by an act like anamnesis, their estrangement from a maternal enclosure as from the vernacular, and their exile in a world of harsh divisions, borders, and separations (an exile, and sometimes an estrangement as in the case of Eliot and Pound, from the mother country as well). The dialectic of the sentimental and the serious looks like a family romance: pathos returns to make its argument, the reader is affected, and yet this maternal indulgence must be denied; made visible (Millay), it is rejected as popular, sentimental writing.

The story of desire for American critics has had an Oedipal shape— the subject gets over his imaginary attachments in order to take his place in culture as a man.[20] American modernists make the struggle to outgrow a sentimental (and banal) literary past homologous with the struggle to grow up. This narrative of criticism constructs a systematic misreading of women's writing which gives it inordinate coherence and stigmatizes it at the same time.

Maturity for modernist critics such as John Crowe Ransom—as for Freud—involves a separation from the sentimental (m)Other. Therefore when Ransom evaluates the work of Edna St. Vincent Millay, he finds her immature, all too womanly, "fixed in her famous attitudes." The story of the male mind seems to him so obvious he needs no argument: it has become a matter of biology, not culture or history. In 1930 Ransom wrote:

> The minds of man and woman grow apart, and how shall we express their differentiation? In this way, I think: man, at best, is an intellectualized woman. Or, man distinguishes himself from woman by intellect, but it should be well feminized. He knows he should not abandon sensibility and tenderness, though perhaps he has generally done so, but now that he is so far removed from the world of the simple senses, he does not like to impeach his own integrity and leave his business in order to recover it; going back, as he is often directed, to first objects, the true and tried, like the moon, or the grass, or the dead girl. He would much prefer if it is possible to find poetry in his study, or even in his office, and not have to sit under the syringa bush. Sensibility and tenderness might qualify the general content of his mind, if he but knew the technique, however "mental" or self-constructed some of that content looks. But his problem does not arise for a woman. Less pliant, safer, as a biological organism, she remains fixed in her famous attitudes, and is indifferent to intellectuality. I mean, of course, comparatively indifferent; more so than a man. Miss Millay is rarely and barely very intellectual, and I think everybody knows it.[21]

At the same time that Ransom would seem to deny that a woman could be anything more than "indifferent to intellectuality," he maintains that a man at his best is "an intellectualized woman." As the story goes, sensibility and tenderness belong to an earlier stage than the intellectual, and women never quite grow up. This narrative psychologizes the modernist history of the literary sentimental. It accounts for the successful cross-dressing of the male poet, at his best "an intellectualized woman," and suggests that the cross-dressing could not easily go the other way. Women and their sensibility belong to tenderness—they should stay under the syringa bush rather than write poetry. This naturalizing of gender as subjectivity denies the power of discourse to position subjects, but it works to establish the difference of intellectuals. The woman, precisely, seems indifferent, incapable of entering into the play of differences.

The new criticism split the female into the sexualized textual body and the conventional feminine lady, into a revolutionary and erotic object and a derided maternal or hysterical subject. The term *sentimental* makes a shorthand for everything modernism would exclude, the other of its literary/nonliterary dualism. The feminization of culture as content allowed modernism to avoid responsibility for its most questionable exclusions, and its most notoriously reactionary violence.[22] It is neither the feminization of culture nor the return of an unholy maternal that is responsible for formalist affinities with fascism, but the dogmatic mystification of these powerful forces associated with literature and politics, including the maternal and the aesthetic, the imaginary and style.

The horror of the sentimental helped to define the good male poet as the prostitute once defined the good woman.[23] In the literary world defined by modernism, the writer who wrote for women, whose audience included "the ladies," opened herself to the most terrible critical scorn. Morton D. Zabel characterized the awfulness of what he called "Popular Support" for the arts in a "Comment" for *Poetry* in 1930. Subtitled "Cattle in the Garden," Zabel's piece made the connection between bad taste and writing for the ladies. Exemplary of "Popular Support" were items from the Herald-Tribune Books, where "week after week, poetry is plucked from every bush that grows by the effusive Miss Taggard, that energetic specialist in Immortality" whose "style (and incidentally her critical standards) derive largely from Queen Marie's testimonials for Pond's Facial Creams" (269). Genevieve Taggard did not deserve this invective. But note that Ann Douglas also blames women writers for consumer advertising. The importance of this example as a habitual trope which works to define the new criticism may be suggested by Cleanth Brooks's appearance at the 1989 Modern Language Association, where he reiterated his notion of the importance of separating poetry from "laundry lists and advertisements for face lotion." Needless to say, the gracious old gentleman did not recognize the gendering inherent in his categories. These categories of thinking are still strongly at work in critical discourse at its least conscious.

The apparently contemporary and ungendered judgment enacted today when we make distinctions about a poem or book or drama or television show by calling it "sentimental" has an uncanny resonance with the history of writing by women. When a female literary history arises out of the generations of women writers, it appears as a reviled past: the anxiety of influence appears as the threat of the Mother (nature, love, tongue, muse), powerful in several guises. This maternal-seeming past is what modernism denies in the name of intellectuality.

Sentimental discourse participates in the psychology of abjection, a psychology related to the formation of social and cultural groups, as Julia Kristeva defines it.[24] The abject is involved in rejecting the maternal. Western culture has developed a logic which is at work constantly to purify itself of unreason. At the level of culture, of an anthropology, this creates scapegoats, strangers, groups representing the unreasonable other: women, Jews, slaves, peasants, working class, blacks, Arabs—together with the transgressive carnivalesque. At the level of psychoanalytic narrative, this creates the abject, which appears in conjunction with the sublime, in a borderless state logically prior to Oedipal cuts, where the process of delineating borders between an undifferentiated self and the maternal other is marked by horror and disgust. At the level of discourses, literature is the abject. The discourses of religious power (of self and other) generate the scapegoating logic, but so does the binary thinking (of identity and nonidentity) associated with the rise of scientific logic. Poststructuralism has—from Jakobson to Kristeva—worked together with feminist criticism to challenge this polarized thinking, which is associated with claims for the superiority of male reason over female emotion in philosophy. The sentimental is the representation of an abject struggle over female emotion. By its banal rhetoricity, the sentimental reveals the struggle to be about representation.

The feminine stranger produced by rational rejection of the sentimental is not only the object of disdain. This discursive otherness is tinged not only with horror or disgust but also with love, longing, and sublimity. The psychology implied by sentimental narratives has to do with transference— not only the transference operating in the relationships of characters within the texts, but also with the reader. It appears, with its emphasis on *sympathy*, to be narcissistic. Certainly it is implicated in the melancholic by its suffering beyond language.[25] But as a quasi-literary discourse, the sentimental encloses narcissism and melancholy within a feminized linguistic domain. Thus what psychoanalysis will categorize as belonging to the pre-Oedipal—narcissism, melancholy—also belongs to a degraded discourse, the sentimental, which is the object of rational paranoia. The literary history of the sentimental could be characterized by that dialectic of narcissism and paranoia.

Is it possible to talk about women writers and the sentimental without eliciting the modernist response? It is a knee-jerk reaction without parallel in literary criticism. Ann Douglas wrote before most of the feminist history appeared which has clarified the extent of women's writing and contributions, but that might make little difference to her readers, to all of *us*, who still respond to the way the word *sentimental* is loaded. The word does not mean just an emotional fakery. It marks the limits of critical discourse as if they were natural. As an epithet, *sentimental* condenses the way gender still operates as a political unconscious within criticism to trigger shame, embarrassment, and disgust.

A brief pause for a look at the way the word operates right now will suggest the powerful opprobrium the "sentimental" continues to evoke. Is it fair to take a single issue of the *New York Times Book Review* as a representative sample of literate usage? The following are all from the November 6, 1988, issue. Todd Gitlin makes the sentimental a pivotal term for defining antisentimental postmodernism, which "regards 'the individual' as a sentimental attachment, a fiction to be enclosed within quotation marks." "In the global shopping center . . . local traditions have been swamped by the workings of the market; anything can be bought, and to speak of intrinsic value is mere sentimentality" ("Hip-deep in Post-modernism"). Eva Hoffman, in "Taking a Chance on Pathos," worries that Andre Debu "is sometimes too closely adjacent to the sentimental" (7). Natalie Angier approves of David Hull's competitive model for science, even though "casual and sentimental observers may wish that society could somehow encourage scientists to cooperate more" ("Nice Guys Don't Win Nobel Prizes" 14), and Ben Logan also approves of realism about competition: "In asking what will become of his aging father and the Kohn land, he strips sentimentality from the words 'family farm' and shows us that traditional ways of farming are in grim competition with large-scale farms that use polluting chemicals" ("The Flip Side of Dad" 17).[26]

Even though the postmodern seems different from modernism, and Gitlin occupies a somewhat ironic relationship to it, the "sentimental" continues to call up an image of critical agreement that makes further elaboration seem unnecessary. The sentimental is here connected loosely to a version of liberal humanism: valuing the individual, intrinsic value, emotion or pathos, the endorsement of niceness and cooperation, and the family farm. The involvement of gender in this individualism is deeply hidden. As a literate audience, we are expected to agree—we are reconstructed as agreeing—that it's a weakness to wish for any of these; it's part of being in the discursive community of the tough and the critical. Thus Todd Gitlin expects our agreement when he criticizes American politics for becoming personal rather than political.[27] Becoming an intellectual in America is sort of like being inducted into the army (or maybe the first grade) and learning not to be a sissy.

The intellectual is separated from the ordinary as the feminist is separated from the feminine. What is there about the posture of serious literature that makes the honorific "writer," or worse, "critic," or worst, "theorist," an embarrassment for women who think of themselves as ordinary? Why are ordinary women an embarrassment for feminism? What makes Frank Lentricchia sound so reasonable when he argues that feminist literary history such as Sandra Gilbert and Susan Gubar's doesn't really speak for his mother "who would laugh, embarrassed, at the idea that she might write something besides letters to family and grocery lists"?[28] To what kind of knowledge, what kind of limits, is he appealing? This is not just a matter of critiquing the notion of an essentialist subject, the mistaken idea that women are all alike.

Women *are* alike by being the subject of an unwarranted discourse. The threat of embarrassment keeps women in our place, but it also defines that place, turning issues of the political—of gender, class, and ethnicity—into personal emotion. On the other hand, "serious" literature embarrasses the popular by its discriminations, even as it is renewed by the popular, and women's writing is always turning out to be popular. What will be the fate of Alice Walker's *The Color Purple*? Will this enormously influential work continue to promote a radical critique of cultural convention, or will the continuation of formalism emerge within postmodernism, also repressing women writers as not experimental enough?[29] Will *The Color Purple* seem too interested in moral instruction to endure as "serious" literature?

When the critic makes a distinction between important literature and letters to family—especially when he attributes the distinction to his mother, rewriting the political into the personal—the modernist effect continues, at the very moment when Lentricchia thinks he is questioning it. We might note that just as the domestic list occurred to Cleanth Brooks, it comes into Frank Lentricchia's mind when he uses his mother as an example of the ordinary woman. What texts are we to take seriously? Modernist sanctions against the personal and the sentimental continue as a political unconscious of criticism.[30] And Lentricchia points to the way feminists themselves are implicated in modernism. As intellectuals, feminists often find themselves painfully cut off from the sentimental community of women, even though feminism itself is caught in the gendered unwarranting.

In this book I will follow the traces of the sentimental to open up narratives of literary history and the politics of criticism, to reveal the doubleness of sentimentality and the critical. The modernist innovation depended upon a rewriting of woman's image that resisted the sentimental and troubled women writers. This was a rewriting that women writers have struggled both for and against, desiring freedom and authority as serious members of the avant-garde but also needing the traditions of emotional identity they have been pressed to abandon. Modernism created a rhetorical battlefield for women. As writers, they have had to rethink the entire range of gendered relationships between authors and their characters, between authors and their readers.[31] My study examines women's writing for the effects of the modernist revulsion against the sentimental, and their strategies for recovering bonds of emotional identity. The effects of modernism, in other words, included not only denial but also recuperation. Reading these works, I hope we can make use of the strategies of recovery in these texts.

I hope as well to make women's powerful role in modernism more visible. The authority of Emma Goldman and Edna St. Vincent Millay was far from invisible in their time. Modernism was anarchic, and Goldman embodied its challenge of the conventional. She and Millay both represented the politics of free love as well. Like suffrage, the right of women to be public poets marked radical cultural shifts, and Millay was the most visible of all. But Goldman and Millay both vanish from view by the way the field of literature has been defined. Their involvement with politics and with women's causes was frank and largely unaffected by the revolution in style which was beginning to erupt. Their contributions to the revolution reveal its openings into a previous culture; their unabashed sentimentalism recalls the femininity which joins their discourse to their audience.

Women who identified with the modernist revolution and were part of the avant-garde, such as Louise Bogan and Kay Boyle, define their experiments in terms of the struggle between sentimental attachments and the violence of writing. These women found themselves caught in the contradiction of needing to recuperate a woman's tradition and yet participating in a revolution against forms that included gender. Bogan, writing as both poet and critic, marked her love poetry with the bitter loss of authority, of the very warrant for her subject: woman, love, the lyric. Internalizing modernist attitudes, she wrote critically of the sentimental past: "Women, it is true, contributed in large measure to the general leveling, dilution, and sentimentalization of verse, as well as of prose, during the nineteenth century."[32] At the same time she argued that "the wave of poetic intensity which wavers and fades out and often completely fails in poetry written by men, on the feminine side moves on unbroken" (19). Her mixed feelings about the woman writer and her painful toughness seem less than sisterly—but surely sisterhood involves just this struggle of affiliation, rage, and alienation. The scorn of Bogan's critical modernism seems more harshly directed against her own work (and the volume of what she accepted is slender) than against the poetry she reviewed as critic for the *New Yorker* so many years. Perhaps this reflexivity itself, this self-wounding, has to do with the feminine in her work. Was she haunted by the figure of Edna St. Vincent Millay?

Kay Boyle, whose stories are filled with female heroines, refuses to this day to identify herself as a woman writer and rejects feminist criticism. Boyle has characterized herself as "a dangerous 'radical' disguised as a perfect lady."[33] She maintains her credentials as a social activist the hard way, accompanied by personal sacrifice—but she believes that revolution has a problematic relationship to the community of women. Her writing shows a kind of experimental form that works so softly, her important innovations were long overlooked. Yet, I will argue, she crafts a feminist perspective by her politics of style.

Under postmodernism, women have flourished; they have, indeed, come to serve as a new avant-garde. Women have learned from the solutions of earlier writers, and the issues of style and gender continue to inform women's writing. Annie Dillard and Alice Walker both work out successful relationships to popular culture and yet position themselves within dissimilar versions of a marginality which calls both genre and gender into question. The modernist Dillard replaces subjectivity with style, practicing, I think, not a genderless discourse but the *gynesis* Alice Jardine describes, withdrawing from political attitudes at the same time that she displaces scientific nonfiction with poetic language and with laughter. The resurrection of the epistolary novel in Walker's *The Color Purple*, on the other hand, frankly calls up the old sentimental traditions. Writing and advocating a "womanist" prose, Walker reconnects with the community of women and braves the condemnations of serious literature by turning to the vernacular.

I am writing this book with the conviction that we need to restore the sentimental to modernist literary history—with all its banality and also all its connections to subversion and ethical appeal. Doing so, we restore literature to its place within a history of rhetoric. Acknowledging the sentimental, we might also readmit all the questions about progress and modernity that we still need to raise. What is the relationship between intellectuals and a feminine sensibility? We need to reconceive the question of a feminist authority. Now that feminist scholars have given us back so many of our ancestors, it is time to elaborate our critique of the modern, restoring the old progressive discourses to modernity together with the other versions of the secular, the vernacular. Perhaps we can take advantage of the provisional, rhetorical, and parodic element of the sentimental. This is not an antimodernist position. My critique of modernism is not outside or in opposition to it but rather an extension of attention to the uncanny sentimentality it has always tried to deny.

Is there something wrong with the rhetoric of pathos? Even though Douglas has been seen as attacking feminism, there are many feminists who are in agreement, whose discomfort with the sentimental is a matter not just of embarrassment but of seeing the sentimental as complicit with patriarchy, rather than with the oppressed. Modernist women shared the same revulsion. It is, in part, a revulsion against the history of capitalism, liberalism, and the middle-class individual. On the level of psychoanalysis, it is associated with resistance to the woman of authority, the phallic mother. But we are still caught in this gendered system of representation, and so we are premature if we dismiss the sentimental as an aspect of bourgeois thinking which we can escape through a purified critical logic, whether the logic is conservative, liberal, or Marxist.

Each of the deliberately disconnected textual moments in Roland Barthes's *A Lover's Discourse* calls up a sentimental past in literature, like the ghost of Young Werther. And the lover's discourse constitutes not Barthes but the lover, a figure with whom Barthes may then be identified. This imaginary lover unsettles the intertextual reservoirs. Embodying a subject of a discourse within literary history, the lover speaks the conventions which define the conduct of the lover. By removing all connecting explanation, narration, exhortation, and commentary, Barthes emphasizes the disconnection between this rhetoric of pathetic figure and the arguments of political and economic history, a disconnection that had through the eighteenth and nineteenth centuries come to separate the gendered realms of public and private knowledge.

An important step in our understanding of pathos and modernism is, therefore, to problematize the sentimental, to open it up and to recall the variety of traditions, images, tropes, conventions, and ideological implications that modernism reduced to the single, gendered, and awful other defining literature by its absence. Judgments about value, discourse, and authority need to be made, but judgments were made about the sentimental as if it were a feminine aesthetic, free from cultural context and inferior to a modernist aesthetic which was also free from history. No rhetorical judgment comes from form alone, without a history. Thus a certain resistance will be necessary to the genealogy that has accompanied the concept of sentimentality, but also to the rejection of the past that continues as a trope of modernism. It is important to explore the possibility that the sympathy extended to a community of readers might coexist as rhetoric with the emotional power of style.

Modernism excluded whatever was associated with the fatally popular ladies. Doing so, it represented an exaggeration of the split between popular and elite culture in American letters. Can feminist criticism discover a rhetoric which might address this mutual estrangement, recuperating style in the service of a wider purpose? Have women writers been at work on such a rhetoric? Let us be instructed.

THE MATRIX OF MODERNISM

The Sentimental and the Modern
A Common History

They had no words to express the
sublime emotions they felt.

—ANN RADCLIFFE,
THE MYSTERIES OF UDOLPHO[1]

I

The sentimental has a strange existence as a discourse, with its coherence defined by opprobrium. Making
a narrative of its history would in-
volve rewriting the history of literary criticism, a task beyond the scope of
my inquiry. I can only suggest how the "serious" constitutes itself again
and again—not as a continuity but in a series of repetitions—against a
feminized "other" discourse which functions like woman herself to make
the binary definition possible. The specific contents of these oppositions
change, but the gendered difference is renewed. For example, romanticism
arose as an opposition to a feminized sentimentality and its accompanying
natural sublime. But modernism constituted itself by conflating the romantic with the sentimental and the popular. The private discourse of
feeling and the public community of women, guardians of feeling, are,
under modernism, both sentimental. And postmodernism, apparently, is
conflating modernism with a sentimental humanism, if Gitlin's character-
izations are to be believed. In retrospect, no discourse is without emotional
appeal or pathos, and so, in retrospect, the sentimentality becomes evident.

A host of dissimilar discourses have been assimilated to the feminine
by the ongoing construction and denial of the sentimental: working-class
vernacular, peasant dialects, the bawdy and the carnivalesque, the rhetoric
of religious dissenters, but also the refinements of aristocratic poetry and
the aristocratic lover. Defending writers against the kind of dismissal that
classifying them with the sentimental might imply involves disentangling

them from this conflation and making distinctions. For example, Carol McGuirk, in her study of Robert Burns, restores the sense in which he might be called "sentimental" and defends the eighteenth-century senti- mental poetic: "Being sentimental required a pursuit of intense respon- siveness that always created some pathology of feeling in a text. . . . the text solicits intense reader reactions to dire events that probably would have been averted by protagonists committed to the normal social world of sur- vival and compromise."[2] McGuirk wants to reassert the value of a rhetorical literature: "when the writer happens to be adept at manipulation . . . classic literature results." She also wants to assert the value of the vernac- ular. The fact that Burns writes in a dialect—solidifying a Scottish time and place—does not mean he is a minor writer. The case of Burns exposes the politics of the sentimental. Even though the stakes are obviously high for women writing, breaking open the undifferentiated otherness of feeling releases everyone else in the vernacular margins as well.

The discourse is not called "sentimental" because it takes a position even though the position seems clear enough: in favor of a gendered in- dividual, one who would have a heart, who could draw on feelings of sympathy, an individual who could, therefore, make moral judgments grounded in a private realm which oppose the developments of urban industrial society. The early, positive representation of the sentimental soon came under fire. The sentimental has been composed since then not only as a writing about the feminine but, more important, by judgments about it. In Western culture, the discourse of reason denies that its unconscious enters through style. The reason denies that the text functions as a hys- terical body, communicating through symptoms, and tries to eliminate the marks of pathos. Reasonable histories have produced the sentimental ret- roactively as the effect of their judgments about emotion in discourse, and their efforts to eject it. So the history of the sentimental in literature is a history of these judgments as well as of the fragmented body and conven- tions that both serve as examples and make the woman a stranger to lan- guage. Its kinship with melodrama on the one hand and with the psychoanalytic discovery of hysteria on the other suggests that the senti- mental operates to translate the relations of gender and the body's gestures into drama.

The word *sentimental* came into being in eighteenth-century England, together with the sentimental novel, as a term of approval.[3] It was con- nected to the pathetic appeal—the appeal to emotions, especially pity, as a means of moral distinction and moral persuasion. The seemingly ahis- torical critical term *sentimental* as we use it now refers obliquely and dis- paragingly to its historical roots in a literary tradition dominated by women. The disparagement has served, indeed, to repress the fact that writing women were beginning to dominate the history of writing and that their domination was far from being a sign of escapism. Writing women crossed the borders between the domains of production and reproduction. Dale Spender points out that this writing by women started with a sense of great transgression: "by the time of the Restoration when more and more women were earning their living by the pen, the distinction between the prostitute and the woman writer was so blurred as to be almost non-existent and it is possible that the opprobrium associated with both is more closely connected to the *selling* and *money making* than it is to any particular commodity they were trying to sell."[4]

The sentimental is a turning point for narratives of sociability.[5] Radcliffe's *Mysteries of Udolpho* and Wollstonecraft's *Maria* do not argue the idea that there are overwrought emotions. The gothic begins with that assumption and then works to classify and make distinctions. In the eighteenth-century concept of sociability, for example in Hume and Adam Smith, the place of the passions undergoes a change, a decline. In Richardson, Sterne, and later novels such as Goldsmith's *Vicar of Wakefield*, there is a development from sympathy, from a conception of passion as the basis of sociability, into a conception of passion as hypochondria and hysteria— that is, a turn from pathos as a rhetorical asset to pathos as not only diseased, and isolated, but feminized. The development of the gothic novel from the late eighteenth century to *Wuthering Heights* testifies to an ambivalence about the emotions, marking precisely this turn from that which is the basis of the social to that which threatens the social.

This represents the narrative sequence of the common critical judgment about the sentimental as a lower, degraded mode. We might recognize the premonitions of a Freudian form. Critical philosophy appears to correct the hysteria and pathos. But in fact this narrative with its privileging of the critical represents a recurring dialectic of male/female, reason/passion, city/country, public/private, and serious/popular which has reappeared again and again in various guises. The intense emotional response of a sentimental figure generates its critical opposition almost from the beginning. First the new woman appeared—Clarissa—fixing the object of desire, and in response developed the whole structure of middle-class man. But the response to Clarissa also redefines other forms of desire and introduces gender as a means of social oppression. Sentimental elements appear in all periods of literature. Pathos in the eighteenth century is distinguished by being made *central*, so that literature is defined together with other kinds of nonliterary texts in terms of its instructional and moral value, and other fictional elements, such as plot and character, play a secondary role to the often static tableaux of domesticity, virtue, bliss, and suffering.[6] This centrality means that pathos was organizing social change as the appeal to emotion mobilized not only the domestic but also democratic revolutionary sentiment.

Sentimental writing in the eighteenth century established a recognizable, highly conventionalized style. Its normalizing mannerisms are thoroughly intertwined with skeptical resistance to the sentimental. Thus the nineteenth-century "poetesses" seem sentimental because they make lyric expression a convention of feeling. The question of style is critical, for its abstraction and/or repetition both assumes and re-creates a *community* of like-minded readers.

In the eighteenth century, the vocabulary itself often presumed the reader's agreement. Sentimental expression is fragmented, illogical, a rupture of narration by static tableaux evoking the melancholy and the sublime. The scenery in Radcliffe's *Udolpho* delays the reader's progress constantly:

> During the first days of this journey among the Alps, the scenery exhibited a wonderful mixture of solitude and inhabitation, of cultivation and barrenness. On the edge of tremendous precipices, and within the hollow of the cliffs, below which the clouds often floated, were seen villages, spires, and convent towers; while green pastures and vineyards spread their hues at the feet of perpendicular rocks of marble or of granite, whose points, tufted with Alpine shrubs, or exhibiting only massy crags, rose above each other, till they terminated in the snow-topped mountains, whence the torrent fell and thundered along the valley. (168)

Emily combines the images coming to her mind into a sonnet, which also appears in the text, interrupting the narrative.

Tropes of sympathy argue through embodiment and an appeal to experience: the sentimental locates moral values in the (feminized) heart and denies the importance of external differences. Thus the sentimental also grounds the moral appeal to respect individual differences. The terms are hyberbolic and abstract: *benevolence, virtue, esteem, delicacy, transport, weakness, sweet, delicate, grateful, cruel, base, unkind, ungenerous, unfeeling.* Furthermore, phrasing itself is predictable. There is both extreme conventionality and extreme fragmentation. All the resources of the page are summoned to heighten—by punctuation marks, typographical devices, and gaps and breaks in the text—the often declared insufficiency of words to express the feeling described.

Sentimentalism is international, but like the history of modernism, its history takes form in ways specific to each culture. In England, sentimentalism is connected to the rise of Methodism and to religious dissenters. Methodist hymns reveal the patterns of a spirituality which is disconnected from established institutions and makes its appeals "directly" to the heart.[7] The English sensibility is distinct from that of other countries in its relationship to the bourgeoisie. When Rousseau takes up the epistolary forms of the sentimental in *La Nouvelle Heloïse*, he makes those love letters the basis not only of pedagogy and domestic and religious doctrine but also of political change.[8] The sentimental enters into French literature with its radical politics evident, appealing to avant-garde intellectuals in the formative years of the French Revolution.

In the United States, the history of sentimentalism and women's writing carries pervasive religious connotations at the same time that it is connected to the politics of social reform. The rational and theological versions of scapegoating are joined in Puritan rhetoric. Perhaps the modernist revolution of language in the United States seemed much closer to a battle of the sexes than elsewhere because American intellectuals (always the colonized) indeed, in some sense, fear being more "feminized." Women writers in the United States have not only the question of conduct to negotiate but also the legacy of Puritan threat and feminine heresy. Ann Hutchinson's notorious challenge to the Puritan priesthood was based on claims for the validity of religious emotion, or "enthusiasm"; her figure connects radicalism with female hysteria.[9] Her story suggests the violent prejudice of Puritan rhetoric. American Puritanism was able to be severe about religious dissent. The English Puritan ascent to power under Cromwell necessitated some degree of compromise with religious enthusiasts, a sort of coalition politics that encouraged tolerance. The American tradition of extremity together with the symbolic weight of the Salem witch trials provides evidence of a rhetorical paranoia which had to do with the dangers of trusting women's emotions. Americans had an early history of demonizing the female body and condemning female hysteria which presses questions of social virtue into theology. By the time of American modernism, women writers had a sentimental past which allied them not only with weakly ineffectual claims for the powers of sympathy, as Ann Douglas portrays it, but also with the strongest (most threatening) elements of social revolution and anarchy.[10]

A brief characterization of the history of women's rhetoric in America may help to make the point. In the nineteenth century an American discourse had been forged which combined the political appeal for social change with the religious and emotional appeal to personal experiences of sympathy—a discourse emerging in the 1830s with the first public expression of women's voices and the growth of antislavery movements, identified with the democratic ideals of American progress. The young Harriet Beecher Stowe probably participated at her father's dinner table in the early debates about women's right to speak in the western New York great revivals.[11] The increasing public influence of women—what Ann Douglas documents as "the Feminization of America"—depended on the immense success of this discourse with its combination of religious affiliation, a rhetoric of sympathy, and liberal appeals for change. After the Civil War, this discourse separated into specialized strands of women's rights and temperance, theological modernism, national progress, and moral reform. One could argue that the strong joining together of the various elements into the antislavery movement suffered disintegration and decline after 1865, as the rise of the industrial machine—the "dynamo"—and the adventures of the frontier captured the American imagination, and the feminine appeal to sympathy became a matter of convention, "genteel." But this would mean overlooking the rise of feminism and reform movements based on the moral appeal which grounded the sentimental.

Sentimental writing provided overt connections with sociocultural ethics that modernist criticism made it difficult for women to express. There are many qualities of the most sentimental fiction that we might want to endorse. That first best-selling American novel, *Charlotte Temple*, rehearses the sentimental situation which must at the date of its publication in 1791 already have been quite familiar. Late-twentieth-century readers will find elements of it so conventional that it seems like parody. Perhaps this parodic quality will now help make it attractive again. During the nineteenth century the story appeared in every form of publication; by the time *Charlotte Temple* appeared in a corrected, scholarly edition, in 1905, it had surely been learned "by heart."[12] It emphasizes the vulnerability of women, and it also expresses the pressure of women's desire. The innocent Charlotte is lured away to America by a rake, who abandons her after she becomes pregnant, and she dies pitifully upon the birth of her child, reunited at last with her grieving father. The message seems clear: smart ladies resist their sexuality because motherhood makes them vulnerable. (Is the message really out of date?) But the scenes of high emotion do their cultural work (as Foucault has taught us) to produce a dangerous female sexuality, its power the more alarming because it is seen only in its effect, the wrenching scenes of debasement, loss, and regret.

The author, Susanna Rowson, does not intervene to condemn Charlotte. As readers, our sympathy is all with the heroine, even though she plays a willing role in the seduction. What Rowson condemns is the cool greed and self-promotion of several villains. There is the calculating Mr. Lewis, who loans a Mr. Eldridge money for his son's advancement and forces the father into ruin when he protects his daughter from Lewis's seduction. Superfluously, the villain also kills the son in a duel. There is the French teacher, Mademoiselle La Rue, who lures Charlotte into the seduction and then, having made her own way into a good marriage, repudiates her. And there are the faithless friend, Belcour, who ought to have given Charlotte the money left for her but tries to seduce her instead, and even the landlady who throws poor Charlotte out into the cold when she has no rent money.

All of these villains are people who misuse the power of money and position, who fail to help another in need. By contrast, the heroic figures are defined by their social morality. Charlotte's father, who is not rich, rescues Mr. Eldridge and lives a good life frugally in the country. And Mrs. Beauchamp extends her care to the pregnant Charlotte without blame. The seducer himself, Montraville, is not really a villain but a man of feeling, who finishes out his days "subject to severe fits of melancholy" and makes frequent visits to "weep over the grave, and regret the untimely fate of the lovely Charlotte Temple" (118).

The moral of this sentimental story might well outrage Puritan morality, testifying as it does to the power of feeling. It suggests why the sentimental has become the obscene; *Charlotte Temple* locates evil not in sex but in the unfeeling. Early in the story Mr. Eldridge formulates what Mr. Temple calls the "true philosophy": "Painful as these feelings are, I would not exchange them for that torpor which the stoic mistakes for philosophy" (17). This book is meant to teach an ethic of social responsibility which respects both passion and suffering. Why should women writers deny themselves access to this ethos or the force of such an appeal? Modernist literature allowed writers such as Kay Boyle and Louise Bogan to acknowledge women's sexual desires. But they write about narratives of desire as they intersect with the painful issues surrounding love and domesticity. The modernist refusal of the sentimental has obscured their wider concerns.

The practice of separating literature from rhetoric and hence from ethics is recent in American culture, and in some ways antithetical to its Emersonian traditions. But getting rid of sentimentality has made it hard to restore the place of rhetoric as well. In his *Philosophy of Rhetoric*, first published in 1776, the Scottish theologian George Campbell endorsed the sentimental at the same time that he recognized its connection to ideology, to "the moral powers of the mind."[13] According to Campbell, the sentimental "occupies, so to speak, the middle place between the pathetic and that which is addressed to the imagination, and partakes of both, adding to the warmth of the former the grace and attractions of the latter." Campbell, like Hugh Blair, assumed the importance of appeals to passion. The pathetic works best, he says, "by some secret, sudden, and inexplicable association, awakening all the tenderest emotions of the heart. . . . it will not permit the hearers even a moment's leisure for making the comparison, but as it were by some magical spell, hurries them, ere they are aware, into love, pity, grief, terror." The description suggests the kinship of sentimental and sublime. The description also suggests, perhaps, the kinship of the sentimental with power, loss of control, and female sexuality.[14]

Although Campbell wrote in the eighteenth century, his was the dominant rhetorical text for much of the nineteenth century in America. In spite of romantic turns against this rhetorical doctrine, it was not so bad to be sentimental, then. What has happened to the once-positive connotation of the word? Campbell joined two things together which were firmly separated by modernism: he considered poetics to be a "particular mode" of rhetoric, and he considered both reason and passion to be legitimate parts of persuasion. This larger view of the rhetorical situation disappeared from departments of literature in the wake of modernism.

However, the fate of the sentimental in America is not a matter of a straightforward chronology. Serious romanticism opposed sentimental moralizing, and the instructional intention. Hawthorne's influential reformulation of sentimental philosophy in *The Scarlet Letter* breaks with rhetoric by condensing theological, sexual, and political heresy into a single emblem and affixing the moralizing symbol of the scarlet letter on the free-thinking woman Hester Prynne. The book has evident affiliations with sentimental and feminist traditions. Richard Chase points out the book's close likeness to a "feminist tract" (and Hawthorne's debt to Margaret Fuller's rhetoric), and Leslie Fiedler calls Hester "the female temptress of Puritan mythology, but also, though sullied, the secular madonna of sentimental Protestantism."[15] But Hawthorne denies that he moralizes and denies responsibility for the rhetoric of judgment which he calls up from the ghosts of a Puritan past. His novels, he claims, are not conduct books or moral tales but rather acts of imagination, romances. His Puritan ancestors would say he was "disgraceful": " 'A writer of story-books? What kind of a business in life,— what mode of glorifying God, or being serviceable to mankind in his day and generation,—may that be? Why, the degenerate fellow might as well have been a fiddler!' " (89).[16]

Thus does Hawthorne stage the separation of art from morality. His works represent not only a borrowing of the women's sentimental but also a struggle against the sentimental community, against their scribbling women and their feminists. Hawthorne calls not on his readers' sympathy so much as on their horror at the uncanny aura of crime surrounding women's sexuality and women's power, exemplified not just by Hester Prynne but by one female figure after another in his writing. He is haunted not just by lady novelists but by a powerful rhetoric—perhaps associated in his mind with Margaret Fuller. Hawthorne repudiates rhetoric. Henceforth the severity of a Puritan judgment will be directed toward a rigorous separation of art from life.

Modernist critics welcomed him as an ancestor. Rewriting elements of the sentimental into the form of the romance (Richard Chase says *The Scarlet Letter* is "almost all picture") and withdrawing from the hurly-burly of prose into a more poetic, more literary discourse, he does not violate the plain speech of the Puritans so much as he withdraws literature from the common house of political discourse; Chase claims Hawthorne has no politics (70, 74). The romance does not speak directly to its readers to instruct them. Like the sentimental heroine, the book does not speak for itself. It practices, indeed, a rhetoric of embodiment which transfers the sexuality of the woman which appears in *Charlotte Temple* to the body of the book, to an uncanny textual criminality, *The Scarlet Letter*. When modernist criticism at last theorized the ontology of the text, it is not surprising that it also reached back in literary history to canonize Hawthorne and to discard Susanna Rowson's *Charlotte Temple*. At the same time that Hawthorne denies the real power of the book, he takes up certain elements of the sentimental into *style* and perhaps inaugurates the politics of American symbolism.[17]

The relationship of the sentimental to the romanticism which follows it, in so many ways takes it up, and yet separates its powers from the femininized rhetoric of pathos, has much to do with the vexed history of the sublime. Samuel H. Monk, in his influential classic of critical history *The Sublime*, details the connection of literary women with the development of the eighteenth-century taste for the sublime, which was, of course, not separated as an aesthetic from natural emotion.[18] Thus he cites Mrs. Elizabeth Carter's " 'passion for the sublime' " and her " 'taste for the terrific' which impelled her to seek out ocean storms on nights when people of less fine sensibilities were content to remain at home" (212). Anna Seward represents an "epicurean pursuit of sensation" (214). He suggests that these tendencies appear earliest among women—Carter, Montagu, Vesey, Chapone, Seward, Radcliffe—because women did not have the education in the classics which men had. This was an advantage for the development of the sublime, Monk says: "They were . . . by virtue of their sex, somewhat outside the tradition, and if they had intellectual tastes, they might be able to criticize more independently than could men" (216). Monk means to compliment the women: Mrs. Carter's report of her experience of the sublime scene is "remarkably similar to Kant's conception of sublimity." But women were not able to carry it beyond mere sensibility, as Kant and the romantics would do.

In Monk's history, Wordsworth rescues literature from the women's imitative art, and from the inadequate aesthetics of Burke and of Blair, by the "high seriousness" which integrates the sublime experience of nature with religion:

> If one contrasts Wordsworth with any or with all of the enthusiastic admirers of nature in the last decades of the eighteenth century, he will observe that the basic difference between them is that while the Blue Stockings and the picturesque travelers strongly resemble faddists, and were concerned with the resemblance of natural scenes to paintings, Wordsworth was mainly interested in his aesthetic experience of nature as it offered support for his religious intuitions of the reality of the One in the Many. (228)

Like Allen Tate, Monk finds women lacking in "high seriousness." Like other modernist critics, he associates women with "faddists." First published in 1935, his history of the sublime is also a history *within* critical modernism, concerned to separate the merely sensible from aesthetic sublimity. His narrative follows the familiar sequence from an immaturity of women's writing to the mature male romanticism.

Modernist women, even more than a male writer such as Hart Crane, faced difficulties invoking the romantic tradition. Kant's attachment of the aesthetic sublime to the masculine, and beauty, the lesser category, to the feminine, had refigured the silences and the sublime emotion associated with female sensibility by the sentimental. Romanticism brought the representational shift away from a mimetic aesthetic to the romantic concept of the *imagination* and left women seeming inadequate to the figures of authorial transcendence and original genius. Female romantics might confront the sublimity of the creative identity as Gilbert and Gubar's "madwoman in the attic," or as a selfhood become monstrous, from Mary Shelley's *Frankenstein* to Louise Bogan's "Medusa."

If we think of the romantic individualist as inherently male, then women were not romantic.[19] They could not, at least, appear as unique and singular identities, since women were the other of the individuating logic. Even though the romantic poet appears to continue the tradition of the sentimental Man of Feeling (and the ideology of gendered individualism which women's writing from its gendered point of view was also constructing), the poet does not belong to the low culture of the novel. Women played a role in developing the romantic sense of self, and it would distort their contribution to think otherwise. At the same time, however, the cultural consensus developed quickly to exclude men from the interior, domestic space. The male romantic poet could have feelings, but they must be philosophically significant, and he must express them in the domain of high culture if he was not to seem laughable.[20]

The sentimental tradition was always dialectical, made up of writing by men and by women, and likewise criticized by both men and women— that is, by the very men and women who were making use of the convention. Jane Austen's *Sense and Sensibility* gives us the two sides, with feminine sensibility already under criticism. As Mary Wollstonecraft exemplifies, a recurrent theme is that women should stop being—by situation and by choice—like children, dependent on their fathers and husbands. In particular, their subjection seems to Wollstonecraft to be caused by women's attachment to sentiment rather than reason. "Another instance of that feminine weakness of character, often produced by a confined education, is a romantic twist of the mind, which has been very properly termed *sentimental*," Wollstonecraft declares: "Women subject by ignorance to their sensations, and only taught to look for happiness in love, refine on sensual feelings, and adopt metaphysical notions respecting that passion, which lead them shamefully to neglect the duties of life . . . " (157).

Adopting an ideal of rationality which would deny that the sentimentality associated with domestic life has anything to do with important pleasures and would abhor everything to do with the domestic, Wollstonecraft here defines women's sensations as aberrant, thus condemning her own emotional life. In other words, this notion of the superiority of the rational over the sensible had a long history before modernism: it was, of course, fundamental to liberalism and to the history of liberal feminism. The modernist innovation was to challenge the representability of the sensible, to try to stop the dialectic and end history.

A century after Wollstonecraft, many modernist women also rejected the domestic tradition on similar grounds, seeing an antiintellectualism in the sentimental. Yet nineteenth-century liberalism fed into the modernist rejection of the woman's emotional and communal life. In *The Subjection of Woman*, John Stuart Mill provides us with the epitome of the liberal argument as it seems to be prowoman.[21] Yet in Mill we can see the problem of liberal rationality more clearly. Mill splits women into rational, free (masculine) individuals and inferior, unconscious individuals embedded in the matrix of feeling and ordinary life—like mothers. What Mill has done is to invent "the exceptional woman" who chooses to be different from the ordinary. The woman who "chooses" housemistress as her profession, however, cannot be free to do anything else.

The Other that Mill thus constructs as the unconscious feminine is associated not only with domestic chores but with all of the messiness of sentiment and sexual desire, including motherhood. Cultural reproduction, including the work of writing the domestic, is separated from production and occupies a diminished and secondary terrain, not the primary arena of political and philosophical issues. Mill assumes that women's cultural production is inferior. He says that "their sentiments are compounded of a small element of individual observation and consciousness and a very large one of acquired associations"—women are inferior in literature and art because they are not modern; they suffer from a "deficiency of originality."[22] The argument idealizing rational will and the freedom to change represses issues of feeling together with the facts of economic deprivation. The working classes, the poor, the foreigners, as well as women, are consigned to represent the irrational. Emphasizing originality, Mill denies the cultural work of women's writing and mystifies the way serious (male) writers imitated, for example, the feminine sublime.

The modernist oversimplification of a mixed history made the traditions of women's writing seem univocally sentimental and uncritical. But the sentimental was not only complicated by the ongoing conflict of liberalism and romanticism; it was also fractured by the construction of sexuality. In the nineteenth century, the idea of free love, arising at first as the idea of a freedom to choose one's mate separate from patriarchal arrangement, began to involve feminists in an ongoing struggle to define sexuality from one generation to another. Feminists have often taken limited definitions of sex as their starting point, accepting the idea that the domestic and sentimental traditions have nothing much to do with sex. Feminists in the nineteenth century did not often endorse free love outside marriage, but they rather generally emphasized the dangers of sex and emphasized "social purity." They did not think of the strong feminine friendships they developed as sexual; they thought sexuality belonged to men and prostitutes. Nevertheless radical women, in particular Victoria Woodhull in the 1870s, took a "prosex" position. In the twentieth century, feminists have increasingly asserted women's right to pleasure, but this often takes the form of advocating the old ideas of free love. The problem for this debate is that neither feminist tradition questions the gendered construction of sexuality.[23]

The "free love" doctrine was adapted in complex ways to the logic of anarchy by most modernist women, by Emma Goldman and Edna St. Vincent Millay when free love was part of the Greenwich Village credo, but by Louise Bogan and Kay Boyle less as a belief than as a separation from ordinary expectations about the constraints of marriage. Lesbian women such as Natalie Barney and her fortunate circle of friends were able to free themselves from the woman's role and find support and love in the company of women, which offered some protection against the violence of attacks on women who broke sexual codes.[24] At the turn of the century, just as Ferdinand de Saussure was discovering the arbitrariness of the linguistic sign, the avant-garde was also discovering the arbitrariness of gender and asserting, like Oscar Wilde, the freedom to violate the conventions not only of dress but of desire. This freedom turned out to be a dangerous and difficult exercise, however, for both lesbian and heterosexual women. Women such as Louise Bogan and Kay Boyle were isolated, not in spite of their heterosexuality but because they challenged the conventions of marriage and family, and they felt the force of social oppressions in the everyday difficulty of their lives.

Modernist notions of sexuality were of course very much influenced by Freud. But Freud's theory enacts what it describes, repressing and denying its attachments to a maternal matrix—not only the influence of mothers, but also its origins in the nineteenth-century romantic literature's advocacy of feeling and desire. In order to assert male independence in the postures of a scientific attitude, the law of the father and the influence of science are fully acknowledged. This amounts to a rejection of certain kinds of discourses: the sentimental because it insists on maternal power, the religious because it encourages weakness and self-abnegation, the ro-

mantic when it hysterically embodies the unconscious rather than subli-
mating and projecting and objectifying.

Narration in the twentieth century would become a struggle over how
emotion is to be regulated and distributed, where feeling can be allowed.
The word which marks a passing over the limits of acceptable feeling for
Freud is not *obscene*, but *sentimental*. But from another point of view, the
sentimental made unrepresentable becomes the unconscious. Freud introduces the sentimental—that is, love—into the heart of reason where
mother love is forbidden, and so he sets the scene for the return of the
repressed.

II

Modernist literature (like Freud) shattered the pure, proper, inviolable
"I." This splitting of the identity of the speaking subject unsettled gendered
individualism and promised a kind of liberation for women—but the anarchy of the word was confined to the text. T. S. Eliot's "Love Song of J.
Alfred Prufrock" articulates a split subject of ambivalent desire, where the
retreat from the woman as object elicits a greater intensity for questioning
of imaginary identity, turned back in narcissistic self-reflection upon itself.
But the separation of poem from author protects Eliot's status as a critical
intelligence; the separation protects a conservative propriety from the unsettling effects of poetic language.

Ernest Hemingway's *The Sun Also Rises* distributes the power of desire
ironically, with Jake occupying the psychoanalytic position of the woman,
already castrated, so that he can serve neither as the subject nor as the
object of an eroticism which defines Lady Brett's identity. Jake's ironic
response to what might have been, "Isn't it pretty to think so," locates the
action in a discredited imaginary.[25] The book unsettles the male plot of
desire with its female objects—shouldn't it have been written by a woman?
But the struggle with the objects of desire is less important than the struggle
to separate from a maternal past and the mother country where it is located,
and in the experience of war, a violent and painful separation from optimism about the future. These texts work at the borders of identity where
the other is not an object but is ambiguously mingled and rejected from
the self, where what is evasive is not the object of desire but a desiring
subject, and the problem of intersubjective relations is paramount.

In the texts of modernist women writers, such an erotics is also apt to
govern—arising also as an ambivalent refusal of the mother and the sentimental past, also ambivalent about the woman as object of desire, but
often without the leverage of symbolic irony mediating the social impact

of their questioning, and perhaps with different relationships both to freedom and to pleasure, or *jouissance*.

Literary modernism founded itself on an appeal for freedom, but the nature of its conflicting politics has been covered over by the polarization of advocacy for free love against a sentimental gentility that came to seem antierotic. This in spite of the fact that, as Foucault argues, the Victorians articulated a sexuality by their discourse about the repressed.

Modernism is an ambiguous term. In fact, it has been used to identify histories that came to be completely opposed to each other in the first decades of this century. On the one hand, modernity continues the utopian and progressive themes that began to appear in the nineteenth century. This optimistic attitude had been connected to many of women's social and cultural involvements, from fighting for the abolition of slavery through promoting public education to social reform movements and the beginnings of feminism.

The hope for a better future that characterized the narratives of modernity influenced socialism, anarchism, and communism but also, of course, liberalism and the rise of the middle class. Modernism in the church was a liberalizing trend, with figures such as Harry Emerson Fosdick, an important model for Martin Luther King, encouraging believers to accept change.[26] These narratives of progress helped to create a revolutionary pressure for change, but they also came to be associated with a sentimental ideal that the reality of industrialization seemed to contradict.

However, the major public battles of modernist literature were fought over censorship and sex, not over industrialization: think of the confiscation of the *Little Review* when it printed parts of Joyce's *Ulysses*. Gilbert and Gubar have taken up this theme and characterized it as part of a battle of the sexes.[27] In agreement with them that gender is an issue, I nevertheless want to change the focus of attention from authors and characters who seem to be already constituted subjects in the field of sexual battle to the field itself, to discourse, where what is at stake in the erotics of the text is how the subject might enter into discourse and how ideology might be reproduced. The censorship battles were not just proof of American narrow-mindedness but proof that the field of discourse was articulating sexuality together with the political. If Comstock's prosecution of offenses against decency was defining the limits of the field in terms of a Puritanism that would protect women within language, the revolution of poetic language was defining a crisis of gendered subjectivity that might open up the limits. Modernism was transgressing the limits of identity. At the same time, however, the political significance of this crisis was obscured by the separation of art from life.

Women writers in the first two decades of this century entered a well-established female literary tradition which joined art and life, a rich, elaborated, complex, and contestatory tradition which included not only the private realm of letters, diaries, and personal memoirs (many at that time beginning to be published) but also a highly successful, highly visible public record in fiction, poetry, essays, critical and historical analysis, and journalism. In the context of social movements for suffrage and birth control, with writers such as Gilman, Addams, Beard, and Gage providing social analysis, writers such as Freeman, Jewett, and Chopin in the recent past, and Austin, Wharton, and Cather evolving prose forms, women writers before World War I would seem to have entered a literary field of unparalleled opportunity for women in particular. The tradition had through all its development in the nineteenth century become deeply involved both with social progress and with the inflection of gender. But the revolt against the sentimental, after its three or so decades of ascendancy, effectively buried that tradition. Women writers found themselves gradually cut off from the very past that might nurture them—at the same time that they seemed to be gratefully freed from a patriarchal family structure that threatened them, and a sentimentality associated with maternal-seeming ties.

In the matrix of American modernism as it emerged in the years before World War I—beginning perhaps before the 1912 appearance of the "imagists" in *Poetry*, with the immigration of literature from the European avant-garde, or when H. D. was a college-age friend with Ezra Pound and William Carlos Williams and Marianne Moore—the older discourse of progress and reform mixed confusedly with the new revolutionary forms, also associated with political revolution in the minds of participants. Emma Goldman, publishing her *Mother Earth*, and John Reed were political activists *and* literary figures in the Greenwich Village of the *Masses*, with Max Eastman (who was a poet as sentimental as any of the nineteenth-century poetesses). Artists such as Man Ray, John Sloan, and Robert Henri did covers for the radical magazines. Sadakichi Hartman, who had been attending Mallarmé's Tuesday nights in Paris, contributed stories.

But at the same time, T. S. Eliot was already abandoning with revulsion his kinship to an American past, linked all too directly through his grandfather's ministry to New England traditions of Unitarian liberalism and the proprieties of Boston ladies. And Ezra Pound was already advocating a new mode of writing, cleansed of all vague appeal to emotion, of the abstract vocabulary of sentiment—closer to the object-centered scientific procedures of observation exemplified by the story of Louis Agassiz in Pound's *ABC of Reading*. Pound was writing into literary theory an alphabet of misreading which would both appropriate and disconnect the sympathetic rhetoric of women writers, beginning with H. D.

Radicals to the right and the left shared a certain antihistorical fervor with European pronouncements in the arts, such as Marinetti's futurism. The excitement had a carnivalesque quality that would be lost by the later seriousness of the academics. For example, Guillaume Apollinaire posted a bulletin for the Paris artistic community in 1913, shocking for its typography and green color (called "merde") as well as for its program of "destruction and construction." Labeled "L'ANTITRADITION FUTURISTE" or THE FUTURIST ANTITRADITION, the manifesto called for "a suppression of history" without regrets—"a suppression of poetic melancholy, of exoticism, of the copy, of syntax, of the adjective, of punctuation, of typographic harmony, of the tense of verbs, of the orchestral, of theatrical form, of the artistic sublime, of verse and strophe . . . and of boredom."[28] This kind of program of revolt against stylistic convention appealed to Margaret Anderson as she and Jane Heap began their editorship of the *Little Review,* as did Emma Goldman's political anarchy: they featured both the art of futurism and notices of Goldman's appearances in their pages.

After World War I the optimistic mixing of progressive politics and literary revolution came apart, and the use of the term *sentimental* grew as the zero degree of critical opprobrium. For many woman writers in the twenties, poets and novelists alike, the woman's tradition was all too coherent, and they even shared the modernist revulsion against it in some ways. In the era of the 1920s, as literary modernism gained authority, a woman poet such as Edna St. Vincent Millay defied the laws of modesty, obscurity, and constraint when she reached out for her woman readers, and critics such as Ransom unleashed their contempt. It was risky for a writer to appeal to a community of readers which identified her with the feminine.

How in the world, we might ask, could it possibly be a daring or political gesture to write "O world I cannot hold thee close enough"? But the popular appeal was precisely what was risky. Millay had grown so hugely popular by the late 1920s that her kitchen was featured in *Ladies' Home Journal* ("Polished as a sonnet . . . Light as a lyric . . . Must be the kitchen for EDNA ST. VINCENT MILLAY." Only late in the article, at the back of the magazine, was it admitted that her husband was really the cook of the household.) The risk of shaming and exile was especially daunting when the female readership was middle-class, bourgeois, and sentimental, and when the values affirmed had to do with love and motherhood. That feminine community, however populous, was nonliterary and nonauthoritative by definition. Therefore what Millay risked by writing poetry of inclusion rather than of exclusion—risked and perhaps lost—was poetry itself.

In American literature, the political triumph of the new criticism which emerged was to install high modernism as a critical field which obsessively focused on the careers of Pound, Eliot, Joyce, and perhaps Stevens and Williams. High modernism meant that the works of a few male writers stood for a whole period of literary history, with a definition of literature that would seal off the anarchic forces of the revolution of the word. It left women out of the literary canon, and it made *sentimental* into a term of invective. The modernist criticism also posed a problem for feminism which persists to this day, separating literary style from rhetoric and political practice and estranging the serious critic from the popular community: "the high forms of literature offer us the only complete, and thus the most responsible, versions of our experience," asserted, for example, Allen Tate.[29] The high forms of literature came to define a "modernism" at odds with cultural modernity. Part of the double bind for women comes out of this contrary assignment of meaning.

Modernism, literary modernism, the American movement in intellectual politics, was against what not only feminists but also the engineers and churches and social workers and evolutionary biologists thought of as *modernity*. Literary modernism was ironic about progress and critical of the cultural history around it, from Main Street to old Boston.

The modernists were resistant to dominant capitalist culture, but that did not mean they were necessarily radical. The avant-garde was associated with progressive politics for Emma Goldman, Edna St. Vincent Millay, or Kay Boyle. But when Ezra Pound said "make it new," he was headed in the opposite direction. A decidedly reactionary trend developed which emerged triumphant. Many critics followed the lines of T. E. Hulme's influential rejection of humanism and revolutionary optimism, "Romanticism and Classicism."[30] Both a philosopher and a poet, Hulme associated romanticism with the ideals of the French Revolution, in particular the enthusiasm for "liberty." He rejected the metanarrative of Progress, the idea that bad laws and customs had suppressed "the infinite possibilities of man." These hopeful romantic sentiments Hulme identified as "spilt religion," a mistake: "The concepts that are right and proper in their own sphere are spread over, and so mess up, falsify and blur the clear outlines of human experience. It is like pouring a pot of treacle over the dinner table" (118). Romanticism was conflated with sentimentality; Hulme looked to the classical past for his model of reason.

Even when a certain disillusionment with politics set in after the war, modernist writers such as Hart Crane, Ernest Hemingway, Louise Bogan, and Kay Boyle wrote with a longing and sense of loss that suggested utopian critical perspectives, not a rejection of the sentimental. Even *The Waste Land* gains power from its melancholy nostalgia. But T. S. Eliot, taking up Hulme's severity, wrote insistently about the priority of form over content in judgments about art. In a 1928 essay reviewing *Personae* and defending Ezra Pound, he revealingly argued for the idea that Pound's innovation and influence were a matter of his form and not his contents, which Eliot freely admitted were reactionary.[31] This *formalism* connects Eliot to the new critics. Making form the basis of positive value rather than the means of revolution, he shifts attention away from the issues of morality, politics, love, and community associated with the sentimental.

The new critics, many of them poet-critics who greatly admired the early trio of Hulme, Pound, and Eliot, soon took up the banner. Yvor Winters, John Crowe Ransom, Allen Tate, and Robert Penn Warren were part of the artistic community in the 1920s, but they translated the new movement into the universities. Ransom, Tate, and Warren were members of the Fugitives (said to be fleeing sentimentality), and then the Agrarians.[32] They were associated with Vanderbilt University, and with promoting the South as a model of antiindustrial culture. When Cleanth Brooks joined the circle, he and Warren published in 1938 *Understanding Poetry*, a textbook that transformed the teaching of literature from a study of history, authors, and social context to the close reading of the text. In 1939, John Crowe Ransom published *The New Criticism*, formalizing a movement that had been growing out of literary modernism for twenty-five years, a movement that was about to dominate English departments and literature for several decades.[33] Its suspicion remains: of the progressive themes and appeals to feeling Hulme called sentimental, overlapping with the hermeneutics of suspicion, invisible within the rationality of the critical.

The modernism women participated in threatened social stabilities, including the stabilities of intellectuals on the left as well as the formalists. By 1931 Edmund Wilson was worrying, in *Axel's Castle*, about how the new movement seemed, like symbolism, to be withdrawing from political commitments.[34] But he too defined feminine sensibility as the opposition, identifying the feminine with the conservative. Powerful critical antipathy was directed against women writers from the left as well as the right, and they began to be driven out of the canon as modernism worked its way into the literary and academic establishments. Willa Cather, like Edna St. Vincent Millay, saw her credibility decline; Granville Hicks followed Wilson and others to attack her in 1933 for her conservatism, romanticism, and nostalgia.[35]

About the same time Kenneth Burke argued that the aesthetic perspective of modernism was too limited, that from a rhetorical perspective the arts were participating in a wider cultural revolution.[36] Burke wanted to counter the aesthetic claim that art is useless or amoral or merely formal and to restore it within rhetoric—to claim the possibility that art might indeed have an effect on morality and history, even though the effect might be threatening. Burke might have made an opening for women's writing, but he didn't acknowledge that the issue of morality/immorality was gendered. That possible immorality was what got Flaubert into trouble over *Madame Bovary*, at a moment in the history of nineteenth-century France when the avant-garde began to clash openly with the values of the bourgeoisie. Indeed, the trial of *Madame Bovary* in 1857, reproduced by the trial of *Ulysses* so many years later, marks the way that the novel, as Dominick LaCapra argues, might commit "ideological crime," and thus might be connected with "sociocultural transformation, through effects of the uncanny and carnivalesque."[37]

By the thirties, as events in the Soviet Union as well as in Europe made it seem increasingly that "progress" would be accompanied by violence, the distances between the political left and the antipolitical aesthetic criticism had grown painful. Louise Bogan wrote in a 1936 letter: "If revolution is the one means of change, I wish people would stop being sentimental about it. . . . revolution is also hell."[38] Let us take this reversal quite seriously as an argument: perhaps there is a sense in which pitching the site of struggle on the terrain of international politics is also conventional, escapist, a fantasy—"sentimental." The practice of political revolution was even then taking shape not only as fascism but also as Stalinism. But if the individual subject is the site of revolution, that does not make it less painful. Considering her several personal struggles with psychosis, let us also imagine that Louise Bogan knew what she was talking about when she said that revolution was violent. Her experimental writing represents a challenge to the codes of the family romance, not only at the level of theme but also at the level of subjectivity, at the level of the Freudian drama. While stories of free love and narratives of maturing to manhood may only reinforce the power of the family romance, women writers such as Bogan march to a different sense of story. And we need to be cautious about assuming that such a revolution of poetic language was necessarily a withdrawal from combat.

Feminist criticism has made defining and retrieving a women's literary tradition an important part of its critical agenda. Yet in doing so it has discovered the dilemma that situates women's writing in the twentieth century: the past exists as an unwarranted discourse, tied to the sentimental domestic configurations which wrote the modern woman into social existence. This sentimental is affiliated with the domestic discourses which founded the terms of the imaginary worked out across the last three centuries, inventing the modern individual, gendering not only human bodies but the institutions of culture. Frequently identified as the support for patriarchy, the sentimental nevertheless also marks the terrain of ideological conflict and so the site of women's struggle to find a voice.

Feminist critics have often called sentimental literature patriarchal, subservient to a male-dominated middle-class order. Nancy Miller, for example, in *The Heroine's Text*, reads the speeches of women in romantic fiction as finally subordinate to the dominant order of a male authority, a narrator who is looking past them at a male reader.[39] However, others, including Leslie Rabine, have argued that women's voices enter into novels as into a dialogic text, where the power of their discourse is not obliterated even if it is overlaid with a controlling structure.[40] The literary history of the sentimental coincides with what Terry Eagleton labels "the feminization of value."[41] And Armstrong warns us that women need to recognize our own contributions to the construction of middle-class gender.[42]

Women's involvement with the traditions of the sentimental has been a source of rhetorical power and of revolution at the level of the subject. If the sentimental has been an "unwarranted discourse," it nevertheless, as Jane Tompkins has argued, includes the women's fiction which is associated with social and political reform and with assertions of female power. It is also, as Nancy Schnog has added in her analysis of Susan Warner's *Wide Wide World*, a form of fiction which constructs an "emotional landscape" mapping the internal world of female sentiment.[43] And the sentimental has functioned, as Schnog argues, to "ameliorate women's psychosocial needs," to provide a model of mother-daughter and woman-woman relationships which might help assuage the isolation and vulnerability of women produced by history (n. 20, p. 25).

Critical arguments about the function of the sentimental have perhaps overlooked the overdetermination of its forms. Sentimental fiction has functioned in some respects to reproduce patriarchy, to produce it in new forms, and its failure to successfully invent a revolutionary order beyond patriarchy has made the happy endings seem hollow to succeeding generations of political women. However, the sentimental has also successfully functioned to promote women's influence and power, and this rhetorical success continues to be met with a countermovement of criticism and resistance which simply opposes women.

Modernist women writers called upon traditions established by women, the appeal to feeling, their loyalties to the "new woman," their desire for progress, their allegiance to maternal and comforting forms, but they also participated in the revolution of the word. As Louise Bogan recognized, they made an important contribution to poetics, "keeping the emotional channels of a literature open," not in spite of their close association with sentimental conventions but in some respects *because* of it: "women poets share with men the need for some sort of civilized ground from which to draw sustenance."[44] Poets such as Emily Dickinson and Sara Teasdale and Edna St. Vincent Millay trace the lineage. Not only Marianne Moore and H. D., Gertrude Stein and Katherine Anne Porter, but also Amy Lowell, Elinor Wylie, Leonie Adams, Djuna Barnes, Mina Loy, Renee Vivien, and Kay Boyle: they were modernists and they were women, and so they worked to define a new kind of writing, a writing which might unsettle the terms of the cultural gendering which oppressed them. This struggle shaped their writing in ways that I think we can begin to use ourselves.

Acknowledging the necessary dialogue of modernism with the sentimental can give feminism a postmodern identity. This notion of a writing subject acting not to oppose but to unsettle also characterizes Julia Kristeva, suggesting a continuity between modernism and the poststructuralist critique of the subject which is the context of her work. More important, there is a continuity between the presence of the symbolist intervention in American modernism and Kristeva's presence in the scene of American postmodernism—the American Kristeva. She represents the way an apparent internationalism disguises the specifically American form of the opposition of high and low culture, a form that is gendered. American feminists have taken her up as perhaps their most important woman critic for American reasons, precisely because she doesn't (as a French critic) enter the debate as a woman.[45] The fact that everyone overlooks how her Bulgarian origins might function in her work suggests how little nationality is really the issue.[46] As a modernist criticism, her position can function simply to continue the modernist exclusion of the sentimental. But her criticism can also function to carry out the unsettling that modernism inaugurated—particularly if we keep her feminine strangeness before us at the same time: her overlapping of the low-culture novel and the high-culture symbolist revolution, of the low-culture conversation of psychoanalytic clients and her high-culture psychoanalytic criticism.

Kristeva, influenced by Bakhtin, suggests that the subversive dialogic novel, as well as the subversions of poetic language (e.g., of the literary avant-garde), provides means of countering the forms of domination:

> the dialogism of Menippean and carnivalesque discourses, translating a logic of relations and analogy rather than of substance and inference, stands against Aristotelian logic. The novel, and especially the modern, polyphonic novel, incorporating Menippean elements, embodies the effort of European thought to break out of the framework of causally determined identical substances.[47]

Similarly, the poetic function of language is by nature revolutionary; it "has 'musical' but also nonsense effects that destroy not only accepted beliefs and significations, but in radical experiments, syntax itself, that guarantee of thetic consciousness."[48] These effects of language are what Kristeva calls the "semiotic," as opposed to the "symbolic," proposition-making, or "thetic" mode. The poetic function uses the semiotic—in whatever text it might appear—to subvert the domination of the discourse's implied ideology, because it is heterogeneous to *meaning*. Therefore, critical practice needs to take account of the poetic.[49]

This accent on the revolutionary potential of style rather than reason is modernist and runs the modernist risk of an aestheticism. Kristeva does not sufficiently acknowledge the importance of gendered histories in the politics of criticism or in the history of class formations in the West. Her work needs the corrective of sentimental history to be useful to Western feminists. But American women modernists can help us with that corrective. They were already taking the sentimental into account; thus their work can provide us with a dialectical perspective on developments in postmodern theory that is more grounded in American sociocultural history.

Nevertheless I think there are affinities between Kristeva's project and the work of modernist women writers. Modernist women tended to be politically utopian, whether they were politically active or not—to see the revolution of the word as potentially liberative. Kristeva's text is postmodern rather than modern most of all because (for all of its journey through melancholia) it is not unhappy. Her critical practice does not endorse pessimism even though she advocates setting limits to one's labors—as psychoanalysis limits itself to addressing the pain of individuals, rather than taking up all of society at once. Her notion of "revolution" comes out of a sense of possibility that is nothing short of utopian when compared to the massive resistance against notions of progress characteristic of modernism. She and American modernist women share, in that sense, the same modernity.

The revolution of the word was a revolution in style which challenged conventional expression, including the sentimental. The new criticism, however, exploiting the antihistoricism of modernist poetics, limited the destabilizing effects of philosophical perspectives—the threat of Nietzsche, the sexuality of Freud—to the interior of the poem, just as psychoanalysis condensed and displaced the effects of modernity on society to the interior life of the individual subject. Advocating an impersonal poetics, Pound and Eliot paved the way for the new critics who would separate literature from the personal self, inaugurating a logic excluding "intentional" and "affective" fallacies.[50]

Thus the revolution of the word worked by a double movement to both claim and deny the political significance of private experience. Authenticity was relocated in the word, not in the persons of author or reader. Modernist poetics addressed Baudelaire's estranged reader, the "hypocrite lecteur" invoked again by T. S. Eliot in *The Waste Land*. American individualism was under assault, but a new polarity replaced the old essentialism of gendered subjects. Private experience came to seem the final political reference point for the anarchical revolt against convention: even Emma Goldman thought so. However, modernist art separated the work from the person; "the symbols of Symbolism were metaphors detached from their subjects," said Edmund Wilson, and the modernist poem seemed to represent authentic experience precisely because of its ironic distance from personal feeling.[51] That ironic distance segregated art from a personal subjectivity that in the United States seemed increasingly feminine and sentimental. But style itself was in the feminine domain.

The separation of literature and everyday life replaced the separation of male and female traditions, so that women writers, like today's feminist critics, were cut off either from the serious or from the community of women. Modernism wrote itself out on a metaphor of the subject, the body of a textuality that was already gendered, the text itself—Rimbaud's "hallucination of the word"—feminine, hysterical, a rhetoric of embodiment, in ironic relationship to the symbolic mastery of other languages. Literature took over the domestic space of emotional language and the hysterical body of the text, repressing the historical body of gendered discourse and the genealogy of the personal. Contemporary writers of what Alice Walker calls "womanist" prose reconnect with that community but may still endanger their status as serious writers by doing so. The modernist revolution generated a new aesthetic theory which saw poetic language as a rupture of an oppressive social logic, surely a sentimental claim. But the voice of a revolutionary femininity was disconnected from power, as literature structured itself upon the exclusion of a banality identified with women.

And yet, is not this question of the banality of the subject precisely what postmodernism must still address? The movement of desire in language is at issue, and the question of emotion. Deconstruction locates the motor of rhetorical invention in the gaps of difference. But the sentimental by its excess of both feeling and conventionality displaces the power of desire from a never-attainable object to discourse as the object of sociability.[52] The love letter exposes the crisis at the level of identity: the incapacity of rhetoric to guarantee authenticity, and yet the importance of the reproduced formula.

The sentimental, that unwarranted discourse, constructed by negativity, inhabits the very notion of authenticity. As I will further explore in the chapters to come, the uncanny reproduction of the letter of love—by its very claim to authenticity in the middle of a negation—guarantees that literature will continue to exhibit the symptoms of a rhetorical subject, maintaining embodied, hysterical powers. When woman appears as the author, the discourse may be always already discounted, parodic, rhetorical, and estranged from the warrant of historical truth, at the same time that its pathetic appeal elicits our banal responses. But for postmodernity this represents the return of an author counted as dead. Barthes argued for antihumanism in "The Death of the Author," Foucault for the "ethical" principle of an "indifference" about who is speaking in "What Is an Author?"[53] The unexpected rebirth of the author, or ethos, through the feminine subject will return in my conclusion as sentimental modernism, a maternal irony.

Anarchy as a Literary Figure,
Anarchy as a Female Form
Emma Goldman

I

In lectures all over the country, from the 1890s to 1917, in articles and pamphlets, in her magazine *Mother Earth*, and finally in her 1931 auto-biography, Emma Goldman staked out a claim for anarchy in the resistant hearts of American audiences.[4] Goldman translated the European histories of class opposition into an American version of antagonism, using herself as free woman to mark the limits of middle-class ideology American style. Goldman as anarchist exposed the histrionics about patriotism and the narrowness of Puritanism, even in progressive movements such as temperance and women's suffrage. She went to jail for confronting the oppression of women revealed by laws against birth control, and she was jailed and deported when she continued to speak against conscription and war itself after America had entered the First World War. But Goldman's anarchy was less

[42]

a matter of specific issues than an attack on the very systems of conventional narratives which articulated oppression in the United States. Her anarchic rhetoric, her distrust of mass consciousness, her rejection of majority rule, and her convictions in favor of free love were positions defining a new kind of revolution in culture which the literary movement emerging as modernism associated with the revolution of the word.

To return to Goldman is to return to the crossroads where the revolution of the word intended the revolution of the world, where poetic language is imbricated in the political practice of revolution, and/or revolution instead of tradition came to articulate the literary. In the important early years of American modernism, we find a figure at this intersection, a figure divorced for us from literary texts, who apparently has left no traces of interest to literary history. This figure takes the form of a person, Emma Goldman, but it is also the figure of anarchy itself, the very attitude of crisis, a relentless undoing of convention, and the paradoxical turning on whatever seeks to establish a totalitarian governing of discourse. The relationship of literary modernism to the political becomes visible in this trope of anarchy.

As the very figure of resistance, challenging the genteel conventions of decent silence, Goldman's lectures took up as topics whatever might seem unspeakable, especially opening up the nexus of virtue, chastity, domesticity, and marriage which placed woman in the position of safeguard against the double anarchy of free love and the free circulation of money.[5] So threatening was her speech that she was at last imprisoned and then deported, but not without leaving an enduring and contentious place for the anarchy of discourse as "free speech." Like a character out of the Ibsen plays she loved so well, Goldman saw herself as one who would change the world by challenging the ghosts of ideology, by changing the consciousness of individuals thinking about the world. She moved the stage of anarchic action from politics to culture.

Emma Goldman personifies the extremities of a resistance which has as its ground an individual subject as speaker. This individualism is at once native and alien, as central as the female subject of virtue to the American tradition, as familiar as Thoreau and Huck Finn, and yet opposed not only to the past but to history itself as a narrative of external, public events. Goldman's individualism addresses a long tradition of American revolt that seems part of the American male character and yet invokes the moral sympathies for children and for the oppressed that belong to the sentimental. Her anarchy makes a familiar individualism reappear as something foreign, strange, uncanny.

Anarchy enjoys a peculiarly invisible history in the culture of the United States, even though (or because), as Sacvan Bercovitch has concluded, radicalism is conventional in American ideology.[6] Warren I. Susman suggests that the history of American modernist revolt is quite native, that the figure of the Bohemian outcast, such as Jack London or John Reed, belongs in actuality to a tradition reaching back to Whitman and Mark Twain's Huck Finn, a tradition gradually "brought to stand in the service of a counterculture dedicated to overturn . . . the sterile Genteel Tradition."[7] And David De Leon argues that anarchism *is* the American radical tradition, tracing its origins back to Roger Williams, Anne Hutchinson, and William Penn.[8] But this seems somewhat surprising, given the small number of radicals identifying themselves as anarchists and the narrow attention paid to anarchy as a political force in our history. The discourse of anarchism in American cultural history has been disconnected from its historical continuities with European radicalism. The energy of extremity somehow becomes identified as part of the social order. Bercovitch writes:

> To be American for our classic writers was by definition to be radical—to turn against the past, to defy the status quo and become an agent of change. And at the same time to be radical as an American was to transmute the revolutionary impulse in some basic sense: by spiritualizing it (as in *Walden*), by diffusing or deflecting it (as in *Leaves of Grass*), by translating it into a choice between blasphemy and regeneration (as in *Moby-Dick*), or most generally by accommodating it to society. . . . In every case, "America" resolved a conflict of values by reconciling personal, national, and cultural ideals.[9]

American ideology takes up the anarchy of capital and invests it in the hegemony of capitalism: modernity, change, and a ceaseless antagonism to the past are conventional. It is traditional to innovate, an American anxiety to prove the culture original, not a colony. The implications extend all the way into poststructuralism: the Americanization of deconstruction has been a critical success, but it has removed the symptomatic reading from its material consequences, as if the ceaseless irony of the mass media were material enough. Repressing its own femininity, the origins of individualism in sentimental fiction; finding abject the feminine, colonized dependency of American gentility on European and British models, and the dependency of American heroes on a feminine matrix of material support; denying the presence of collective misery, the American ideology of individualism hides its continuities with subversion as well.

Emma Goldman threatened this manly autonomy in part because she grounded her appeals in a sense of continuity between her anarchic community and the values of an American past. She published articles in *Mother Earth* which argued the case explicitly. For example, Lillian Browne's "Emerson the Anarchist" called Emerson's advocacy of *self-reliance* "the trumpet call of the emancipation of the individual; emancipation from the bondage of customary and traditional virtue; from the spiritual slavery of family despotism, from the chains of superstitions and popular standards."[10] William M. Van der Weyde discussed "Thomas Paine's Anarchism," locating the foundation of both European anarchism and American values in "The Rights of Man," particularly in Paine's critique of government.[11]

Adding Emma Goldman to the line of American anarchists may seem, however, to be a questionable claim, since she was opposed to the values of capitalism, she was an immigrant—and furthermore, she was finally deported. In the American twentieth century, perhaps partly because of Goldman and Berkman, we have made strict distinctions between American and un-American activities.

But this insistence on the American has created an artificially pure history of anarchy in this culture. Not only is there the continuous influence of immigrants, but European revolutions and radical social movements profoundly influenced American literature. Larry Reynolds, who looks in particular at Emerson, Fuller, Hawthorne, Melville, Whitman, Stowe, and Thoreau, argues that the "Red Revolution" of the mid-nineteenth century had marked effects on our culture through these writers.[12] For example, Harriet Beecher Stowe "used the prevailing fear of and hostility toward the 'Red Revolution' in Europe to dramatize her antislavery themes. Knowing that her readers anticipated future uprisings of the masses abroad, she played upon their fears to get them to consider the possibility of similar events in the United States if the Negroes were not freed" (52). Reading the "Concluding Remarks" of *Uncle Tom's Cabin*—"Every nation that carries in its bosom great and unredressed injustice has in it the elements of this last convulsion"—Reynolds goes on to argue: "From such a point of view (which has much to recommend it), one can regard the Civil War (which Stowe's novel helped precipitate) as the final disturbance of the earthquake that convulsed Europe in 1848–49" (53).

Margaret Fuller became a socialist after she saw the wretched conditions in England, France, and Italy, and she sent reports back from Italy of her convictions about the new revolutionary movements. But of course, Fuller is at once the most likely figure as a predecessor for the contributions of Emma Goldman, and the emblem of how thoroughly repressed she might be. Fuller has been the most forgotten major literary figure of her own times.

Goldman's attack on Puritanism and the ideal of chastity was shocking, but she grounded it too in the enduring themes of American letters. The horrors of Puritan New England, she pointed out, "have found their most supreme expression in the American classic, *The Scarlet Letter*."[13] As we imagine the small, plump figure of Emma Goldman on the stage, with the crowd below and policemen at hand, does she reproduce the scene of Hester Prynne upon the scaffold? She must have thought so herself. Yet she went far beyond the freedom of mind about gender that Hawthorne imagined with such ambivalence for Hester Prynne. She said that women are the "victims" of chastity, whether unmarried and thus forced to repress their sexual desires, or married and thus forced to "incontinent fruitfulness." Prostitution, together with venereal disease, was thus "the greatest triumph of Puritanism." Goldman changed the terms of the discussion in order to produce a new notion of the subject, portraying the individual as a product of social conditions. Her arguments about prostitution were in favor not of reform but rather of rethinking. "An educated public opinion, freed from the legal and moral hounding of the prostitute, can alone help to ameliorate present conditions."[14]

At the same time that Goldman brought the accent of the Russian Jewish immigrant to American anarchy, her speeches, invoking Hawthorne, Thoreau, Emerson, and Whitman, repeated other moments in American literary history. But this is a connection that would be rendered invisible by the modernist literary revolt against the romantic past. If American modernism had deep affiliations with the Emersonian past, they were repressed, indeed forbidden. Even Hart Crane's dramatic poetic ambition to acknowledge his (our) debt to Whitman encountered trouble. Critics such as Yvor Winters were not willing to let him get away with it: Winters used Crane as his object lesson in his major diatribe against the influence of Emersonianism.[15] If Goldman articulated a continuity with the American literary tradition, she failed to address modernism's resistance to the humanistic language of the past. She tried to make a connection between a certain notion of the individual and the anarchy of the avant-garde at the moment when that would come to seem as unacceptable and sentimental as the "spilt religion" of romanticism.

The events most responsible for confusing the future treatment of anarchy itself in the United States arose in the 1880s. First, there was the association of anarchism with bombing and terrorism, an association that set aside the influence of the nonterrorist anarchist. Public opinion fixated on four incidents: the Haymarket bombing of May 4, 1886; Alexander Berkman's assassination attempt on Henry Clay Frick of Carnegie Steel in 1892; Leon Czolgosz's assassination of President McKinley in 1901; and the Ludlow Massacre in Colorado in 1914, which prompted three anarchists to retaliate against Rockefeller by setting off a bomb that killed a woman instead. The other source of great confusion was the splitting of anarchists in the 1880s into individualist and socialist-communist factions. While the chief difference in ideology seemed to be that individualists believed in private property, the more significant effect was to separate "American" anarchism as individualism from the "un-American" anarchism influenced by Kropotkin and Johann Most.[16]

The crises in Emma Goldman's career center around these two issues, for she would reject violence and endorse the individual as the source of radical change rather than the masses. She had what she calls "My Social Awakening" when she heard of the Haymarket executions and began reading Johann Most's newspaper, *Die Freiheit* (9–10). Goldman herself would have been involved in the *attentat* against Frick if Berkman had not insisted on going alone. As it was, her life story turned on Berkman's act and his subsequent imprisonment, since she herself was accused of complicity, and she plunged into speechmaking and writing initially in Berkman's defense (85–107ff.). Goldman had met Czolgosz, and she tried to organize a defense for him after the assassination. She herself was accused by the newspapers of complicity in the crime, but she had had no knowledge of it (310–17). When she heard the news of the massacre at Ludlow, Colorado, Goldman set aside her drama lectures to write in *Mother Earth* and give lectures to raise funds. But she was "aghast at such irresponsibility" when she heard of the bomb exploding in a crowded tenement, and she mused:

> I remembered a similiar event in my own life. . . . my little room in Peppi's flat . . . Sasha experimenting with a bomb, and me watching. I had silenced my fear for the tenants, in case of an accident, by repeating to myself that the end justified the means. With accusing clarity I now relived that nerve-racking week in July 1892. In the zeal of fanaticism I had believed that the end justifies the means! It took years of experience and suffering to emancipate myself from the mad idea. . . . though my sympathies were with the man who protested against social crimes by a resort to extreme measures, I nevertheless felt now that I could never again participate in or approve of methods that jeopardized innocent lives. (536)

Goldman combines the American individualist and the un-American communal strains of anarchism in the impossible position of the passionate woman. She reveals the anarchy of free love and the sense in which a desire freed from loyalties to the hierarchies of social order can serve not to endorse the institutions of capitalism but to critique them. If her strong feelings about this are not to be simply dismissed as a romantic and sentimental weakness, what are they? Her meditation reveals another ground for what she would later call her own "fanaticism":

> he had no need of me in his last great hour. The realization swept away everything else—message, Cause, duty, propaganda. What meaning could these things have compared with the force that had made Sasha flesh of my flesh and blood of my blood from the moment that I had heard his voice and felt the grip of his hand at our first meeting? Had our three years together shown him so little of my soul that he could tell me calmly to go on living after he had been blown to pieces or strangled to death? Is not true love—not ordinary love, but the love that longs to share to the uttermost

> with the beloved—is it not more compelling than aught else? Those Russians had known it, Jessie Helfmann and Sophi Perovskaya; they had gone with their men in life and in death. I could do no less. (88)

She suffered through his long and terrible prison term and worked to carry on their mutual fight for freedom. They would always be the closest friends, even though not lovers. But she changed her mind about the usefulness of violence.

Goldman's anarchy did not fit the standard readings. Perhaps her American focus on changing individual consciousness and her un-American rejection of capitalism made her seem almost outside history, in some sense. Goldman repudiated the socialism of Most as, shortly after the Russian Revolution, she later repudiated the results of communism in the Soviet Union. She was against external authority of any kind. But if history in the public imagination is a battle of contending spectacles, surely the small female figure of Emma Goldman asserting the outrageous right to free speech put the older images of bombs and bearded foreigners into question for a brief moment, and helped put anarchism back on the American agenda in the important years before World War I. It was then that American literary modernism took up the antagonism to bourgeois culture that had been in European poetry since Baudelaire. To take Goldman seriously is also to take seriously the cosmopolitanism in the cultural history of the United States—a cosmopolitanism which contributes to explaining both the energy of literary modernism and the source of its alienation.

II

Goldman's anarchy opened up a space which resembles the heroic position of literature itself in its antagonism against middle-class certainty. Her rhetoric, Margaret Anderson argued, was above all Nietzschean.[17] Goldman had argued that artist and anarchist met under the sign of Nietzsche years earlier, in 1897, in a conversation with the critic James Huneker, who was arguing for the separation of art and revolution:

> "Nietzsche himself is the proof of it," he argued; "he is an aristocrat, his ideal is the superman because he has no sympathy with or faith in the common herd." I pointed out that Nietzsche was not a social theorist but a poet, a rebel and innovator. His aristocracy was neither of birth nor of purse; it was of the spirit. In that respect Nietzsche was an anarchist, and all true anarchists were aristocrats, I said.[18]

Before T. E. Hulme attacked romanticism and religion, Ezra Pound rejected poetic abstraction for imagism, and then Pound and Wyndham Lewis denounced futurism in the name of Vorticism in *Blast*, Emma Goldman set out a public rhetoric of extreme discontinuity and resistance which functioned to critique the authority of any convention. Like literary modernism, Goldman allied herself with the freedom of negativity, not with the older reform movements, and so not with traditional movements for women's rights, or with progressive or socialist or even communist movements to construct programs for the future. Like Pound and Eliot she was influenced by European literature which engaged in a cultural critique.

Goldman promoted a mutuality of revolutionary art and revolutionary politics that drew on European intellectual traditions. In 1907, her story about Grandjouan's new cover for *Mother Earth* criticized American artists for their "money-getting genius": "That the artist must serve the highest bidder is an American axiom. Practicality is our most essential trait" (358).[19] By comparison, Grandjouan told Goldman, in France "there is not an artist of consequence who is not also a revolutionist" (358). Goldman believed that the originality of art is tied to revolutionary politics, and that is the problem with American art:

> Therein lies the fundamental difference between France and America. Delaunoy [sic], Yossot, Herman Paul, Toulouse de Loutrec [sic] and Grandjouan are idealists, responsive to the efforts of oppressed humanity; therefore their art gains in originality, strength and beauty. With us, most artists are matter-of-fact men, practical people; thus their creative faculties become stultified, and their work commonplace. (359)

She recruited American artists before she was through, including members of the Ash Can School, and the covers of the August and September 1914 issues of *Mother Earth* are by Man Ray.

She was convinced that anarchy's revolutionary principle would work to free individuals as it worked to free the language of art, even though this was a political confidence which the avant-garde perhaps did not deserve. Goldman maintained her hopes for the liberative powers of art even after World War I and the disappointments of the Russian Revolution. She wrote from abroad for the final issue of the *Little Review*, in May 1929:

> Inasmuch as I consider modern art in the experimental stage I welcome its restlessness, its discontent and its desperate effort to find itself. Above all, I admire the arrogance and the reckless indifference of the modern artists. My world-view is Anarchism—a social arrangement where each can express himself to the fullest without fear or favor from his surroundings.[20]

Anarchy as Goldman practiced it makes sense only when oppression works from within, hegemonically, in the forms of culture. When her career began, she had not yet developed this notion of politics working within individual consciousness. Her early audiences were workers, who saw themselves in opposition to the bosses, and immigrants, whose marginality was enforced by overt acts of prejudice and violence. She followed the anarchic principles of Bakunin, Kropotkin, and Most. But she saw the importance of culture in history and opened up the drama as subject for her anarchist lectures. She began to address women's issues, demanding free speech for information about birth control, advocating free love, and she redefined anarchy as she redefined the nature of oppression. She gave lectures on Nietzsche. Her opposition to the war and to conscription appealed to women and men who were not only from despised and neglected classes. Her audience became the hegemonic subject of internal oppression, of force psychologized and made personal as ideology—the middle class.

In mounting a resistance to the genteel culture of love and virtue and marriage, she also participated in the modernist rejection of woman's domain. Her advocacy of free love was, of course, one of the characteristic stances of modernism, but literary representations of free love were less threatening than Emma Goldman, even though they prompted censorship, because they were literary, separate from the ordinary individual. Goldman's work made the dangerous connection between the private domain of the middle-class American individual and the anarchy of the avant-garde.

It is not surprising that Margaret Anderson and the readers of the *Little Review* would feel an affinity with Goldman's anarchy. The interest of Eliot, Pound, Stevens, Crane, Bogan, and other modernist writers in French symbolist poetry put them in touch with anarchic poetics that were entwined with avant-garde politics. Symbolist practice opened the revolution of poetic language by its radical turn to musicality, raising the question of language's referentiality. As precursors, however, the French symbolists also had connections with political anarchy.

Unlike American (and British) Victorians, who had obscured or denied any connection between modernity and radical cultural politics, the European avant-garde grounded itself, and not just metaphorically, in the violence of the *attentat*. Matei Calinescu traces the use of *avant-garde* back to a 1794 military journal titled *L'Avant-garde de l'armée des Pyrenées orientales*, which revealed its Jacobin sentiments by addressing French patriots with the call for "la liberté ou la mort." The notion of an avant-garde soon extended analogically into French culture. Calinescu argues that, in fact, the cultural avant-garde is inherently anarchistic (even when professing Marxism), because "anarchism as an attitude implies a veritable mystique of crisis."[21]

Julia Kristeva tells us there was a crossing of paths between that master of withdrawal, Stephane Mallarmé, and French anarchists, including Louise Michel. At an evening sponsored by Anatole Baju, founder of the review of the *Décadents*, to which Mallarmé, Moréas, and René Ghil, among others, had been invited, Michel spoke of their common practice. She said, "Les anarchistes, comme les décadents, veulent l'anéantissement du vieux monde. Les décadents créent l'anarchie du style" ("Both the anarchists and the decadents want to undo the old world. The decadent poets are creating the anarchy of style" [my translation]).[22] Of course, Louise Michel and the French anarchists did not take up the anarchy of style into their rhetoric. Their discourse appeared not as a symbolist new word but rather, as Kristeva says, "spontaneous, naive, and humanistic." That is to say, the anarchists were not practicing a revolution of poetic language. However, both the symbolists and the anarchists engaged in a practice which would undermine authority. Furthermore, they acknowledged a commonality of interests. Even so, both the anarchists and the symbolists worked from within a dominant ideology constructed by the bourgeoisie, the larger modernity, an ideology which used gender to construct power and the separation of literature and life to disguise its work.

The perspective of Goldman's long rhetorical productivity and political leadership calls attention to the questionable relationships between the avant-garde and twentieth-century politics. For a time, in the years before the war, Goldman seemed, like John Reed, Max Eastman, even Floyd Dell, to represent the political program of the new literary and artistic movements. She was a familiar figure among modernists. Margaret Anderson filled the pages of the *Little Review*'s first year with essays and announcements about Goldman.

Together with other members of the left in the Greenwich Village of the *Masses*, in the time of the Provincetown Players, Goldman felt herself a part of the literary culture. She edited *Mother Earth* and wrote drama criticism. Robert Henri, John Sloan, and George Bellows worked with Goldman on the progressive Ferrer school, Sloan did illustrations for *Mother Earth*, and Henri painted her portrait. However, by 1929, when Goldman's response to a questionnaire appeared in the final issue of the *Little Review*, she was growing impatient with certain elements of the lost generation: "I look forward to a time when human beings will be engaged in creating beautiful things rather than being satisfied with the substitute of publishing idle magazines full of idle questions."[23] Like the socialist critics who followed her, she advocated a literature which would promote a progressive social philosophy, even though—like many modernist writers—she thought of revolution as the creative breaking of oppressive convention, not the establishment of yet another oppressive state.

Like other modernists, influenced by Nietzsche, Goldman distrusted the rule of the majority who emphasize quantity over quality: "public opinion is the omnipresent tyrant in American society," she said. The mass "clings to its masters, loves the whip, and is the first to cry Crucify! the moment a protesting voice is raised against the sacredness of capitalistic authority or any other decayed institution."[24] But such a distrust of the majority also has the deep American roots Goldman found in Emerson and Thoreau. Goldman's Emerson uses the idea of individualism to distinguish difference, and the distinction begins with gender: "The calamity are the masses. I do not wish any mass at all, but honest men only, lovely, sweet, accomplished women only" (78).

If this is such standard American rhetoric, why did Goldman raise such a furor? In spite of her Emersonian justifications, a critique of the "people" delivered by a woman such as Goldman was regarded as so inherently subversive that William Buwalda, a young soldier who went to hear her, was court-martialed for treason and sentenced to three years in prison. There was something about Goldman that was not easy to assimilate, that threatened the stabilities of everyday life.

As times changed in the twenties, and the freedom of the flappers began to look more and more superficial, a freedom of haircuts and hemlines, perhaps Goldman found her analysis of mass culture as basically resistant to change still warranted. Paralleling the literary revolution, Goldman had distinguished her appeals to the individual from appeals to the masses and based her rhetoric on confronting the mass antagonism to innovation:

> Without ambition or initiative, the compact mass hates nothing so much as innovation. . . . The oft repeated slogan of our time is, among all politicians, the Socialists included, that ours is an era of individualism, of the minority. Only those who do not probe beneath the surface might be led to entertain this view. Have not the few accumulated the wealth of the world? . . . Their success, however, is due not to individualism, but to the inertia, the cravenness, the utter submission of the mass. ("Minorities versus Majorities" 70–71)

Like modernist writers, Goldman targeted an audience of those who would consider themselves gladly "different," and hence in that respect "individualized" as a minority of the more courageous. As she claimed, there was a certain kind of Nietzschean aristocracy involved.

However, Goldman's pedagogical stance differentiated her ideological position from the increasing withdrawal of the literary. Anarchy would not be indifferent to ideology but would replace religion with a communal individualism. She preached that individuals are in conflict with social instincts because they believe themselves dependent on the powers described by religion. These stories all "sing the same refrain: Man can have all the glories of the earth, but he must not become conscious of himself."[25] "Anarchism is therefore the teacher of the unity of life. . . . There is no conflict between the individual and the social instincts any more than there is between the heart and the lungs" (52). Thus Goldman redirected conflict from the sphere of mass politics, redefining anarchy in terms of the individual subject. She quotes Emerson: "The one thing of value in the work is the active soul; this every man contains within him. The soul active sees absolute truth and utters truth and creates." What anarchy as thinking can do, Goldman says, is produce the "reborn social soul" (52).

Through Emerson, Goldman borrows the metaphor of spirituality, the language of the soul, to talk about a revolutionary change that is dependent on consciousness. Emerson, Irving Howe says, had a "devotion to *inwardness*" but "succeeded in escaping doctrines of the sacred without having to suffer the penalties of desacralization."[26] Howe argues that Emerson was a cultural revolutionary, with the revolutionary aim to transform humanity, that "Emerson speaks for a permanent revolution of the spirit, he who in no ordinary sense could be called a revolutionist" (21). In that sense—though she *would* be called a revolutionist in any ordinary sense— Goldman is simply going on with the agenda for change already set out by Emerson. Furthermore, Howe suggests that it is Hawthorne who "provides the first persuasive portrait of Emerson's new American: a woman named Hester Prynne who, if not quite a 'seeker with no Past at my back,' stands ready to pay the price for her self-reliant assertions" (38). If Goldman's anarchism blends in with the native American strain, grounded in the ideal of the Emersonian free individual, with the figures not only of Hester Prynne but of Margaret Fuller behind her, perhaps she makes evident how high the price was. Goldman does not just imitate the soon-to-be-repressed idealism of American romantics; she recalls the profound ambivalence with which the American tradition had received these figures of womanly assertion. Goldman exposes the subversive possibilities of Emerson, and especially of the free American woman.

Although her speech was always self-consciously avant-garde in pressing for the annihilation of the old regime, Goldman's language was not like the symbolist or the modernist practice, not experimental, not the anarchy of style. But that does not mean that she was captured by the monologic of bourgeois ideology. Her rhetoric in lectures was dialogic, her autobiography dialogic in a Bakhtinian sense, with a multiplicity of voices entering into the text, not subjected to the totalizing subordination of any singular consciousness but anarchic. Refusing to use problem solving and reformist modes of argument that offered persuasive "solutions" to the crisis she exposed, she constructed her speeches and lectures according to the strategy Kenneth Burke calls "perspective by incongruity."[27]

Martha Solomon charges that Emma Goldman lacked effectiveness with American audiences because her politics constituted a critique, rather than a positive program for the future. This led to her use as the chief forms of her rhetoric of "perspective by incongruity" and "embodiment"— enacting anarchy by her own performance, rather than explaining and persuading.[28] Why does Solomon accept the conventional attitude that only a problem-solving argument has validity? This is, perhaps, to say that Goldman's effects are literary. Indeed, Goldman's rhetoric of embodiment dramatizes the rhetorical power of literature in culture. It is not true that Goldman lacked effectiveness with American audiences. The effects of the controversy she inevitably stirred up generated not only antagonists but also adherents, not only for anarchy but also for free speech. Rather than looking right now at the immediate impact of Goldman's political theories and her activities, however, let us think about the revolutionary impact of her nonprogrammatic practices, especially the part of her rhetoric which seems only to raise questions, and the part related to women's issues and literature and not to the "real world" at all.

Her speech worked to make her audience self-conscious; she shattered the larger rhetorical structures of middle-class ideology. Goldman confronted her audiences with a new and intolerable conjunction of anarchy and American individualism, joining in her person the revolt of the wife against marriage, of the mother against enforced childbirth, and of the free individual against the authority of church and state. She at once refused all the social roles of woman and took a place that defines a *womanly* relationship to the nonprivate world, the place of a teacher, a pedagogue, a nurse, of one who works directly on the subjectivity of her audience— whose mission is not to create a new world but to create *new subjects* fit to make a world for themselves.

Goldman therefore defined anarchy in terms of the individual subject's resistance rather than in terms of collective programs. She said:

> Anarchism can not consistently impose an iron-clad program or method on the future. The things every new generation has to fight, and which it can least overcome, are the burdens of the past, which hold us all as in a net. Our most vivid imagination can not foresee the potentialities of a race set free from external restraints. . . . We, who pay dearly for every breath of pure, fresh air, must guard against the tendency to fetter the future. If we succeed in clearing the soil from the rubbish of the past and present, we will leave to posterity the greatest and safest heritage of all ages.[29]

Although she was so thoroughly identified with the values of the left that she is still known as "Red Emma," Goldman did not hesitate to extend her critique to the new state forming after the Russian Revolution. After she had been in Russia for a number of months, she confronted Lenin with demands for decent treatment for anarchists and the right of free speech: "His reply was that my attitude was *bourgeois* sentimentality."[30] Subject to the social codes that pressed her to marriage and motherhood, Emma Goldman resisted and made outrageous resistance into an avant-garde act. Her advocacy for women and for passionate commitments to others is easily lost in what followed.

Anarchy, with this vision of cleaning up the wasteland for the future, a metaphor that seems ever more literally appropriate today, may nevertheless sound like another story we cannot tell in the perspective of postmodernism. On the one hand, there is the suspect connection to an individualism that so often has served to oppose collective activity, and to deny the positionality and complicity of subjects. On the other hand, there is the suspicion of programs and solutions. Martha Solomon's charge against Goldman is similar to the charge made against poststructuralism. Anarchy, indeed, seems to precipitate the critical crisis, making all alternatives equally guilty, equally illegitimate.

We don't know how Goldman sounded, except that she talked very fast and was obviously a speaker who could control large audiences of people—in the thousands—under extraordinary conditions. But we know something of how she looked: small, increasingly plump as she aged, with iron-rimmed glasses. Her appearance was unexpected, for she looked more like a soft peasant woman than a rebel. Her pictures are always unsmiling, with the corners of her mouth turned down as if in refusal to smile as a woman is expected to do, or to make things easier in any way. Margaret Anderson thought her expression was of a maternal sadness. If the crowds who came to hear her expected exhortations to violence, they did not hear them.

But Goldman was a demanding speaker, violating conventions and expectations. She resisted the processes of mass audiences—at the same time that she worked them expertly. She appealed to continuities between American culture and anarchy, but she did not allow her audience to identify with her. She broke their most sacred codes of womanly behavior. She did not smile; she did not defer; she insisted on talking about forbidden subjects, such as birth control. She kept them constantly on edge—not only by her attacks on conventional mores but by her attacks on their ignorance.

Her essay "Anarchism" demonstrates her strategy. She begins with a narrative frame situating the progressive point of view which her listeners might—with some previous faith in progress—be expected to share. Her version connects the older modernity of the Enlightenment to the modernist revolt against tradition. It is the Goldman version of Ezra Pound's dictum "make it new," and it suggests the way that early literary modernism was associated with a sense of the need for change.

> The history of human growth and development is at the same time the history of the terrible struggle of every new idea heralding the approach of a brighter dawn. In its tenacious hold on tradition, the Old has never hesitated to make use of the foulest and cruelest means to stay the advent of the New, in whatever form or period the latter may have asserted itself. Nor need we retrace our steps into the distant past to realize the enormity of opposition, difficulties, and hardships placed in the path of every progressive idea.[31]

What conspires against the progress which anarchy advocates? Ignorance. "Both the intelligent man and the ignorant mass judge not from a thorough knowledge of the subject, but either from hearsay or false interpretation" (49). Goldman did not allow her audience to be comfortably reasonable. If you knew little of anarchism, you had no excuse.

Goldman described the pedagogical scene of anarchism as a fight against ignorance. "How is the ordinary man to know that the most violent element in society is ignorance, that its power of destruction is the very thing anarchism is combating?" (49–50). Characterizing ignorance not as a lack but as a destructive force, Goldman makes anarchy a paradoxical kind of knowing—one which by its resistance to ignorance forces it into view, where it can be known, or seen as a willful not-knowing. Thus Goldman *resisted* the assumptions of the mass—that anarchy is violent, that anarchy is negativism. If anarchy is resistance in practice, it is also the way out of present impasses and into the future, because thinking provides a way to escape the constraints of ideology, to get out of the story. This practice of defiance and resistance in Goldman took the form not of resisting capitalists or presidents or priests but of resisting the most familiar, closely held of shibboleths—patriotism, chastity, motherhood. Patriotism is a superstition, she said: "the people at large are like children: an army and navy represents the people's toys."[32] Even though avant-garde poetry reflects similar anarchic attitudes and attacks on mass ignorance, the rhetoric of modernist poetics, hidden in its denial of rhetoricity, differs from Goldman. She took up a practice of revolutionary *instruction* through defiance and resistance.

Her rhetoric is not reformist or liberal feminist: Goldman did not work for equal rights. She acted as if she were equal; she embodied defiant equality. Her speech was a performance of equality. She upset her listeners' recourse to the conformities of gradual reform in American politics. Like Thoreau, she was against the vote, against majority rule, and called suffrage "the political superstition." "Anarchism . . . stands for direct action, the open defiance of, and resistance to, all laws and restrictions, economic, social, and moral. But defiance and resistance are illegal. Therein lies the salvation of man."[33]

Such an ideal of resistance to the law found its embodiment not only in Emma Goldman but in the recurring figure of the artist as criminal (from Villon to Rimbaud) that many modernists—Louise Bogan, for one—would endorse. Genet would perhaps understand this mounting of revolt without ramparts or barricades as *theater* like the performance mounted in the seventies by the Black Panthers, on which he reports: "Les Panthères vont s'employer à terroriser les maîtres, mais avec les seuls moyens dont ils disposent: la parade" ("The Panthers exert themselves to terrorize the masters, but with the only means at their command: the parade"). The emotional power of the spectacle of Emma Goldman similarly arose from a real risk of jail and violence, a real closeness to suffering and death. Genet's judgment of the effectiveness of the Black Panthers may serve as well for Goldman.

> Les Panthères allaient donc soit dans la folie, soit vers la métamorphose de la communauté noire, soit dans la mort ou en prison. Le résultat de l'entreprise fut tout cela, mais c'est la métamorphose qui l'emporta, de loin, sur le reste, et c'est pour ça qu'on peut dire que les Panthères ont vaincu grace à la poésie.[34]

> (The Panthers advanced, then, into madness, or toward the metamorphosis of the black community, or into death or prison. The result of the enterprise was all of that, but it was metamorphosis which prevailed over the rest, and it is for this reason that one can say that the Panthers overcame thanks to poetry.)

Did Goldman's exile not usher in the metamorphosis of artistic exile? What Goldman can remind us of is the instructional power of resistance, and how embodiment and incongruity—points at which a poetic may become rhetorical—are ways that poetry becomes political.

Her audiences came to count on her dramatic critique, her rhetorical promise to tell them what they did *not* want to hear, defying their mass desires. In Goldman's audience there was the double play of shock and recognition. The stitching together of anarchy with a foreign accent and the familiar American refrains from Emerson and Thoreau meant that her speech was always paradoxical. In the name of resistance she called up the familiar. As an act of defiance she carried on with a revolution already recognizable as American. Her anarchism became revolutionary as the police confronted the crowd, and as the papers unleashed their tirades. J. Edgar Hoover started his career with a raid on *Mother Earth*'s files and the prosecution of Goldman and Berkman. Roger Baldwin started the ACLU to defend the free-speech movement which coalesced around Goldman's lecture tours. Goldman's authority as an anarchist came not only from the victories for free speech but from the opposition. Her enduring effective-ness may be traced in the legacy of resistance which artists and writers have represented, a threat to authority written in the paranoia of Hoover's files. She left us with a community of advocates for free speech.

III

The question is how Goldman's "individual" self is related to this discourse. Is she just an apparition of the anarchic drama? Can the subject-in-crisis of this critical power be identified with the agents of democratic struggle? Can the "subject" of a discourse against totalitarian discourse be "different"—be, for example, female? Can the female subject, eliminated from conventions of subjectivity, be the subject of subversion, even of a subversion undoing humanistic constructions? And, finally, can the fan-tasies and utopias dreamed by such a subject be taken as serious programs?

These questions were already appropriate for the case of Emma Gold-man because the problem appeared, if in a form that was not quite post-modern, from the beginning of this century, with the advent of modernist literature and avant-garde texts. Jonathan Dollimore has argued that in-dividualism was associated with a "transgressive aesthetic" in the work of Oscar Wilde, associated with difference and with a radical separation from bourgeois propriety.[35] Dollimore is arguing that both postmodern decen-teredness and modernist depth go to make up the subject of late capitalism. "In Wilde's writing, individualism is less to do with a human essence, Arnold's inner condition, than a dynamic social potential, one which im-plies a radical possibility of freedom 'latent and potential in mankind gen-erally' " (27). Modernist writers fought for the literary freedom to "make it new" and endorsed the critique of the middle class. However, their politics did not necessarily support a better life for the oppressed; the operations of individualism need to be historically specified.

The subject of anarchism as Goldman evoked her resists the domi-nation of the monsters of authority—*religion*, "the dominion of darkness, the greatest obstacle to all progress"; *property*, "the dominion of man's needs, the denial of the right to satisfy his needs"; and *the state*—"the dominion of human conduct." Most of all, the individual must resist the ghosts of opinion, prejudice, and coercion that are embedded in thought itself. At the same time that she advocated self-consciousness, however, Goldman did not seem to distrust the ghosts in language that the symbolists were already aware of, and that the modernists were about to exorcize, together with romanticism, the hope for progress, the ideal of Emersonian individualism, and the naive belief that words could make a difference in the public sphere. What makes Goldman an anarchist rather than a transcendentalist is that she confronts the ghosts of past opinion in their living avatars—her internal struggle is projected upon the lecture stage and appears embodied in some of the resistant persons of her audience, most especially in the form of the police. This is not argument but theater. However, it is not entirely modernist precisely because it *is* Emersonian, pedagogical.

Goldman's free speech became a verbal symptom of that which violated respectability and propriety—the anarchy of free love—making the defenders of respectability emerge from their hiding places and appear in new guise, as policemen and enforcers. Sometimes the respectable emerged as allies instead. Louise Bryant (who later would go to Russia with John Reed) reported the events of Goldman's appearance in Portland, Oregon, in 1914 for the *Little Review*.[36] Goldman was arrested for distributing obscene literature (that is, pamphlets on birth control) despite the city's pride: "we have free speech in Portland." There was public outcry, but the "fair-minded" Judge Gatens dismissed the case. Bryant finds his remarks so "refreshing" that she quotes the judge:

> Now it seems to me that the trouble with our people today is that there is too much prudery. Ignorance and prudery are the millstones about the neck of progress. Everyone knows that. We are all shocked by many things publicly stated that we know privately ourselves, but we haven't got the nerve to get up and admit it; and when some person brings our attention to something we already know, we feign modesty and we feel that the public has been outraged and decency has been shocked when as a matter of fact we know all these things ourselves. (26)

In other words, Emma Goldman was not speaking to issues alien to American culture but to what "everyone knows." What Goldman insisted on was violating the gendered segregation of private and public; her speech about women's condition without birth control meant that repression which seemed to be only private would take its place on the public scaffold. Repression which seemed to be simply moral, a matter of individual belief rather than ideology, of free choice rather than law, was exposed by Goldman as a matter of violent public force, the violent force represented by the police and the agents who tried to silence her. As the judge's response suggests, her appeals to free speech and democratic law did not always fall on deaf ears. The spectacle of her daring attracted large crowds, and her confrontations over free speech left an enduring record. Her supporters included free-speech advocates such as William Marion Reedy of the St. Louis *Mirror* as well as the literary avant-garde reading the *Little Review*.[37]

Again and again Goldman worked against the opinions of her audience, live ghosts, who embodied a concrete array of prejudices and preconceptions which she could turn into paradox. She would make the hidden violence appear, all that is arbitrary and not a "natural law." "That governments do not maintain themselves through such harmonious factors is proven by the terrible array of violence, force, and coercion all governments use in order to live."[38]

And to the objection one might bring, that no one knows what "human nature" might mean, she responds, "With human nature caged in a narrow space, whipped daily into submission, how can we speak of its potentialities?" (62). Furthermore, though she seems by her stories to hold out an ideal future of harmony and unity, she gives us anarchy not so much as a story but as a *method*, a process of learning:

> Anarchism is not, as some may suppose, a theory of the future to be realized through divine inspiration. It is a living force in the affairs of our life, constantly creating new conditions. . . . Anarchism does not stand for military drill and uniformity; it does, however, stand for the spirit of revolt, in whatever form, against everything that hinders human growth. (63)

Goldman's dramatic attacks on the conventions of domestic morality figured forth a new woman, emblem of subversive desire, the free woman, subject of free love. This image of the passionate individual located excessive desire just where domestic discourse—and Freud—said it would be found: in the place of the woman. But Goldman did not respect the absolutes of gendered identity the way Hawthorne did and Freud seems to have. She did not separate sexuality and motherhood, or love and political work.

Even though, like many of the modernist writers, Goldman made free love a pivotal position for the attack on conventionality, she believed utterly in the importance of loving attachments and commitments to others. The intensity of her feelings for those she loved had nothing in common with later superficial versions of free love, such as the *Playboy* philosophy. In many ways her strong attachments were most of all maternal. She was a motherly woman, she said, and so did others: Ben Reitman called her "Mommy." But the maternal as exemplified by Goldman was not complicit with a patriarchal family structure but rather with woman as powerful. In 1935, when both were in their sixties, she wrote a birthday letter to her lifelong comrade Alexander Berkman. Even though she was at the time deeply involved in political activism in England, her letter expresses her sense that her most enduring loyalties were personal rather than political or institutional commitments: "I know of no other value, whether in people or achievements, than your presence in my life and the love and affection you have roused. . . . Yes, I believe my strongest and most compelling feeling for you is that of the mother" (*Nowhere at Home* 246–47).

This maternal attitude unites the personal and the political in Goldman's career. It shaped her work as a nurse, among prostitutes, in prison. It led her to take an intense interest in new kinds of schooling, including the Ferrer school. She advocated schools such as the "Modern School" in Paris, founded by anarchist Louise Michel, which would encourage the "free spontaneity" of the child, where "impressions of life will replace fastidious book-learning," for "discipline and restraint—are they not back of all the evils in the world?" (164–65). Such a school would also challenge the resistance of respectability to invention. The serious metaphor of motherhood guided her choice of *Mother Earth* as title for her anarchist magazine, which was, she and Berkman editorialized, "a child born of love" who must grow: "And it shall do all that as far as is in the power of its parents, whose main aim it has been to instill in their child the meaning of true love and harmony which grow out of universal parenthood."[39] The baby reproduces the mother; the baby is *Mother Earth*. This extension of the parental attitude to others was precisely what her anarchic community was about:

> That is the beauty of a universal baby; it is not dependent only on its parents. Because of that the parents are even more eager to care for it. True, the mother must forego the comforts of a home, exposing herself to many hardships while racing about the country, seeking new friends for her child. But love overcomes everything. Besides, when the mother can choose the father of her child, she need never fear to leave it to his care and affection. (2)

Does this story of motherly love and personal commitment reinforce the patriarchal ideology she worked so hard to attack? Is Goldman participating in the cultural imaginary, the fantasy of love, at the same time that she critiques woman's position? How might we talk about this doubleness? As Nancy Armstrong points out, the power of bourgeois domesticity is in the fantasy, not the facts of marriage or divorce. The disintegration of the modern family is accompanied by our ever-stronger preoccupation with imagining stories about the family drama.[40] However, Goldman's emphasis on the maternal analogy and the experience of individual love should not simply be dismissed as a remnant of bourgeois ideology.

Goldman's most controversial stands constitute a dismantling of the ideal woman as constructed by the nineteenth century, a shattering of the domestic space. Not only does she claim that chastity, far from being a virtue, is bad for women; she goes on to agree with Nietzsche that women endanger freedom by their support of religion, of war, and of the "fetich" of home. "Woman clings tenaciously to the home, to the power that holds her in bondage."[41] Goldman opposes women's suffrage, not only because she is in principle opposed to government by majority vote but also because "woman's narrow and purist attitude toward life makes her a greater danger to liberty wherever she has political power" (204). After a century of accumulating power around the virtues of chastity and purity, the angel in the house had gained clear dominion over not only private life but also cultural values. Goldman therefore argued against woman's emancipation because "as understood by the majority of its adherents and exponents, [it] is of too narrow a scope to permit the boundless love and ecstasy contained in the deep emotion of the true woman, sweetheart, mother, in freedom."[42] Free love for Goldman demonstrated freedom from internal tyrants. And at the same time, Goldman thought that the "new woman" was leaving love behind. "The demand for equal rights in every vocation of life is just and fair; but after all, the most vital right is the right to love and be loved" (224). Goldman's version of individualism does not envision personal isolation but the context of a community.

Goldman thought especially of the case of women when she argued that changing individual consciousness was more important than freedom from "external tyrannies": "the internal tyrants, far more harmful to life and growth—ethical and social conventions—were left to take care of themselves" (221). In this emphasis on the importance of individual consciousness, Goldman of course inherited the problems of the humanistic subject. Yet she insisted on passionate engagement—not the centered ego—as the basis of political discourse. Her sense of individualism may be continuous with the critical subjectivity Judith Newton attributes to contemporary feminism: "it was the grounding of insight in intimate personal experience that made critiques of 'objectivity' and analyses of the construction of the subject so passionately a matter of concern—it was our subjectivity after all! And it was our passion that put these matters first on the theoretical agenda."[43]

It is important to remember the ongoing historical connection between the avant-garde and anarchic individualism as communal politics. Alan Ritter argues that anarchy as a philosophical concept continues to offer the possibility of a "communal individuality."[44] Goldman thought of herself as belonging to the avant-garde, and to a politics that preceded and would outlive her own efforts:

> An avant-guard of many years of public activity? How discouraging. Yet if we consider that Anarchism is the only social theory that has undertaken to transvalue all values, we will see at once that the position of its exponents must needs remain that of the avant-guard, for some time to come.[45]

She was writing in her regular *Mother Earth* report of her tours, "Light and Shadows in the Life of an Avant-Guard": "The police, like the forest beasts, at the sight of blood become mad for more. Who but the avant-guard of Anarchism could be better prey? Anarchist meetings were closed, and Anarchist speakers suppressed. . . . The avant-guard, like the wicked, finds no rest" (384). Her wording suggests how she thought of herself as the subject of the avant-garde.

But the passionate woman is a particularly difficult figure for American politics to take seriously. By the time Goldman wrote her autobiography, in 1931, the split between the serious individual and the subject of love had grown so large that Goldman left much of her ten-year love affair with Ben Reitman out of her story. (And how do we take his calling her "Mommy"?) It was not that she worried about confirming that she had lived out the ideals of personal and sexual freedom, but that she feared the "pathologically curious reading public" would turn it into "a sensational sex story."[46] Goldman's love letters express her anguish over feeling "weak and dependent, clinging to the man, no matter how worthless and faithless he is." Candace Falk speculates that Goldman felt embarrassed at revealing herself overwhelmed and powerless with such feelings (4). Goldman had been party to the dismantling of sentimental power, party to the repudiation of the female psychology, but the critique turned into a denigration of the lover's discourse so pervasive that she feared it would extend to her own revelations.

Goldman occupies a discursive position that becomes impossible for literary modernism. Her political rhetoric conjoins anarchy and the sentimental. The revolutionary potential of a passionate appeal and the subversiveness of women are precisely what became too dangerous to countenance. Passion would appear as an embarrassment. Goldman was prosecuted and exported at the same time that this "foreign" element in American thought was being repressed and denied. Pretending that the sentimental appeal was merely a romantic, subjective rhetoric, critical modernism showed itself to be complicit with the larger cultural effort to deny the status of speaking subject to the groups Goldman addressed: women, foreigners, workers, the avant-garde. This walling off of literary innovation from progressive rhetoric, and not the sentimental, was reactionary.

If her language was not poetic, Goldman's story was nonetheless modernist in other ways. It was her gesture to repudiate what the "compact mass" would say, to counter authority, to resist in the name of an individualism which is not the productive and romantic ego but which is post-Freudian, shaped of civilization—an individualism which finds its authorship only in the structure of resistance.

That is, Goldman herself functions like a work of art, like a dramatic production, to educate and to teach anarchy as a semiotic principle—to teach the form of revolution in overthrowing the conventional. In becoming the story rather than writing it, she takes up the position of the woman in modernism, within the spectacle, rather than removing herself to the impersonal distance of the author. Hence the story she *is* produces history in its address, calling up the subject of anarchy to carry on with critical thought, but also calling up the dramatic others, the actors of history: the rescuers of free speech such as Roger Baldwin and the persecutors such as J. Edgar Hoover.

Goldman's life is exemplary. But isn't an exemplary life itself another kind of narrative that is not innocent? What are we to think of this individualism, the person-centered story which Goldman herself made of anarchy? Stories of individual lives serve at once to organize discourse so that individuals rather than story-telling mechanisms seem to be the cause of events, and to appeal to identification, a rhetorical figure of coherence bodied forth, as if organic, in the image of a bodied subject.[47]

The imaginary coherence of this figure has much to do with the ideology of American individualism, grounding free enterprise in the practice of self-reliance. But the critique of individual stories may not always be politically progressive: in American history, the position of the free individual has also provided moments of resistance, a place for anarchy to enter into discourse. That is, the story of the individual locates a position from which the illegitimacy of transparent histories can become visible. Goldman as individual refuses the allegorization of the female body—she is a "foreign body," setting up an ambiguous dissonance in the smooth separations of the two modernisms, her unsmiling visage representing a catastrophe of challenge to the commodified woman as to the commodified work of art.

Modernism's long critique of the subject, from Freud and Nietzsche to postmodernism, has not functioned altogether innocently, for it has not worked simply to expose the falseness of romantic individualism, but also to cut off discourse about personal experience from politics and history. In effect, first the political was made personal, feminizing the position of the literary, and then the personal was reduced to the objectivity of the text. When W. K. Wimsatt and Monroe C. Beardsley collaborated on "The Intentional Fallacy" in 1946, they said: "the design or intention of the author is neither available nor desirable as a standard for judging the success of a work of literary art."[48] They wanted to segregate literature from biography.

Omitting the authorial subject from both literary and critical texts so that the close reading of the text would provide objective warrant for the inferences of criticism, the new criticism replaced the individualism of the romantic author with the singular, organic body of the literary text, which, if it is "successful," springs into eternal life as a poem. But "The Intentional

Fallacy" was not about cleaning up the logic of literature so much as it was about legislating discourse so that certain generic intersections became invisible and unspeakable. Literature—and criticism—repressed ideology (and the power which canonized certain authors) by disconnecting from the subject. Separating literature from biography, the new criticism had the effect of eliminating great numbers of authors, especially women writers, from the canon. Close reading could afford the time to scrutinize only a carefully limited selection of texts, and women's texts—other texts—seemed interesting only for biographical or historical reasons. Under the regime of the new criticism, Goldman's connections to literary history became unspeakable, and forgotten.

But if the subject is problematic and her story incredible, what good is a revolutionary woman? What can we make of women who appear as strong characters with stories to tell? Some continue to insist that, whatever else it is, Goldman's *Living My Life* is not literature, that we need not give "Anarchy" a close reading. The addition of semiotics and rhetoric to poetics can still help us in departments of literature to talk about the intersection of revolution and poetic language. But then, should we not go on to think about the story and the individual not only as modes of identification which are suspiciously regressive but also as a mode of resistance? *Living My Life* was the title, after all, of the anarchist's story.

Goldman wanted to present the figure of a strong, revolutionary woman whose power exemplified the possibility of such an individual. That is, she wanted to demonstrate the power of the private sphere, the speaking individual, to affect public events. Her argument for the social significance of the drama could as well be extended to her own life: "It is the purpose of the modern drama to rouse the consciousness of the oppressed."[49] What Goldman demonstrates is what happens to literature when the boundaries drawn between public and private, history and literature, are crossed—why modernism might both encourage anarchy and deny that literature has anything to do with politics. In her essay on Yeats and the Irish drama, Goldman rejects the modernist apolitical stance, the repudiation of "any implication of a social character" which she thinks Yeats himself might make, and asserts: " 'Where There Is Nothing' is of great social significance, deeply revolutionary in the sense that it carries the message of the destruction of every institution—State, Property, and Church—that enslaves humanity."[50] Goldman claimed that "the drama is the vehicle which is really making history, disseminating radical thought in ranks not otherwise to be reached" (243). That is, the drama, like Goldman herself, brought anarchy to the middle class.

Emma Goldman, the very person who clearly articulated both the challenge of modernist literature against the middle class and the challenge of modernity against tradition, thereby made a connection between style and politics that would be severed in the name of literariness. The anarchy of style would not lead to a revolution, would become safe, because it was separated from the question of the gendered individual. The narrative of the federal bureau versus the subversive was installed, and literature retreated to the English department to hide out. J. Edgar Hoover stayed here, and Emma Goldman was deported.

Goldman liked to enunciate the final, fearful question about anarchy which one might ask, one in her American audience not quite willing to embrace ignorance but worried about thinking as well. That question about anarchy was: "Will it not lead to a revolution?" Her answer came as a paradoxical reassurance: "Indeed, it will."[51] If the audience was not reassured, it had not yet understood.

Jouissance and the Sentimental Daughter
Edna St. Vincent Millay

The effect was at first, to embarrass
me: it was a little as if a Shakespearean actor were suddenly, off the
stage, to begin expressing private
emotions with the intonations of the
play.

—EDMUND WILSON,
I THOUGHT OF DAISY[1]

Long ago, when I was mooning and
dreaming through the pigtail period,
I used to think how fine it would be
to be the greatest woman poet since
Sappho. The audacity of youth—the
near-childhood—would have scorned
any lower goal. . . .

—HARRIET MONROE,
"COMMENT: EDNA ST.
VINCENT MILLAY"[2]

I

The story of growing up, as
Freud tells it, does not set forth a clear
sequence for women to advance to
maturity. Teresa de Lauretis gives us
a version of the tale which underlines
its difficulties: the girl must accept
sacrifice, a lack of power, and passivity, because growing up means becoming the sacrificial mother.[3]

The contradictory versions of the
Mother we have inherited from the
nineteenth century at once give wom-
en intolerable power (from her symbiotic relationship with the child)
and a secondary, almost obliterated
place in the power structure of the
culture, as represented, importantly,
by Freud's handling of the Oedipal
narration. Monique Plaza, among others, argues that Freud's Oedipal dra-
ma must be seen in the context of the history of Motherhood.[4]

Millay's poetry is caught up in these issues.[5] For her (passive?) repetition of conventional literary forms, the former gestures of power, is
somehow feminine, slavish. When the modern father abandons his rituals,

religions, perhaps the departure of the father leaves the structure to be maintained by the mother; the pain, then, of submitting to a love sonnet is the pain of the powerless, of repeating an ideological surrender to that which gives no power, except over the child. As Sara Ruddick says in her essay "Maternal Thinking," "Central to our experience of our mothers and our mothering is a poignant conjunction of power and powerlessness."[6]

Millay's poetry frequently seems to lure us into an easy, symbiotic merging, an identification. This identification may be usefully seen (as Teresa de Lauretis suggests) in terms of a narrative rather than the specular image.[7] Freud conceived of masculinity and femininity in the narrative development of the Oedipal drama, and only secondarily in visual terms. The reader, like the spectator of the cinema, may take up the position of the subject constructed by the drama. For a female subject, however, as for a female spectator, this position is crossed by contradiction.

One of the problems for readers of Millay is that there is a constant obtrusive slippage about the position of the subject, a slippage which threatens to violate modernist conventions of literariness. Do we see the "I" of Millay's poems as linguistic, objectified, dramatized? A persona? Or as a self, a subject, a proper (historical) person? The Poet? The Poetess? The object of fame? Millay? Of course all of these questions are bound up in various ways with the question of gender: is the subject of the poem male or female, masculine or feminine? Millay's refusal to be "consistent" in developing some universal perspective, an attitude, or even a metapoetic (about which modernist critics of Millay complained) may force her reader to abandon differences, to take up the position of the spectator at the drama of character. Then Millay's poetry becomes a gesture of definition enacted at the margins of identity, and the self she does and does not define— does and does not seduce us into taking as the *subject* of poetry—is the borderline character of the adolescent, not Woman as Poet but the Girl, whose chief subject is love.

Are there no grown-up pleasures in the texts of Edna St. Vincent Millay? Can we only resist as we read her, more firmly than she resists in the drama of her theatrical poetry, an embarrassing, seductive—annihilating—identification, an imaginary coalescence with the poet, or Art, or the Other? Or as she is mastered by the mastery of form, submitting deliciously to be consumed by the convention, the language of poetic traditions, do we too abandon ourselves to the clever, childish play? If so, if we become thus un-self-conscious, there are moments then of public exposure, when the spectacle is penetrated by a refusal (which may itself be phallic, patriarchal, perhaps a revised Puritanism) demanding that such play at least be new, productive, intellectual—profitable. We wish above all not to be embarrassed—not to be immature or "sentimental."

This context helps us to understand the antagonistic critical reception given Millay as she grew in popularity during the thirties and forties. John Crowe Ransom criticized Millay for her sensibility: "Miss Millay is rarely and barely very intellectual, and I think everybody knows it."[8] Allen Tate said, "Miss Millay's success with stock symbolism is precariously won; I have said that she is not an intellect but a sensibility: if she were capable of a profound analysis of her imagery, she might not use it."[9] And Cleanth Brooks simply picked up Ransom's theme to conclude that Millay was "immature." She failed to be a major poet because she lacked irony: "Miss Millay has not grown up."[10]

In the age of Eliot, defined by the failure of relationship and the antiheroics of the poetic loner, Millay was writing most of all about love, and her sentimental subject was only the beginning of her crime: more than that, she was writing in a way that is easily understood, that invites the reader in, that makes community with the reader and tries to heal alienation. Millay was of course flagrantly engaged during the twenties in the bohemian leftish lifestyle of Greenwich Village, with its tenets of free love and support for the working masses. She worked on behalf of Sacco-Vanzetti and chaired the committee to raise funds for Emma Goldman's autobiography. But her radical lifestyle never put off her readers the way a radical poetics might have.

Millay does not practice the modernist anarchy of style: her poetics are founded on commonality. She may shock her audience, but she does not separate herself from them. The accessibility of her work seems from the beginning of her career more important to her readers than her bohemian attitudes. In Millay, we see that the gestures of social revolt don't always sever ties. She could write "My candle burns at both ends" and take a flippant attitude about her lovers, but the fact that she did it in sonnet form kept her credentials as the poetess of the American middle-class consensus in order. The epithet *bourgeois* or *middle-class* in the mouth of a modernist critic was meant to be as devastating as the charge of sentimentality. But some continuity with the middle class was for Millay as for many other women writers a prerequisite for maintaining a woman's tradition and for creating a community with women readers.

In the following pages, I will look at a couple of poems by Millay to see how she negotiates the contradictory demands of a modernist art and the appeal to a powerful community of readers. As we talk about the large impact of modernism and its elevation of intellect over sensibility, let us not forget the small numbers of its audience. Millay had a popular and sweeping success as a "poetess." Her sentimental readers were in the majority, and they recognized her immediately. I found an early piece on Millay appearing in a 1922 volume called *Flames of Faith*, written by a New York evangelist popularly known as "Wild Bill" Stidger.[11] Remembering the long-term connections between revivalism and feminine rhetoric, I was not so completely surprised, even though Millay's reputation as a "new woman" would seem contrary to attracting such readers. Stidger is responding to Millay's sentimental rhetoric, which he reads as an expression of feeling: "Whose heart will not be won by these lines," he asks by way of introduction to Millay's little poem "Tavern" (48).

A poem about a tavern may not seem a likely topic for the sentimental reader. But this one is about a congeniality that is a remembrance of motherly hospitality. The tradition may go all the way back to matrilineal Celtic materials; in any event it takes advantage of the fairy-tale tradition which identifies "gray eyes" with the "old people." It goes like this:

> I'll keep a little tavern
>   Below the hill's high crest,
> Wherein all gray-eyed people
>   May set them down and rest.
>
> There shall be plates a-plenty
>   And mugs to melt the chill
> Of all the gray-eyed people
>   Who happen up the hill.
>
> There sound will sleep the traveler,
>   And dream his journey's end,
> But I will rouse at midnight
>   The falling fire to tend.
>
> Aye, 'tis a curious fancy,
>   But all the good I know
> Was taught me out of two gray eyes
>   A long time ago.

Stidger goes on to say, after quoting as well from "God's World" ("O World, I cannot hold thee close enough!") and "Renascence" ("The soul can split the sky in two, / And let the face of God shine through!"), that "her first message was one of a great, groping sense of suffering. So men and women sing who have lost some loved one" (49).

The loss, one might argue, is a loss of female community itself, although the community of suffering and of loss is not simply female. It is the loss of a hearth which is tended. By Millay's time, the codes of pathetic appeals, together with the literary inheritance from sentimental narratives which had been associated with female writing, were under attack by literary modernists. Millay's "Tavern" is about a love, but the beloved of the "gray eyes" is more motherly than romantic, and the speaker's response to loss is to found a hospitable retreat, not to withdraw from sociability.

What we have in Millay is in part at least a writing which unites rhetoric and poetics, appeals to conventional ideas and appeals to feeling. Speaking from a place of authority which is female, Millay refuses the separation of the subject from social convention. Her work is at once personal and conventional. It's easy enough to call it sentimental.

Modernism has given us an ideal of an impersonal, serious art, a poetics severely separated from rhetoric. This modernist poetics is indeed at odds with Millay's poetic practices, as with any text which fails sufficiently to separate itself from the personal or from the drama of its performance. Modernism assumes an estrangement between the poem and the reader—difference, not familiarity. Exile, not community.

The marginal subject has difficulty participating in the modernist revolution of poetic language. As we see with Millay, the marginal speaker must do something familiar. Difference is different if you're in danger of never being listened to in the first place. Millay's poetry may be read rhetorically, as an argument that she is to be considered a real poet. However, the very fact that this persuasive appeal is going on keeps the poetry from being read as poetry, as a modernist text. Because she is accessible to readers, she is "marginal" only in a special sense, though it is a sense that she cared about very much. Millay is only as marginal as her readers—all the readers of *Vanity Fair* and *Ladies' Home Journal*, and all the high-school students who have put her poems to memory, and the former students who can recite them still, generations later. Because this powerful community, influenced by women as readers (and teachers), is invisible to literary criticism, it does indeed inflict on Millay a literary marginality. To this day she seems not quite interesting, not really subversive, her passion perhaps even a little nauseating to the ironic reader.

In spite of the reputation for rebellious marginality she acquired by her penchant for dramatic gesture, then, Millay wrote poetry which appears to do the opposite of demonstrating female difference. Far from subverting the masculine tradition by using poetic conventions in new ways, in the very age of "make it new," Millay was writing sonnets. She subverts male modernism by appropriating conventional male poetics from a more classic past, speaking a colonized discourse.

Does Millay's rhetoric betray feminine discourse, then? More popular and more widely read to this day than Pound or Williams (but not, of course, by readers who can be classed as "literary"), Millay disappears into the crowd. She writes within conventions so much a part of the dominant culture that she is easily assimilated by it. Millay's poetry celebrates the failure of independence even in its defiance, seeming to advocate a return to the domain of the natural, the simple, the pastoral order—to the myth which joins Christian sacrifice to nature in the figure of the mother. Thus Millay uses the rhetoric of sentiment on behalf of aspirations admittedly bourgeois, to a kind of power women were already used to claiming in the early years of this century—a power over human feelings and community which, in fact, modernist male writers rejected as they rejected all rhetorical and political ambitions for poetry. Readers could recognize immediately that she speaks as a poet in favor of interests long supported by the middle class—interests of importance to women because they had been established through the whole of the nineteenth century by female writers as the best means for women to exercise power, as Tompkins's work on *Uncle Tom's Cabin* demonstrates.[12] The alienation of affection and the personal which was modernism was bound to reject Millay, as it rejected in a larger sense the claims of women and sentimentalism to power and value.

Millay confronts the modernist tradition over the influential poetry of Charles Baudelaire, whose *Flowers of Evil* she helped to translate. If we look at how Millay reads Baudelaire, a regular pattern of choices emerges which I think can be categorized as sentimental, and which may also be characteristic of writing which is very concerned with audience identification. The fact that she is a woman may have shaped her translation, for she is very much concerned with creating communal understanding, not an aesthetic object. We can usefully contrast her translation with a recent one by Richard Howard which is very different in effect, though not necessarily closer to the literal, and more distant in form. Here is the original poem:

> Sous les ifs noirs qui les abritent
> Les hiboux se tiennent rangés,
> Ainsi que des dieux étrangers,
> Dardant leur oeil rouge. Ils méditent.
>
> Sans remuer ils se tiendront
> Jusqu'à l'heure mélancolique
> Où, poussant le soleil oblique,
> Les ténèbres s'établiront.
>
> Leur attitude au sage enseigne
> Qu'il faut en ce monde qu'il craigne
> Le tumulte et le mouvement;
>
> L'homme ivre d'une ombre qui passe
> Porte toujours le châtiment
> D'avoir voulu changer de place.[13]

Richard Howard's translation:

> Under black yews that protect them
>   the owls perch in a row
> like alien gods whose red eyes
>   glitter. They meditate.

> Petrified, they will perch there till
>   the melancholy hour
> when the slanting sun is ousted,
>   and darkness settles down.
>
> From their posture, the wise
> Learn to shun, in this world at least,
>   motion and commotion;
>
> impassioned by passing shadows,
>   man will always be scourged
> for trying to change his place.[14]

Edna St. Vincent Millay's translation:

> The owls that roost in the black yew
> Along one limb in solemn state,
> And with a red eye look you through,
> Are eastern gods; they meditate.
>
> No feather stirs on them, not one,
> Until that melancholy hour
> When night, supplanting the weak sun,
> Resumes her interrupted power.
>
> Their attitude instructs the wise
> To shun all action, all surprise.
> Suppose there passed a lovely face,—
>
> Who even longs to follow it,
> Must feel for ever the disgrace
> Of having all but moved a bit.[15]

There are two central contrasts between the Millay translation and the Howard translation to which I would like to call attention.

First, Millay's work demonstrates a very different relationship to form. She maintains the eight-syllable lines and the rhyme scheme, as if an attention to that structural convention would also come closer to translating the voice of Baudelaire's poem. That is, she keeps the connection to traditional forms rather than emphasizing the modernity of Baudelaire's poem. Howard abandons the rhyme and interposes six-syllable lines— shortening them enough to threaten making the poem more slight than it is, and losing the poem's abbreviation of the sonnet form.

But the second contrast is the more startling. While Howard makes a translation that is fairly close to the literal, Millay introduces vocabulary which might be called "stock symbolism"—several words which by their combined effect, I would argue, move the poem out of the category of symbolist poetry and make it popularly romantic—or "sentimental," if you will. Her use of the "you" in the third line sets up a speaker of the poem who has a casual, personal relationship to the reader—the opposite of the distanced, impersonal speaker of the symbolist poem, the "I" who is an "other." She overspecifies: the strange, foreign, or alien gods become "eastern." Again it is, perhaps, a move to make the reader more comfortable, the kind of specifying a storyteller might invent, and it makes the poem seem to be about some familiar romantic themes. She adds a personification of night in the second stanza, surely a humanizing touch Baudelaire would not have considered. Finally, and most strikingly, she changes Baudelaire's "ombre" or shadow to "a lovely face," so that it is no longer the mysterious, multiple, undecidable reference to the other but specifically a reference to a love affair with a woman.

Owls, then, in Millay's version, tend to remind us of the opposition of love and reason, as of male and female. In Baudelaire's poem, the owl as text or word seems to generate something else which is mysterious, nonverbal, intoxicating, absent—the very lack pursued by desire. The female is entirely repressed. What Millay does is to reinsert the female into the text. This makes the absence or lack seem conventional, familiar. Instead of writing a new word or rupturing the language, she makes Baudelaire seem part of a known history. There are relations, connections. We all share the same story. The motive is communal, the opposite of a making strange, or defamiliarization. The poem becomes more rhetorical, less poetic. Baudelaire's poem marks difference; Millay's rewriting works against alienation. This working toward the remembrance of love and loss is, in fact, likely to be one of the very qualities that seem negative about writing we call sentimental. Baudelaire is practicing another kind of poetics, decidedly not personal, undermining convention. No maternal connections appear in the poem. Baudelaire's poem mystifies and depersonalizes the repression of the feminine.

How are we to judge Millay's translation? A contradictory response by the reader may be characteristic of the legacy of modernism. We will not recognize as legitimate or serious either the pathetic appeal to feelings, love stories, or the conventionality of images drawn from the rhetorical stockpile. Yet the magic of authority, of the mastery over literary forms, depends upon being recognized as some kind of conventional speaker, within the context of a discourse. Marginal writers have trouble with authority in their writing. Millay, marginal as a woman poet in the age of modernism, writes her own authorship into her poems as the speaker of a community-making creation, daughter of a motherly tradition. It is a stance of contradiction, including her in the readership of women as it excludes her from the critics.

The very gesture of hospitality, inviting the reader to join her, inscribes the female in Millay's text and marks her poetry as unacceptable for male modernist critics. And as literary readers we are forced to reject the female or the literary.

Millay lets us see our readerly dilemma. We can be cold and lonesome critics, or we can join in the circle where "There will be plates a-plenty / And mugs to melt the chill." Tough choice. Maybe instead we should reopen the question of the sentimental.

II

Although the differences between Julia Kristeva and other French feminists such as Hélène Cixous and Luce Irigaray are significant, they reflect a similar hope of joining feminism and the avant-garde in a literary practice which would rupture the phallogocentricity of language from within the discourse of the Western tradition. The historical reading it might receive, however, makes a difference in the kind of rupture and renewal which may be effected by women's writing. In the twenties, the question of whether to "make it new" by writing in free verse and abandoning traditional forms did not simply involve women writers in a debate about new and old *forms*. The choice of form, convention, and style had consequences that were ideological and that propelled women writers into professional impasses at all levels of their work.

The impasse which confronts us now has to do with the separation of literary considerations from the devaluing of women's history. It is important to keep before us the problem of how such evaluations interact with ideology and the history of gendering. Thus Earl Rovit, writing in 1980, is not helpful even though he aims to call attention to "Our Lady-Poets of the Twenties."[16] He seems, in fact, to blame feminist criticism for their neglect: "Current evaluation has condescended egregiously to these women, grossly overrating them by sentimental standards which patronize or upbraid them for their failures to incarnate the feministic consciousness that today's militants require as the sole token of female integrity" (72).

The phenomenon addressed by Showalter in her review article "Critical Cross-Dressing" is very "interesting" to us as women.[17] After years of being marginal, we find marginality in style; after the pain of difference we hear difference itself valorized. Liminal, split, founded on the personal as political and so on contradiction, the female subject is because of these one-time shameful flaws now the very model of subjectivity. Feminist criticism seems the very model of criticism—for many male critics now—offering, as Showalter says, "the mixture of theoretical sophistication with the sort of effective political engagment they have been calling for in their own critical spheres" (117).

But Showalter raises important questions: "Is male feminism a form of critical cross-dressing, a fashion risk of the 1980's that is both radical chic and power play? Or is it the result of a genuine shift in critical, cultural, and sexual paradigms? . . . What is the sudden cultural appeal of serious female impersonation?" (120). What has warranted this feminist discourse—does the warrant include the female subject? Teresa de Lauretis has asked us to remember that the story of female subjectivity is a history of contradiction; that what we mean by woman must be referred to cultural codes which mark the private body, specifying sexual identity, in the flesh, as part of the public, feminine self. The marked and contradictory female subject enters history as an ongoing experience which is political. What de Lauretis would have us remember is the female experience of power.[18]

If a "fantasy of power" is the repressed content of women's writing, then we ought perhaps to look at a critical response such as Ransom's for its corresponding denials. Freud limits the wishes of women to erotic longings. Ransom allows us "sensibility." Women should be interested only in feelings or love, not the intellect. But, as Barthes says, "love falls outside of *interesting* time; no historical, polemical meaning can be given to it; it is in this that it is obscene."[19] Making herself a poetess of love, Millay took up a position which would not be interesting and which, indeed, would take on a certain obscenity.

As Barthes signaled, the figures which make up the lover's discourse are not connected by plot—"interesting" or historical time defines the love story from outside it, so that the lover's discourse is made up of figures which must be recuperated by the master narrative. These figures of love— these lyric moments—appear then as episodes of the imaginary, something to be gotten over, grown out of. They are the figures of a discourse without warrant:

> the lover's discourse is today *of an extreme solitude*. This discourse is spoken, perhaps, by thousands of subjects (who knows?), but warranted by no one; it is completely forsaken by the surrounding languages: ignored, disparaged, or derided by them, severed not only from authority but also from the mechanisms of authority (sciences, techniques, arts). Once a discourse is thus driven by its own momentum into the backwater of the "unreal," exiled from all gregarity, it has no recourse but to become the site, however exiguous, of an *affirmation*. (1)

The figures of love in Barthes have some qualities of the Lacanian "imaginary," articulated by the master codes of history, a symbolic order, but they partake as well of the Kristevan semiotic, that motility which is before meaning. Sensibility inhabits the figure. Jane Gallop has already looked at some of the difficulties presented by the differences between the Kristevan "semiotic" and the Lacanian "imaginary," and by our rejecting stance toward the imaginary: "The symbolic is politically healthy; the imaginary is regressive. . . . Since the imaginary embodies, fleshes out the skeletal symbolic, it is possible to see the Lacanian devaluation of the imaginary as related to a hatred of the flesh, of woman and of pleasure."[20] This devaluation of the imaginary in the name of history may also imply a refusal to recognize the conventional power of the feminine, love, the psyche, the sentimental. It is a refusal to recognize that these very categories are not timeless but the creations of the time-bound. Barthes, like Ransom, inhabits modernity, and so to him the relentless renewal of intellectual novelty appears as the master narrative of historical time.

A modern woman poet could not be a woman poet without speaking a discourse which would violate the unconventionality of modernism and seem politically regressive. Edna St. Vincent Millay did not appear to understand these rules; what she conceived as her task was not to create ex nihilo but to recuperate a feminine tradition, as her "Dirge without Music" affirms:

> I am not resigned to the shutting away of loving hearts in the hard ground.
> So it is, and so it will be, for so it has been, time out of mind:
> Into the darkness they go, the wise and the lovely. Crowned
> With lilies and with laurel they go; but I am not resigned.

Karl Shapiro's review of Millay's poetry shows us the critical refusal:

> The poems have an intimacy which makes the reader recoil, even if he is susceptible to this flirtation. What is worse, it is the intimacy of the actress and (off-stage) the *femme fatale*. All this has been said before, and it is said best in the poems. The center of her experience is love, but it is the most desperately middleclass love poetry one can imagine, with neither rough-and-tumble nor courtliness nor high sacrifice. But it rings so true—that makes it worse—and it is so well said, with all its horrid mannerisms; it is such a parody of the great love poets that one is dissolved in tears.[21]

Like the rebellious Jo in *Little Women*, Millay does not escape the sentimental plot.[22] Millay's boyish posturing as "Vincent" scarcely disguises her girlish allegiances to a world governed by women, especially the mother, and her mastery of traditional male literary forms at the historical moment of modernism serves only to put her into a tradition which has lost its cultural endorsement, now become the genteel codes of women writing for women. Ransom says Millay is "the best of the poets who are 'popular' and loved by Circles, Leagues, Lyceums, and Round Tables," and Delmore Schwartz echoes the horror of such fame: "The late John Wheelwright remarked that Miss Millay had sold free love to the women's clubs."[23]

But visibility with the women's clubs was precisely what Millay, "greatest woman poet since Sappho," needed to accomplish. Harriet Monroe's unusually gushy accolade only underscores the great gap between Sappho and any modern poetic tradition for women. As Susan Gubar has suggested, the influence of Sappho on modernist women shows their need for precursors, some kind of literary ancestry, a "fantastic collaboration" with a missing past.[24]

How does one grow up to be a woman and a poet? What kind of transformation or conversion is required? What is the female version of the plot? The famous poem which won Millay a place as "poet" with her first publication (perhaps too soon) is a liminal narrative of rebirth, "Renascence" (3). It is a poem of adolescence, but it is also a narrative which announces the major issues of Millay's future poetry, the issues of separation and identity.

In "Renascence," the speaker, in what begins as a kind of romantic experience with nature, is soon overwhelmed by the natural intimacy. The encounter makes the speaker recoil, leads to burial in a womb/tomb, and the rebirth of the subject involves an escape from an engulfing, undefined female body, as from the immersion (underground) in nature. The anxiety of influence is not Oedipal but is related to the ambivalence of being a mother's daughter. We may read such a plot again and again in Millay's poetry, for it involves her historical encounter with the difficulty of the woman as poet. The particularity of the poem's speaker is overwhelmed by the scene of poetry. The imaginary figure of the cultural Feminine (Mother, Nature, Sympathy) looms threateningly over the girlish hyperbole, transforming the childish excesses, the imitations and the mimes, into the oracular musings of a Goddess, Lover of Art, Poetess.[25]

What appears in this poem as a private encounter with the transcendental turns out to represent public events, for the poem tells the story of the same capture by an ideology which equated Woman/Other/Nature/Poetry and sometimes God which was Millay's fate from the moment of that poem's publication in the 1912 *Lyric Year*, with its attendant "discovery" of her, and the publicity's ensuing creation of her image as the American Poetess. Millay's great success with this poem, making the rest of her career seem an anticlimax, came in part because the poem fit the hopes of middle-class readers. But can a woman poet afford to reject precursors when her struggle is all toward entering the lineage of poets? And, notoriously, the woman's plot does not sever maternal connections.

What is left over from "Renascence" once we have acknowledged the familiar (frequently anthologized) comforts of what appears to be a feminized version of transcendental resurrections? There is, perhaps, a *differ-ence*, something besides the threats and reassurances of inspiring verse. The Oedipal struggle of child and parent is translated into several regis-ters—the self and Mother Nature, the sinner and God, the poet and ro-mantic precursors—and at every level the seductions of identification contend against successful separation. The *difference* of "Renascence" as it enters literary history is a failure to become fully "different" or reborn.

The plot of "Renascence" engages the speaker of the poem in a death and rebirth which may be read in Oedipal terms, as a crisis in the rela-tionship of a child to a maternal principle. However, the daughter/poet of "Renascence" cannot simply solve the problem of identity by separating from the other. From the beginning of the poem, the reciprocity of speaker and world is both threatening and necessary, an enclosure of the senses, immediate. The circular boundary of the horizon is also a temporal return "Back to where I'd started from," to a womblike enclosure. Distance be-tween self and the world collapses—"things seemed so small," even the distance to the sky, "I see the top" and "reaching up my hand to try, / I screamed, to feel it touch the sky."

Critical to Millay's struggle in "Renascence" is an ambiguity about the gender of the Other. She undergoes what seems at first to be a Leda-like rape by the Infinite: "I screamed, and—lo!—Infinity / Came down and settled over me." But in the middle, the overwhelming is an imaginary identification with an Other which, rather than violently establishing dif-ference, enforces sameness, a joining to the Other (a mother?) which at once defines her and forces her knowledge of a universal poisonous (or poisoned?) wound. The encounter suggests the mirror stage in its visual mode of identification:

> And, pressing of the Undefined
> The definition on my mind,
> Held up before my eyes a glass
> Through which my shrinking sight did pass

The Universe is "cleft to the core," not phallic, and the "undefined" is like a great female body of the Mother. The self's return is not to the breast, however, but to a "great wound" she must suck (the vagina? the place of the female "castration"?):

> The Universe, cleft to the core
> Lay open to my probing sense
> That, sickening, I would fain pluck thence
> But could not,—nay! but needs must suck
> At the great wound, and could not pluck

> My lips away till I had drawn
> All venom out.—Ah fearful pawn:
> For my omniscience paid I toll
> In infinite remorse of soul.

The sucking at the wound is an identifying with pain—self as suffering and compassion, a universal sympathy: "All sin was of my sinning, all / Atoning mine, and mine the gall / Of all regret." The other side of the sentimental promise appears here—the reminder that the pleasures of the ecstatic and the abject are akin, perhaps even incestuous. The speaker's omniscience is the opposite of a differentiated and mediated selfhood. It is an "Atoning" or "At-one-ing" which makes castration the universal principal. There is no "masculine," or "symbolic" order, no limit, no finite, no mediation.

The look of the other constructs a self with a wound, a lack: it is the recognition scene of the sentimental.

> A man was starving in Capri;
> He moved his eyes and looked at me;
> I felt his gaze, I heard his moan,
> And knew his hunger as my own.

This scene of sympathetic identification has a long literary history, and in particular a strong connection with women's literature, because it is the very type of the sentimental moment. It has the chief characteristics described, for example, by R. F. Brissenden in his work on the sentimental novel.[26] The encounter resembles the sympathetic pause of the sentimental traveler to be found even in Wordsworth, but it is an emotional witnessing which the modernists rejected. And we ourselves, postmodern readers, perhaps feminists, feel uneasy about this familiar scene. The site of recognition, where lack appears, is also the site of what Ransom calls "the limitation of Miss Millay. . . . her lack of intellectual interest, or masculinity." This lack is not just "feminine" for him but is connected to the sentimental:

> I used a conventional symbol, which I hope was not objectionable, when I phrased this lack of hers: deficiency in masculinity. It is true that some male poets are about as deficient; not necessarily that they are undeveloped intellectually, but that they conceive poetry as a sentimental or feminine exercise. Not deficient in it are some female poets, I suppose, like Miss Marianne Moore.[27]

But in "Renascence," the speaker rejects the encounter with suffering and lack. (Millay thought she was rebelling against the sentimental with her entire career.) However, her efforts to escape the confinement of the feminine all seem to entail her abject return. The maternal moment of omniscience brings contact with the horrible, the abject, the wounded, the suffering. Why would anyone want to have anything to do with the Infinite (or any other Other) after such an experience? Indeed, in Millay's story, the weight of it at last crushes the speaker down into the grave, exactly where she longed to be. However, this "death" (like her rebirth) does not involve rejecting the earth, passivity, or Mother. It is only then (her soul having fled) that she receives the kinds of motherly attention a child might wish for:

> Deep in the earth I rested now.
> Cool is its hand upon the brow
> And soft its breast beneath the head
> Of one who is so gladly dead.

This retreat to the womb/tomb is what makes sound and life desirable again. "A grave is such a quiet place"—and, as the calling up of Marvell's line reminds us, also a place where none embrace. It is a retreat from desire itself, a withdrawal into *aphanisis* which might be associated with the feminine.[28] Again, the plot is from one angle familiar enough—death reminds us how good it is to be alive (and when it is too late we will desire): "I would I were alive again / To kiss the fingers of the rain." The "solution" to the death of desire here appears to be a kind of nostalgia, like the plot of *Our Town* or *It's a Wonderful Life* in miniature. The speaker turns from a horror of being touched to embracing the world, from an identification with all suffering and all lack to—what? An acceptance of suffering? Or the recognition of what is missing, the wounding—to an assumption of lack? The turn and rebirth of Millay's poem may dramatize a questionable *difference*. The abject and the ecstatic seem here to be close, two versions of the same marginal relationship to the world, to the Other. The poem excludes figuration as it allegorizes the process of birth/rebirth on the analogy of mother/Nature. The earth does not provide the poet with a text of objects but rather remains the intimate Other, and separation from this other remains the unresolved issue. For it is the regret, the sense of loss— a desire to return to the past which we might call *sentimental* (or "love")— which motivates the rebirth of this poem, a rebirth as return.

> O multi-coloured, multi-form
> Beloved beauty over me,
> That I shall never, never see
> Again! Spring-silver, autumn-gold,
> That I shall never more behold!

The reader must become as a child to return to this ecstasy—the pleasures of this text—they come from loss of the familiar, and not from the indefinite teasing of desire. At the moment of absence comes the subject's movement—not to control absence by the "fort-da" of symbolicity but to return to the "beloved beauty" of the past, of childhood. The "reborn" subject avoids death by submitting to a "God" who is the earth. It is acquiescence to sublimity, a decisive abjection—schizo-salvation ("like one gone mad"):

> Ah! Up then from the ground sprang I
> And hailed the earth with such a cry
> As is not heard save from a man
> Who has been dead, and lives again.
> About the trees my arms I wound;
> Like one gone mad hugged the ground;
> I raised my quivering arms on high;
> I laughed and laughed into the sky;
> Till at my throat a strangling sob
> Caught fiercely, and a great heart-throb
> Sent instant tears into my eyes:
> O God, I cried, no dark disguise
> Can e'er hereafter hide from me
> Thy radiant Identity!

Is this *jouissance*? Of the writer? Of the reader? If Jacques Lacan had read it, would it seem like the statue of St. Teresa, would it seem obvious that she is "coming"?[29] But no—Lacan finds no female ecstasy in language. Is it impossible for the poetess to act as the statue of herself, portraying for us the event of her own (female ecstasy)? If so, then to whom does the ecstasy belong? To a subject now fixed in the male position? To any "man / Who has been dead, and lives again"? To no one, because it is not material, not in the *writing* (or reading)? To everyone, because, as Julia Kristeva argues in *Powers of Horror*, literature *is* the signifier of the abject?[30] For this poem would make its subject the signifier of literature (a poet).

Kristeva argues that there is an intimate relationship of *jouissance* to the abject, that "jouissance alone causes the abject to exist as such." But in "Renascence," ecstasy follows upon a release from the "compassion" that identifies the poet with all sin and suffering, that is, upon a release from the abject, as "all." Kristeva writes:

> as in jouissance where the object of desire, known as object *a* in Lacan's terminology, bursts with the shattered mirror where the ego gives up its image in order to contemplate itself in the Other, there is nothing either objective or objectal to the abject. It is simply a frontier, a repulsive gift that

Other, having become *alter ego*, drops so that "I" does not disappear in it but finds, in that sublime alienation, a forfeited existence. (9)

Whose existence is forfeited in "Renascence"? The reader's? The maternal enclosure of all? The female poet become male speaker?

In contemporary literature, the sinning word itself lures us into the *jouissance* of abjection, its sublimation, as the sacred once did. Kristeva writes: "At that level of downfall in subject and object, the abject is the equivalent of death. And writing, which allows one to recover, is equal to a resurrection. The writer, then, finds himself marked out for identification with Christ, if only in order for him, too, to be rejected, ab-jected" (26). But in Millay's poem, the abjection from without, not within, points to a structure more archaic than the resurrection of the word. The body of Millay's poem is not a sort of "carnal reminder." In "Renascence," the remainder is a reminder, an excess, the round, not flat, soul. Her word, that is, refuses to sin, re-presents the speaker as the one who repeats dramatically within bounds, within the codes, the one who masters—and is mastered by—the identity of the conventional.

Edmund Wilson, in his "Epilogue, 1952: Edna St. Vincent Millay," says that "Renascence" sets forth the terms of Millay's life, portraying the experience of "claustrophobia" from which she frequently suffered.[31] This eternal return of the sensation of enclosure which appears as the opening of the poem may also be connected to her fame as a "poetess," as a member of the tradition, ably reciting and repeating the forms of literature. If Millay appears to be torn between a loss of self to an archaic maternal principle and a loss of self to an identification with the literary fathers and a male tradition, it is perhaps because she maintains herself on the borders of literature, in the position of the extra one, the child, the girl, at the limits of inside/outside where she is that which exceeds the experience, that which is more than the (circular and repetitive) plot.

Associated with the turn and return of the poet's rebirth is a transformation of both poet and God to masculine positions. As she comes to life again, she sounds a cry like a man, "a man / who has been dead and lives again." And the final lines of the poem may almost be read to declare that a masculine soul is required to keep from further scenes of obliteration—distance and difference and the pronouns *he* and *him* must be maintained:

> But East and West will pinch the heart
> That can not keep them pushed apart;
> And he whose soul is flat—the sky
> Will cave in on him by and by.

With this hardness "The soul can split the sky in two / And let the face of God shine through."

The issue of her gender as poet defines the staging of Millay's work from this beginning. The speaker of "Renascence" is reborn into the likeness of a poet's soul, one who is not flat—but it is a likeness only. The reader remembers her past. She remains a border character, a girl who writes like a man.

III

Perhaps as a joke, Arthur Davison Ficke wrote in his letter to Ferdinande Earle praising the poem: "No sweet young thing of twenty ever ended a poem precisely where this one ends: it takes a brawny male of forty-five to do that."[32] Millay wrote Ficke:

> Mr. Earle has acquainted me with your wild surmises. Gentlemen I must convince you of your error; my reputation is at stake. I simply will not be a "brawny male." Not that I have an aversion to brawny males; *au contraire, au contraire*. But I cling to my femininity!
>
> Is it that you consider brain and brawn so inseparable?—I have thought otherwise. Still, that is all a matter of personal opinion. But, gentlemen: when a woman insists that she is twenty, you must not, must not call her forty-five. That is more than wicked; it is indiscreet.
>
> Mr. Ficke, you are a lawyer. I am very much afraid of lawyers. Spare me, kind sir! Take into consideration my youth—for I am indeed but twenty—and my fragility—for "I do protest I am a maid"—and—sleuth me no sleuths!
>
> Seriously: I thank you also for the compliment you have unwittingly given me. For tho I do not yet aspire to be forty-five and brawny, if my verse so represent me, I am more gratified than I can say. (20)

Like the poem, the letter shows a doubleness about the gender of the poet. There are the pleasures of girlish cleverness and wit—a real mastery of a certain coquettish use of language, which nevertheless might also be called a clinging to femininity. This cleverness, this mastery, this clinging characterizes Millay in all of the letters she wrote in her life—one could argue, as Elizabeth Perlmutter has in "A Doll's Heart," that she never ceases to be this Girl in her poetry as well.[33] There is also the desire to be in the position of mastery with respect to poetry—that is, to be male. The "compliment" for which she thanks Ficke and Bynner, for which she is "more gratified than I can say," is not that her verse represents her as forty-five and brawny, of course; we must make the substitution of the omitted term and read: "For tho I do not yet aspire to be male. . . ."[34]

In this question of gender and identification, then, let us hesitate, withdraw, and look around again at the rebirth (from what womb?) at issue here. What does it mean for Ficke and Bynner to say she writes like a man? What does it mean to say she writes like a woman? One way of reading "Renascence," and the traditional poetics adopted by Millay, would be to say she has tried to deny the place of the woman, or escape it, and to write from the place of the man, of the male subject. (If so, according to Ransom and the other modernist critics, she failed to be sufficiently masculine.) What relationships to the "phallic mother" are implicated here? The omniscient (motherly) Infinite in Millay's poem generates several complexities of gender. Jane Gallop offers a convenient summary of the differing positions of male and female implied by the Lacanian view of the subject's relationship to language:

> Woman is . . . the figuration of phallic "lack"; she is a hole. By these mean and extreme phallic proportions, the whole is to man as man is to the hole.
> . . . The "whole" in relation to which man is lacking has its basis in what in Freudian terms is called the "phallic mother." The "whole" is the pre-Oedipal mother, apparently Omnipotent and omniscient, until the discovery of her castration, the discovery that she is not a "whole," but a "hole." So the woman (phallic mother) is to the man what the man is to the (castrated) woman. It is not that men and women are simply unequal, but they occupy the same position in different harmonic ratios, at different moments. The effect is a staggering of position.[35]

That is to say, the "phallic mother" or figure of omniscience and the castrated woman or figure of lack represent the opposite poles of male positioning.

The representation of "Infinity: the Undefined" in "Renascence" as an overwhelming experience of closeness, a loss of differentiation, a merging, suggests the figure of the "phallic mother." But in this poem the trauma arises from the self's identification—as if she encounters the mother at the moment of realizing her castration, her wound—rather than narcissistic plenitude; the self as whole is also the self experienced as the universe "cleft to the core."

If the way out is the death of the self, or the ego, does that mean that the way out for the subject of this poem may be read as escaping from identification with the mother? In the conclusion of the poem, the subject seems safely to enter into the literary codes of the symbolic, taking the place of the male subject. It does not matter that we think of the imagery of nature as god in connection with the yearning for the phallic mother—the subject no longer has a relationship with the transcendental of identification or merging, but now occupies the male position with respect to the "whole," which is now *whole*, a "radiant identity." The rebirth of the subject rescues her not from the threat of castration or wounding but from boundless abjection. Kristeva has argued that women cannot escape or refuse the symbolic, even though women's writing thereby is made subject to a phallocentric culture, precisely because women are otherwise (in their writing as in their psyches) made vulnerable to such an identification with the mother.[36]

But the stance described in the concluding lines of "Renascence" has some rather curious features if we are going to read it as an accession to the symbolic, to successful (and male-identified) poethood. In it, Millay returns to the opening difficulty—the relationship between subject (now "soul") and a world which presses in on it.

> The world stands out on either side
> No wider than the heart is wide;
> Above the world is stretched the sky,—
> No higher than the soul is high.
> The heart can push the sea and land
> Farther away on either hand;
> The soul can split the sky in two,
> And let the face of God shine through.
> But East and West will pinch the heart
> That can not keep them pushed apart,
> And he whose soul is flat—the sky
> Will cave in on him by and by.

This precarious ending can be read from different positions. From the point of view of the male subject of the symbolic, who desires (but can never fully have) a return to the plenitude of the phallic mother, soul contact with the Other is a longed-for goal. The closing offers an "inspiring" version of the liberal reassurance that the "free" individual (as soul) has control over its relationship with the world—that it is up to the individual soul to get what it desires. Thus it seems to promise imaginary fulfillment in rather predictable ways which, moreover, would be pleasing to the ideology of the moment. But we know that the particular subject of this poem is interested in gaining differentiation or distance from a mother world which always threatens to again press in and become overwhelming.

The poem closes with the warning to "he whose soul is flat" (but if "he" is a "he," would he need it?) that he will suffer the same fate that the subject of the poem has just recounted—"the sky / Will cave in on him by and by." What is a "flat" soul? Is it the soul in a state of *aphanisis*? That is, is it a soul not satisfactorily desiring, not phallic?[37] Is there an identification with an Other for a girl which is not the mother? Of course—it is the imaginary identification with the nonflat soul, the phallic soul, subject of the symbolic, which is, of course, male. There is a contradiction in the story. The subject of this poem undergoes a double narrative. The feminine rebirth reverses the direction of the Oedipal progression, beginning with the wounded woman (the hole), and proceeding toward a phallic relationship with the whole (that is, desiring it). But the power relations move in the usual Oedipal order—from the "Infinite" to the individual "soul"—from the powers of the Other to the desiring subject.

The poem does not encourage us to notice heterogeneity and contradiction. It is possible to read "Renascence" as a vision of the overwhelming horrors of a total identification with the Other, and a resolution that the principle of differentiation must be maintained, resisting a collapse, even though with great difficulty. But this would be a partisan translation of an earlier code, of "Renascence" as the transcendentalist reassertion of faith after an encounter with evil, its message the credo of liberal individualism. Nevertheless—in any event—what we are recording is a formal and thematic turn toward insertion of the subject (and poem) into a conventional social order. The pleasures of the text, then, are the pleasures of security, of being disturbed in our reading, having our expectations upset, but feeling that everything has turned out all right in the end—what the poem seems to say fits in with what would be expected. These are the pleasures of ideological confirmation.

We can still argue that Millay's poem is far too identified with the dominant ideology to be more than repetition of the same, imitative, the submission of the daughter to the father in order to get out of being overwhelmed by her mother. We can note the kinds of pleasures that seem to be offered here and disdain them. It is perhaps easy for us, in fact, to refuse to be the subject which the poem thus addresses, because these are no longer the kinds of ploys which might seduce us. Readers of Millay in 1912 could still hear masculine resonance to the Emersonian or Whitmanian "I" constructed by certain key phrases and moments of "Renascence." The daughter puts on the fathers' garb, their vocabulary, their form—she dresses for success in a version of American transcendentalism which connects the codes of rebirth from Christianity to a romantic idealizing of nature and the optimistic assertions of a liberal individualism:

> Ah! Up then from the ground sprang I
> And hailed the earth with such a cry
> As is not heard save from a man
> Who has been dead, and lives again.

The climactic reencounter of poet/subject with nature is rewritten in terms which equate nature both with the Christian God and with the more archaic (and motherly) "heart": "God, I can push the grass apart / And lay my finger on Thy heart!" Conventional reading protects the reader from the implications of the poet's place, the uncertainty of the ending.

If the reader, however, takes the final section of the poem as asserting the potency of the individual soul, the rebirth of the speaker is threatened by the natural, outside world. The poem has an ending, with a paean to a familiar optimism, but only as long as it is decoded according to a romantic faith in the powers of the individual soul:

> The soul can split the sky in two,
> And let the face of God shine through.
> But East and West will pinch the heart
> That cannot keep them pushed apart;
> And he whose soul is flat—the sky
> Will cave in on him by and by.

In a gesture of daughterly obedience, the poet takes on the codes of the fathers (or the Father): it is the responsibility of the individual heart and soul to keep the world at its proper distance. In this final section, the "I" of the poem disappears and the code speaks (it is the place of the moral lesson). But the terms in which the code is presented suggest a reading besides the inspirational optimism which the poem allows. We can see the daughterly dilemma: an obedient and duplicitous "rebirth" into the manhood of the free subject, the strong soul, the "individual," defends the poet against a collapse of boundaries, but it also makes impossible the very inventiveness which the role demands. The poetess acts the part of the free subject—but the narrative line of the poem suggests the drama of a different plot.

In "Renascence," then, it is the plot itself which is bound. There is a split between a free subject and a narrative enslaved to return. As the warning of the final two lines intimates, the rebirth of the speaker has not changed the position of the subject—that is, surrounded by a world, an outside, which threatens to "cave in" on "he whose soul is flat." The split is not within the subject but between inside and outside, at the boundary of self and "sky." The borders of internal and external do not reliably maintain difference but are permeable, penetrable. The incestuous moment of recognition leads the poet not to separate from the maternal Infinite but to take on the abject ("All sin was of my sinning . . . "). Thus the "Renascence" of this poem involves a ritual of return, finally to the same boundedness.

The writing appears to be male not only because it exploits the formal traditions of English lyric poetry but also because the drama of the self with which it is invested reinforces the myth of male superiority at two levels, seeming to inscribe the figure of the rebellious female into her "proper" place. She would rather die than identify with the suffering of the powerful martyr-mother (to recapitulate the plot as it appears in "Renascence"), but her rebirth as a free self requires that she masquerade as a man in the old lyric forms of "individual" selfhood—she cannot take an active, inventive part in the speaking, for the terms of her entry into the subject of lyric poetry require a daughterly submission to the role.

The feelings of a lyric poet in the romantic tradition are read as "originally" private—they are reported in (expressed by) her poem. Lyric emotion, in this convention, is personal, and the private becomes public as the reader "shares" the experience of the poet, looking over her shoulder as it were, identifying with the speaker's drama, enacting as readers the gesture of the sentimental traveler who pauses to sympathize. The pleasures are vicarious; we feel someone else's feelings, frequently the painful ones of loss or failed love. Only the assumption of original privacy keeps the poet and the reader safely contained in separate categories, as individuals, and allows Ransom to hold Millay guilty of causing his distress in the role of sentimental reader.

Perhaps one reason sentimental literature seemed quickly so very unacceptable has to do with the threat it poses to this reader/writer relationship. In the sentimental tradition, the "personal" quickly became a clear matter of convention—the tears, the joys, the sacrifices and reconciliations all as predictable as they continue to be in the "soaps" and the Harlequin romances. This overt conventionality erodes the carefully maintained barriers between public and private emotions as between high and mass art. But when Edna St. Vincent Millay wrote, modernism was getting desperate to make those barriers work—excluding "feelings" and "the private" (or autobiographical) and "intentionality" from a poetry that could be "original," could "make it new," only by strictly delimiting the constituting *difference* of the poetic text. The new critics had a considerable amount of interest in devaluing Millay, fixing her position as a minor poet, in the good company of the male romantics. Thus Allen Tate asserts: "Neither Byron nor Miss Millay is of the first order of poets. They are distinguished examples of the second order. . . ."[38]

A number of theorists—importantly Stanley Aronowitz and Fredric Jameson—have argued that the valuing of the intellect, of theory, and of "high" art overlooks the extent to which even the avant-garde participates in the commodification of art, and that the repeated demands for intellectual originality create a kind of consumerism which is like any other fashion.[39] And furthermore, Aronowitz argues, the practices even of mass culture contain the possibility for critique of dominant ideology as well as conventionally reproducing it. Middle-class culture may yet be interesting. Tania Modleski has called our attention to the importance of this critique for women's cultural productions in her *Loving with a Vengeance: Mass-Produced Fantasies for Women*.[40] The critique of the modernist ideal of "serious" art is also important for a poet such as Millay who has been abandoned to the *other* order of poetry—that of "sensibility" rather than the intellect, as Tate would have it.

When a woman writes poetry, her failure to escape the order of "sensibility" may make us uncomfortable to the extent that it seems she should be writing more masculine forms—that is, to the extent that the poetry seems to aspire to the first, powerful, order of language. But the passive female position in narrative will be defined by the Oedipal plot wherever it occurs within a cultural situation which articulates meaning according to such a mythology. If the Freudian Oedipal myth can be taken as a version of the cultural sense of value and purpose—with the woman as object of desire—the same story will appear repeated everywhere. The open narrative is closed by the figure of a woman. Teresa de Lauretis writes of desire in the narrative of films, arguing that "woman properly represents the fulfillment of the narrative promise (made as we know, to the little boy), and that representation works to support the male status of the mythical subject."[41]

The figure of the woman—Millay, poetess—stands behind her poems, provoking a doubleness, a kind of oscillation between an ostensibly male speaker and the image of the female poet, like the doubleness of her nickname, "Vincent," and the very feminine—girlish—figure she presented. There is a gap between sign and meaning, form and (female) content, that theatricalizes lyric poetry and turns conventional intimacy into indeterminacy. The parodic element persists to the end of "Renascence"—without, however, undermining conventional pleasures of the text. The reason for the poem's resistance to closure has little to do with modernist versions of irony. The plot is asserted at the same time that it is undone, as a function not of textuality alone but of *context*, the extraliterary fact: the poet is a woman. At the same time that Millay's spectator is made perhaps all too comfortable by the predictable directions of the drama, the poem has managed to suggest that contradictory elements coexist in the way the subject may be heard, that the female author may identify with both male and female positions, that female readers might do the same. Behind the pleasures of submitting to mastery—mastery of form as of ideology—Millay's spectators might discover a reminder of other pleasures as well, the supplementary pleasure masquerading as mere cleverness or wit, the pleasure of the other which shows itself in rebellious duplicities, the pleasure of the masquerade.

Pleasure for this poet seems to lie in cross-dressing. But how long can one sustain the boyishness of adolescent girlhood as an acceptable persona? Perlmutter's detailed characterization of Millay's Girl, the "unflappable flapper whose sophistication has taken her beyond libertinage and rebellion toward an epicurean balance of urbanity and lyricism,"[42] leads her to conclude that the poetry is not serious enough: "Capable of moving readers and hearers, the skillful, charming verse through which the Girl had life was even so too dependent on implied gesture to be taken seriously as meant speech" (164). Millay has, that is, developed a poetry of persona, which is simply too theatrical: "It is all so staged, so visible, so temporary. . . . " Geoffrey Hartman says, "writing simplified into *image of voice* is no danger: it merely reinstates the "Greek desire for visibility."[43] What we can already see, however, in the story outlined by "Renascence" is the maternal shape of the maturity Millay must keep on avoiding.[44]

Millay's theatricality enacts the "Greek desire" for visibility. But as the place of the subject is made problematic, so is the structure of desire and the nature of *jouissance*. The question of feminine sexuality, the phallic function, and *jouissance* has notoriously been taken up by Lacan in *Encore*, where he argues that the subject of desire is masculine. The woman is "excluded by the nature of things which is the nature of words." The side of the woman is *not all*. That is,

> when any speaking being whatever lines up under the banner of women it is by being constituted as not all that they are placed within the phallic function. It is this that defines the . . . the what?—the woman precisely, except that *The* woman can only be written with *The* crossed through. There is no such thing as *The* woman, where the definite article stands for the universal. There is no such thing as *The* woman since of her essence . . . she is not all. . . .
>
> There is woman only as excluded by the nature of things which is the nature of words, and it has to be said that if there is one thing they themselves are complaining about enough at the moment, it is well and truly that. . . .
>
> It none the less remains that if she is excluded by the nature of things, it is precisely that in being not all, she has, in relation to what the phallic function designates of *jouissance*, a supplementary jouissance.[45]

What does a girl like Millay have to do with a man like Lacan? Especially when what she seems to wish is to escape the feminine and mimic the phallic function (or assume it)? Or, on the other hand, when she seems at times not to grow up to adult sexuality at all:

> The sky, I thought, is not so grand;
> I 'most could touch it with my hand!

This regression, this cuteness approaching baby talk—can we even give Millay credit for a mastering of mimicry when she allows herself this " 'most?"

We might ask, taking these words up again, to what does this absence, this elision, of "all" lead us? Instead of showing her adolescent, "almost"— that is, close, near to the edge of a boundary (or maturity)—this elision gives us "I" as the excess, "most," that which is—if childish, nonetheless— *over all*. A few lines earlier there appears a rather superfluous "after all." This is the time "after all"—the post-all experience. The plot may be summarized: "After all I becomes the excess of all." It is a belatedness, but a narcissistic version.

The earlier moment of the abject in Millay's poem is not written; rather, it is narrated in a totalizing style which achieves a paranoid reversal of the abject—it is the *all* which is repugnant, not the "I," whose separateness has been lost to the engulfing All:

> All sin was of my sinning, all
> Atoning mine, and mine the gall
> Of all regret. Mine was the weight
> Of every brooded wrong, the hate
> That stood behind each envious thrust,
> Mine every greed, mine every lust.
> And all the while, for every grief,
> Each suffering, I craved relief
> With individual desire;
> Craved all in vain! And felt fierce fire
> About a thousand people crawl;
> Perished with each,—then mourned for all!

It is the *all* which causes her fall, reversal of religious and literary versions of abjection. The important question of the subject's relationship to "all" is thus revealed with all as an absence, disguised or hidden, before the masquerade of abjection, when "All sin was of my sinning, all / Atoning mine, and mine the gall / Of all regret." What remains after all, most of all, is the girl who must speak, a " 'most" whose place at the borders of dependency, of master/slave or parent/child relations, depends on keeping the all elided and asserting the one (child, woman) who remains.

Since Millay practices no subversions against the linguistic forms of the fathers, she offers no challenge against the phallocentrism embedded in those forms, except by the small incongruity of her girlish figure, whose person says the same thing with a difference. In *Woman and the Demon*, Nina Auerbach argues that the potent female figure of the nineteenth century loses power in the hands of twentieth-century modernism in part because it depends on a valuing of *character* which modernism rejected.[46] But Millay's poetry is the play of a character, the girl become poet-prodigy, loving daughter, little woman.

Millay in her person, that is, represents and reenacts the drama of female selfhood with each presentation of each poem—her signature sets the stage for a reprise of the plot never to grow up, to escape the confines of the old images, the models of maternal sacrifice. Carolyn Heilbrun has argued for the pervasive influence of Alcott's "Jo," who "may have been the single female model continuously available after 1868 to girls dreaming beyond the confines of a constructed family destiny to the possibility of autonomy and experience initiated by one's self."[47] Like Heilbrun's, Millay's plot sees freedom in terms of trying to separate herself from the mother's self-sacrifice without rejecting the mother, either in the person,like Jo's "Marmie," or in the myth, like Millay's world. If the great theme of Millay's poetry—love—marks her as a female poet, her great ambivalence about the dependency relationships created by love marks her daughterly character, marks her as the daughter of a strong mother.

Millay's own family history is like a rewriting of *Little Women*—the absent father, the supportive and hard-working sisters, the loving and much-loved mother who exacted loyalty and high aspirations from her daughters. Thus "Vincent" writes to her sister, Norma, from the Ritz Hotel in Budapest of her decision to bring the mother to Europe:

> Beloved Sister:
>
> Bless you forever and ever for your letter. If ever a girl needed a letter, I was that girl, and yours was that letter. You see, it put some things straight in my mind that had been a little cluttered before. Your telling me that mother had been sick, and all that,—*you* know—made me realize that nothing in the world is important beside getting mother over here with me. At least, of course the Russian famine is important, and a few other things like that, but nothing in my life, at least, is important in comparison to this thing. A possible marriage, for instance, is not important beside it. Anybody can get married. It happens all the time. But not everybody, after the life we have had, can bring her mother to Europe. (March 1, 1922)[48]

A slightly earlier letter to her mother shows Millay conscious of how loving (or sentimental?) her correspondence with her family sounds:

> Dearest Mother,—
> You do write the sweetest and the most wonderful letters! They are so lovely that very often I read parts of them aloud to people, just as literature. It was delicious what you told me about the turtle. . . .
> P.S.—Do you suppose, when you & I are dead, dear, they will publish the *Love Letters of Edna St. Vincent Millay & her Mother*?
> P.P. I am sending you a poem I just wrote.—Show it to the girls too, darling.*xx*—V.(July 23, 1921: 120)[49]

More important, perhaps, this letter to her mother shows how thoroughly interwoven were the literary and family relationships for Millay. Elizabeth Hardwick, in her review of Millay's *Letters*, exclaims that they sound like something out of *Little Women*, even the letters to other poets, to publishers (grown-up occasions, that is).

"Vincent" grows up, writes, loves, and lives as a character invented by Edna St. Vincent Millay to fit the circumstances, a character soon legendary, soon providing a model herself for the young flappers of the twenties who eagerly followed her bohemian lifestyle and repeated the defiant lines from *A Few Figs from Thistles*. Griffin Barry of the *New Yorker* reported in 1927:

> her public cohered quickly in 1919 when the boys got back from France. Crowds of them came—boys fresh from the wars, hungrily fierce about love and as trivial as you please and the young women of the day became fierce and trivial, too. It is not an easy way of life for women—not always. The young women needed a poet. Edna Millay became that one, hardly aware of it herself, at first.
>
> Not until 1925 did the author of the love sonnets decide to print them all. But in 1921 I stumbled on a tableful of American strangers in Paris who knew the lot, producing them in scrawled versions from pocketbooks or from memory. Millay couplets had floated by word of mouth for years through colleges.[50]

This is the era when poetry—serious poetry—divorced itself from character to become impersonal, when all serious writing was also seriously objectified, alienated, aloof in its literariness from context. Millay, more than any other poet, male or female, represented the opposite extreme, a merging of public and private identities, of self, subject, and persona, a failure to establish by irony or invention any distance between her writing and the ritualized declamations of mass ceremony, mass selfhood. Millay's poetess was, as Elizabeth Perlmutter puts it, "plucking an ancient lyre." Her achievement was a "hybridized diction we must ruefully call 'poetic' ": "That is, starting with her earliest verses, Millay's style was a resplendent pastiche of Sapphic simplicity, Catullan urbanity, homeless Chaucerian idiom, uprooted Shakespearean grammar, Cavalier sparkle, Wordsworthian magnanimity, Keatsian sensuousness, and Housemanian melancholy. . . . "[51]

Indeed, the slavishly "poetic" reminiscence called up by Millay's style has had a similar effect on many of her readers, prompting them to feel obligated as part of a Millay reading to call out the resemblances and possible influences they recognize. It is as if the figure of the girl prompts her audience to join in the game, as if something about her attention to the sounds of the lyric code theatricalized the lyric tradition—the convention, that is, of identifying "poetry" with the canonical inheritance exemplified by the rhymed forms of elegy, sonnet, or even ballad. Millay's lifelong habit of committing great poetry to memory and declaiming it for her friends hints of the recitation, and the actress; this was frequently her way of composing her own work as well, having it in her memory before she ever committed any of it to paper.

Millay, then—Vincent—however heterogeneous her text, however multiple the sounds of the voices she conjures from the (masculine) lyric past, gives us repeatedly only the singleness of Millay, girl poet, figure of the female "individual," character, chief protagonist in a drama of relationship, female voice marking the imposture of her boyish speakers and male pronouns, speaking in the female body which is the subject of her work. The reader of Millay is not likely to find writerly pleasures in her text, called so frequently from play back to the spectacle of personality. Millay's work addresses the reader, instead, as spectator—as a male or female subject who may be called upon to identify with her, to take a role in her drama, to enjoy the parody and the masquerade.

That is, the pleasures of Millay's poetry may have much to do with the processes of identification, theatricality, and the cultural construction of the gendered subject—pleasures we are growing used to talking about in studies of the cinema, but which (thus attached to "mass culture" and its political unconscious) we reject as a "proper" reaction to poetry. The reader of modern poetry does not want to be soothed or persuaded into unconscious gender identification—modern poetry and the avant-garde writing which encourages an active reader also, precisely, disrupt the unknowing assumption we hold about the subject, especially the assumption of "character" that there is a single individual with whom we can identify, a single plot which will give us happy or unhappy endings. A single, that is, Oedipal, plot. But this discomfort about the subject's identifications, this playing double with the singleness of plot, takes another—supplementary—form in Millay.

One of the pleasures of Millay's poetry, then, is a pleasure we could call "unpoetic," a pleasure that seduces the otherwise serious reader. It comes out of her repetition of conventions, beloved but old-fashioned and "sentimental" (the maternal matrix). And it comes out of the way the dramatic story incarnates a female Other, a feminine voice of lyric poetry. (The Muse?) Since the codes whereby Millay's work accomplishes this process are inscribed not within the boundaries of the poetic text but in the context in which her poetry appeared (that is, they are not all "poetic"), the spectator of her work is seduced by her extrapoetic " 'most,' " by that dramatic supplement which gives us the romantic spectacle: the mere-slip-of-a-girl-poet heroically playing those weighty antique lyres. It is this figure who protests charmingly: "I simply will not be a 'brawny male.' Not that I have an aversion to brawny males; *au contraire, au contraire.* But I cling to my femininity!" The spectator is seduced by the difference: the writing appears to be competently masculine, but not all—the writer is someone's daughter at the same time, '*most* a woman.

Edna St. Vincent Millay does not seem a likely candidate to be called a feminist writer. Does she offer any of the elements Teresa de Lauretis lists as essential to feminism: "a critical reading of culture, a political interpretation of the social text and of the social subject, and a rewriting of our culture's 'master narratives' "?[52] That may depend on how we read her, and whether or not we take seriously her real power during the 1920s and 1930s to represent women's writing as a part of literary history. Her struggle provokes our awareness of the contradictory status of the woman author, whose authority, as de Lauretis emphasizes, comes from a masculine literary language. Her status, then, depends not on any absolute literary value but on a criticism which extends its interest to the difference that gender makes in literature.

WOMEN AND MODERNISM

Medusa and Melancholy
The Fatal Allure of Beauty
in Louise Bogan's Poetry

It is a dangerous lot, that of the charming, romantic public poet, especially if it falls to a woman.

—LOUISE BOGAN,
"UNOFFICIAL
FEMININE LAUREATE"[1]

You only have to look at the Medusa straight on to see her. And she's not deadly. She's beautiful and she's laughing.

—HÉLÈNE CIXOUS,
"THE LAUGH OF THE MEDUSA"[2]

I

Louise Bogan's haunting, melancholy, but fierce poetry challenges me to sort out the question of poetic language and *écriture féminine*. Her experiments with the lyric earn her an important place in the history of writing by women as well as among modernist poets, and the beauty of her work opens the larger historical problematic of art. These strongly contained poems may seem to represent a look that is as alienated as it is aesthetic, the gaze of the artist at the work of art. But if we listen to the affective tone, we hear the insistent changes of sound and repeated chords, a subtle but extraordinarily intense musicality of voice that inhabits the coolly distant look. The poems exhibit and sound out a femininity that is both lovely and furious—in fact, that threatens to be sublimely awe-ful. Hers is a kind of reversal of irony in the unexpected return of body and feeling to the distanced work of art. As I read Bogan, I listen also to the double possibilities of the critical moral to this story. According to Hélène Cixous, men have made women hate themselves; male dominance has created an antilove in language which women must rupture by the laughter of the very Medusa which men figure as monstrous.

Bogan rouses the Fury to speech, but she also shows us how this can release the most terrifying images and unrelenting despair. She shows us the threat of psychosis about which Kristeva warns us. Should she have written more, dared more? Instead of the fragile structures of normalcy that she constructed to keep herself going, should she have challenged the Oedipal versions of maturity taught her by the psychoanalysts who offered her treatment when she broke down? Bogan feared revolution: hers is the conservatism of a politics of interiority, and of a woman who ruptures the stability of gendered subjectivity and finds the woman's antilove goes much deeper than what we usually mean by ideology, deep into the unconscious. In Bogan's work, we live in a fallen world, and it is a fall into gendered sexuality. If the musicality of her work does indeed function as an *écriture féminine* to write the woman into language, what I hear is not a laugh but agony. What Bogan suggests to us is the difficulty of escaping the familial enclosure and the possibility that woman's writing will open up the scene of "my scourge, my sister" rather than the scenes of reconciliation we long to find.

In *Méduse*, his study of mythological representation and the problematic of art, Jean Clair asks if there is a bond between horror and beauty.[3] He points out the doubleness of human and animal traits in the Medusa, of male and female, and also the doubleness of meanings in the history of Medusa mythology. She was not only a monster but also a fascinating and seductive girl, and it was the latter image that prevailed for Hellenistic culture. Her face has much to do with the history of art and seeing, and with the separation of mind and body. By his account, Clair wishes to explore the enigma of *beauty* which neither Marxism nor psychoanalysis has been able adequately to address. He argues that the representation of Medusa took a decided turn in the Renaissance, away from the beautiful girl and toward the monstrous. Clair draws intriguing connections between the representations of Medusa and, on the one hand, other beheaded figures from John the Baptist to Louis XVI (appearing on a revolutionary poster), and on the other hand, fertility images including ancient body-faces and René Magritte's "Le Viol," suggesting as did Freud the possibility that Medusa represents the female genitals.[4] Clair closes his speculations with the uneasiness that modern art raises in the civilized: "The 'dripping' of Pollock [who was nicknamed 'Jack the Dripper'] is no other, in fact, than the blood running out of the cut-off head of Medusa, tracing the aleatory figure of our perdition."[5]

Louise Bogan began to publish poetry in the era dominated by Millay. Unlike Millay, Bogan separates her poetry firmly from the banal. Nevertheless she also cites the women's tradition in style. Her difficult lyricism inherits the symbolist aesthetic and legitimates its defiant hermeticism for American poetics, together with a musicality associated by her with the feminine. Resurrecting the lover's discourse, and at the same time writing in the modernist severity of poetic language, Bogan evokes the mute and melancholy subject of the feminine transgression. The figure of desire that repeats itself is the figure of the fatal look, a trope of reflection, mirroring of the subject as "something awful." Doubling the ironic—there's something awful about a woman poet—is the uncanny resonance with a claim to the sublime, the awe-ful inheritance of Emily Dickinson.

In a sense Bogan returns us to an American lineage not only from Dickinson but also from Poe—via Baudelaire and Mallarmé. Though she was a disciple of Eliot, she renews the question of lyric subjectivity, pressing the material anarchy of poetry within the crisis of representation. She believed that the poet was necessarily a criminal in the modern state, and she connects beauty, death, and the uncanny. Like Mallarmé she practices a formal estrangement from ordinary language—a coldness which distances the intensity of her passion and her fury. Perhaps she nonetheless leaves the cleared path of a critique of gender which recuperates both emotion and the woman's tradition. If so, the difficulty her own criticism had welcoming women's work will come to seem ironic.

How does Bogan resolve the conflict between Eliot's male sense of the tradition and the inheritance of women's sensibility? Do her limited (if impressive) productivity and apparent willingness to see herself as a "minor" writer signal a woman's negotiation of the austerities inflicted by male identifications? Is Bogan's relationship to the great moderns, Eliot and Yeats, like the relationship to Lacan of French feminist critics—Irigaray, Cixous, Clement, Kristeva—what Jane Gallop called "the daughter's seduction"? Perhaps the relationships are similarly problematic. Ruth Limmer's discussion of an early unpublished poem and her edition of the prose memoir *Journey around My Room* tantalize us with what might have been and the sense of an imagination operating within claustrophobic bonds.[6] But is this the restraint of gender, or of a poetics which would break out of gender by refusing all indulgence in the banal? Mallarmé and Valéry also produced a writing surrounded by silence. I agree with Gloria Bowles in calling Bogan a major modernist writer, but I want to go on to claim, as Bowles does not, that the silence of Mallarmé and Valéry *was* like Bogan's silence because the absences in modernism are connected to *gynesis* and defined by the cultural problem of gender.[7]

If I regard Bogan's work in terms of "achievement," by the critical measures for poetry she herself set forth, what I find is the violence of art, the revolution that Bogan thought avoided the political. What Gloria Bowles calls an "aesthetics of limitation" seems to me not quite like a willing of limits. Bogan's modernist poetics arises in the violence of reason's ascetic encounter of the *semiotic* of art—not, in other words, making safe but rather making difficult what might otherwise be too easily resolved. According to Bowles, Bogan internalized a certain version of the modernist aesthetic too thoroughly; she "achieved such control that she could no longer express any emotion at all" (137). What she internalized, Bowles points out, was a modernist hostility to the feminine. Of course, I agree that women writers have had to struggle against this hostility—the scapegoating of the sentimental—and that many have been crippled by it (but have men not been crippled even more thoroughly?). But I am interested in exploring the possibility that women writers such as Louise Bogan in fact explored the dilemma of literature itself in its gendered relationship to the banal world and thus pioneered modernist poetic discoveries which were displaced and contained by male writers who could cover up their threatened subjectivity in irony and retreat. Still, I agree that it is the subject that is the field of struggle here, that Bogan limits her struggle against more overtly political structures of every kind.

Bogan took from Eliot and the symbolists the idea of a poetry based on the music of forms. What this meant for her relationship to the traditions of a feminized American culture was complex. American modernists associated with Sherwood Anderson and William Carlos Williams were in revolt specifically against the borrowed gentility and colonized, derivative language of an English literary tradition. Marianne Moore is of the Williams, not the Eliot, school, and Eliot himself seemed to some a traitor. Kay Boyle says that even American expatriates in Paris wanted to write American speech into literature, that "T. S. Eliot and Henry James we very much resented"—in fact, they burned them both in effigy one night (7–8).[8] Bogan's allegiances to Eliot may seem at odds both with this renewal of an American vernacular and with the assertion of a woman's point of view. As Ruth Limmer points out, Bogan refuses to represent ordinary life, stripping her style of the vernacular.

Yet I want to explore the possibility that Bogan articulates both the pain and darkness of the writer's situation in the particularly anti-aesthetic context of American Puritanism, and the painful difference of a woman's development, both a cultural and a psychic struggle with the gendering of reproduction. As Bogan studied the French symbolists and found kinship with the Irish Yeats, like Millay before her and Kay Boyle after, she represented the seduction of the American in a daughterly relationship to the internationalism of modernist literature. Is not Eliot himself more daughterly than Oedipal in his relationships to tradition?

Bogan exposes the limits of daughterly genealogies as she exposes the conflicted place of *gynesis* in modernist writing. Her poetry occupies an exceedingly problematic position, on the intersection of discourses which are so incompatible that their conflict threatens her with disaster. How is a woman writer, inscribed in a genealogy of "the line of feeling" established by the feminine poets, to play the part of the symbolist speaker of the poem? How can she be impersonal, like Hérodiade, the mysterious and resistant voice of Mallarmé's verse drama? Symbolist poetics installed the text itself as a kind of femme fatale, a female otherness speaking the subject. Does not the place which might be occupied by a femme fatale exclude a woman as speaking subject and make evident how the possibility of such a rupture of the symbolic is dangerous? Bogan's poems should frighten us. At the same time that they seduce us, they open up that which is usually repressed—not only the alienation of art but, especially, the love and hate evoked by a woman speaking to us, looking at us.

The horror and passionate attachment of the daughter locate Bogan's work painfully in a maternal space, while her longing for form and judgment press her toward the great modernists whose courage, detachment, and irony she wished to emulate: W. B. Yeats and T. S. Eliot, and behind them—in part, *through* them,—Stéphane Mallarmé. She attributed her voice to the women's tradition of lyricism, and she held out for emotion in poetry all her critical career, from the pulpit of the *New Yorker*. She has learned how women's writing took up and reformed romanticism, and she passes on that inheritance. "In women, more than in men, the intensity of their emotions is the key to the treasures of their spirit. The cluster of women lyric poets that appeared on the American scene just before and after 1918 restored genuine and frank feeling to a literary situation which had become genteel, artificial, and dry"—she cites Teasdale, Millay, Wylie, and Leonie Adams.[9] But she also holds out for the importance of form, and formalism enters her poetry not only as invention but also as ritual transcendence, the recollection of forms once associated with the Irish folk culture she shared with Yeats, and with the love of high church liturgy she shared with Eliot: it is not the belief but the forms of belief, the sounds of it, that she recalls.

What she would see in the mirror held up by symbolism is the recurring death threatened by the female subject. Does this terror eventually become her silence? Or does Bogan succeed in writing the experience of the woman into style by, as the title of her first collection calls it, "the body of this death"? Do her poems work, in other words, not only to "defamiliarize" ordinary language but to "defamilialize," as Cixous would have it, estranging gender by the refusals of a woman's text which is thereby made avant-garde? Let us take seriously the courage of her violations: she dared to make visible the violent, the severe, and the powerful seductiveness of the sentimental, and its proximity to psychosis. She did this, and no one dared ever call her "poetess."

Lyric poetry and autobiography as well as fiction have a strong tradition of narratives featuring a fatally and demonically attractive Other, a femme fatale. This "belle dame sans merci" figured largely in the development of the nineteenth-century poet, becoming associated with poetry itself, with the doom of heroic male rationality. We find her in the poetry of Stéphane Mallarmé at an important moment for his development of the symbolist poetic. Under the influence of Poe, and also, perhaps, of Flaubert's *Salambo*, Mallarmé wrote "Hérodiade," a poem in the framework not of the lyric but of a dramatic tragedy. The poem represents not an external drama of seduction and betrayal but a rigorously internalized scene between Hérodiade and a nurse in the chamber, in front of the mirror. The speeches of the cold beauty, Hérodiade, refuse the dialogue proffered by the nurse and thus mark the moment when beauty becomes withdrawal and unrepresentability, or death.

The poem itself is a pivotal turn in Mallarmé's depersonalization of the lyric, in which he withdraws poetry from its attachments to expressiveness, subjectivity, systems of meaningfulness, and stories of desire. His Hérodiade withdraws not only from the human touch of her nurse but also from her own cries, " . . . les sanglots suprêmes et meutris / D'une enfance sentant parmi les rêveries / Se séparer enfin ses froides pierreries" ("the supreme and bruised sobs of a childhood feeling its cold jewels at last separate themselves from among its fantasies" [my translation]). As Mallarmé's work defines it, the poem's *new word* separates itself from childhood as from the lyric voice, purifying the female body into cold stone and setting into motion the final cut, the beheading of John the Baptist, the splitting of body and speaking subject. This situates art as a Medusa which continues the seductive power of its gaze even after the head is separated from the body.

The place of the femme fatale is exceedingly dangerous. The female narcissism which becomes an emblem of the poetic word, articulated in the figuration that endlessly seduces desire and refuses meaning, embodies the violence of the word as act. It is also contained by that embodiment of textuality, by its suggestion of an ontology. The poem itself seems to take on being as a *new word*, and the female body fades into text. The poetic language which Mallarmé invents does not have a simple relationship to the body, for the gendered female body of Hérodiade is subject to the symbolic organization of sex, impure. Mallarmé's text withdraws this imaginary body from representation in order to open language to the material rupture of a negativity which is semiotic, which inscribes the subject in the text by the notorious "absence" of sense. Hérodiade's "chastity," her horror at the possibility of a kiss, is a refusal of a sexuality coded by the symbolic systems of gender, hence a refusal of culture, not a refusal of the material, the instinctive, the drive, the natural, or the unconscious—all distinguished from culture only at the stroke of the code. The musical body of the poem, its absence from sense, locates the unconscious as a negativity with respect to the well-defined and gendered body of the woman. The poem disjoins sexual gender from lyric expressivity.

But what is the power of the poem in culture? The symbolist poem does not necessarily rewrite gender or any other cultural category. The "new word" which poetic language, with its rupture of the symbolic, produces is also received within a language, a culture, which positions the poet as a male speaking subject, with access to further symbolic action. And the invention of the new word is all too easily recuperated by the long project of modern reason, the purifying project which casts off impurities by collecting them in the "pseudocenter" of the feminine other. Thus there is an ambiguity at the start about the revolution of poetic language.

Mallarmé's practice ruptures the sign's apparent referentiality. The body of the text is a material sign which opens language to another kind of sense, to the musicality of sound and rhythm. This estranges the referent, which Mallarmé thematizes as chastity and the withdrawal of an imaginary female body, the signified, separated from, and contradicted by, the signifier. Mallarmé is not practicing a musicality which is in the genre/gender of the lyric. Turning to the theatrical for its enactment of aesthetic distance and the split into multiplicity, he is breaking the back of the lyric, of the expressive, and abandoning those too-easy subjective pleasures he discovers within himself as he inherits the tradition, "the pleasures of a purely passive soul who is still nothing but a woman and who tomorrow will be perhaps a beast."[10] However, as Julia Kristeva points out, even though Mallarmé and the avant-garde text put the rhetoric of experience into question and open up poetry to the processes of signification, the avant-garde text can always be recuperated by the cultural categories which limit it to subjective experience rather than practice, and limit its political effectiveness. When Kristeva writes about this in *Revolution in Poetic Language*, she is clear about the constraints on poetic revolution.[11]

Thus there are two ways of thinking about the body and the subject of poetry in Mallarmé. First, reproducing the gendered other of capitalism, there is the passive, feminine subjectivity identified with the lyric feeling, which—whether as object of adoration, disdain, or blame—is already accounted for as the cultural "poetic experience." And second, there is the active negativity which is *not* the thing but the effect it produces, a resistance to the banality of the everyday and what is already understood, and this resistance is the practice of the subject in process which psychoanalysis will open up. Mallarmé, the symbolists, and their avant-garde successors, Kristeva says, "were to become the hesitant and stray defenders of a certain 'truth' about the subject that the dominant ideologies could no longer master and that religions . . . had sealed up. . . . the moment of struggle exploding the subject toward heterogeneous materiality" (211). But this "truth" of the poetic body does not easily enter into ordinary social processes because the literary has been isolated: "the representative system of these very texts brought this moment back within subjective *experience*" (211). The question is whether this resistant body can be socially productive. Can it carry the negativity of poetic language into social practices, beyond the boundaries of the literary, erupting in a strangeness which would be effective? These are the limits Bogan as well must meet.

Writing in the lineage of Mallarmé, writing hermetic and musical poems that extend the symbolist invention, Bogan struggles with the deadliness of a melancholy narcissism which threatens not only the violence of textuality but the withdrawal into speechlessness of the speaking subject herself, the loss of the word. She has, as she notes, no religious rites to protect her, and she has no male exteriority to help project the narcissistic conflict beyond the borders of interior identity. When she became the poetry critic for the *New Yorker*, she took up the discourse of reason and judgment, acquiring at a stroke the patriarchal maturity that might shelter her. But her poetry constantly works to rupture the ideology that lends her judgments credibility. The lack which threatens her psyche with psychosis is the lack of a public position for the poet that is neither patriarchal nor sentimental—a position that could limit the processes of abjection and provide a remedy for strangeness. Even psychoanalysis in American culture had been taken over by the ego. Thus Bogan's estrangement is accompanied by a longing for the "maturity" which American psychoanalysis would urge upon her. Such a maturity would escape the practice of the text and the threat of the feminine, as John Crowe Ransom wished Millay could do, by reproducing intellectual normalcy and mastering the female sensibility. Maturity would provide closure to the subject in process. The temptation of the sentimental is matched by the temptation to escape it. For a woman, to proceed to maturity is to engage in furious struggle against the self represented as feminine.

II

Glimpses of the fatal figure appear as reflections of the speaker again and again in Bogan's poems. Instead of a "belle dame sans merci," the youth of her "A Tale" finds a place "Where something dreadful and another / Look quietly upon each other" (3). In "Medusa," the glimpse of "The stiff bald eyes, the serpents on the forehead / Formed in the air" leaves a "dead scene forever" (4). What the husband discovers in "For a Marriage" is the woman's "barbed heart": "The sullen other blade / To every eye forbidden, / That half her life has made" (43). And the speaker of "The Sleeping Fury" addresses "my scourge, my sister" from the calm of having rendered her into symbol: "You, with your whips and shrieks, bearer of truth and of solitude; / You who give, unlike men, to expiation your mercy" (79).

She shows how the woman's place as imaginary eternal object of the lyric (stopped, still) becomes terrible, "dreadful," Medusa-like if fixed as the mirror image of the self, like the antinarcissism Cixous describes: "A narcissism which loves itself only to be loved for what women haven't got. They have constructed the infamous logic of antilove."[12] Her poetry at once recalls and rejects this imaginary. Bogan seems both to cite the rejected tradition and to inscribe the feminine into language as estrangement. On the cover of *The Blue Estuaries*, Roethke approves her "scorn" of what he calls the usual lyric "caterwauling," and Adrienne Rich praises her committing a "female sensibility" to language. Bogan both constitutes and distances an ideology that is female, situating herself within the struggle of asserting a lover's discourse which is at the same time a forsaken language.

By refusing the "caterwaul," she also accedes to male standards, male codes, male criticism. Like Marianne Moore, Bogan was severe with her own work, pruning mercilessly, and perhaps giving the critical spirit so large a scope that she curtailed her own productivity, unbalancing the relationship between the critical and the creative. Literary history, emerging as American modernism, recuperated the severe demands of Mallarmé in the purifying and defining break between literature and ordinary language. In the post-Eliotic modernist criticism which Bogan practiced, there is a resistance to the more commonplace identification of poets with femininity. Yet this everyday meaning stood ready at all times to capture her, as it had Millay, in the figure of the "poetess." Bogan seems, writing as a woman, to be caught between antinarcissism and sentimentality, between being critically serious and engaged in gendered social practices.

Nonetheless, Bogan's diamondlike poems cut through the looking-glass to a writing which carries the revolution of poetic language into the authority of gender, fracturing the surfaces of narcissisms, introducing struggle into the portrayals of a self. She thought she was trying to do that by struggling toward "maturity." The tragedy, the paradox, or the distance between her self-understanding and her poetic practice, is that her power comes not from the maturity of resignation but from the fury of her resistance to the Oedipal resolution. She opens up a place for hysteria or "emotion" by struggling with the austere retreats of the symbolist text. The retreat itself is, in Bogan, furious.

According to the modernist metapoetic, writing is about writing. An illusion of depth and being is created in a text by a hierarchy of discourses which end in self-reference, with the allegory of desire thematizing the poetic creation itself—under the struggles of male and female passion, of self and other, as if unconscious, the struggle of writing. The image must be objective, concrete, a showing and not a telling, because the meaning of the poem is *poesis* itself. This has the effect not of installing the text as the practice of the speaking subject but of projecting "meaning" outside to the banal exchanges of information, to the ordinary language of communication.

But in Bogan's poems the relationship of theme and form will not hold still—the body of the text will not withdraw into artistic stillness. There is a mutual interrogation of gender and writing, an intertextuality which refuses the modernist priorities by the unsettling operations of rhythm, sound, and repetition.

Bogan does not argue with the dominance of realist ideology, but instead of natural history she gives us the dead body; she gives us the murderer and the victim of the crime. She keeps the violence of textuality in view. If she writes within the sphere of influence of an imagist and objectivist poetics, she also sees its social context as not a relatively benign scientism but the nightmarish constraint of terrorist political regimes regulating not only daily life but the ordinary language which might describe it.

She thought the detective story was the genre in which future great works would be written in this, our time, "The Time of the Assassins."[13] Her reasons are instructive: its origins in the development of the police state, its emphasis on rules which distinguish it from the "surrounding anarchy of form," and its necessary preoccupation with "death and dissolution"—unlike the literary novel, the detective novel welcomes sensation, "does not reject one detail of the macabre," and "openly accommodates fear and aggression." In detective novels, anyone may be a criminal, and "*everywhere* has become the scene of the crime" (84–85). Poe, of course, has played a major role in the development of the still-disdained genre; Bogan notes in particular, rather mysteriously, that he invented the locked room.

Bogan's poems have strong borders, asserting their autonomy and their discontinuity with prose. Are they locked rooms? Locked wombs? Reflective stasis arises as a recurrent alarm. To read these poems as they read themselves is to be seduced by the poetic, to fall into a narcissistic trance. It is a withdrawal into form that sometimes holds sorrow in place so firmly that it emerges only as repetition, often only the repetition of sound, as in "Night" (130):

> The cold remote islands
> And the blue estuaries
> Where what breathes, breathes
> The restless wind of the inlets,

> And what drinks, drinks
> The incoming tide . . .

Nevertheless the figure of desire that repeats itself is the figure of the fatal doubling, a trope of reflection, mirroring of the poet as "something awful," someone who cries, who is alone.

> —O remember
> In your narrowing dark hours
> That more things move
> Than blood in the heart.

In the final collection of Bogan's poetry, *The Blue Estuaries*, the awful figure appears from the first, in the poem called "A Tale" (3). Although Alfred Kreymborg had published "Betrothed" in *Others* in 1917, this poem's appearance in the 1921 *New Republic* marked Bogan's entry into the critical world of modernist poetry and a decade of remarkable work to follow. The poem opened her first book as well as her last, so that it serves as an introduction to the poetry and the poet.

"A Tale" is in a sense autobiographical, Elizabeth Frank says, its source Bogan's experience of her first marriage, to Curt Alexander, who took her to Panama when the First World War broke out and he was stationed there.[14] She was nineteen, four months pregnant, and had abandoned a scholarship to Radcliffe for this marriage. Bogan writes, "The poet represses the outright narrative of his life. . . . The repressed becomes the poem."[15] Perhaps she is saying something related to Paul Valéry's claim about "La Jeune Parque" that he is writing "an autobiography in the form."[16] Like Valéry, Bogan has often been accused of obscurity.[17] The speaker of Valéry's poem is an adolescent woman; the chief character of Bogan's is a "youth." This crossing of gender has different effects, however, because the feminine persona of Valéry shadows the feminine persona of poetic practice, reproducing the understood equation: the (male) poet is like a woman. But Bogan's hero confuses poetry's gendering, reversing the metaphor so the (female) poet is like a man/like a woman. The poem is not only "about" the autobiographical voyage south to marriage, but also about that other autobiography, the change of the poet's life into form. Or, to put it another way that does not seem to make the life prior to the poem, the poem is the autobiography that *produces* the poet's life *as* form. This feminine body is, for Valéry, purely metaphorical; for Bogan, it is inescapable as pregnancy and "the break / Of waters," and so, terrifying.

The fable itself is cast in the third person, "this youth," and develops the ironic perspective of a cautionary tale about the fate of the romantic and symbolist poet who withdraws from the ordinary. The youth "too long has heard the break / Of waters" and goes in search of the "rocky gates" of Mallarméan withdrawal, only to find "something dreadful." The story is about a quest for something beyond change that turns out to be a version of the "belle dame sans merci."

The first stanza of the poem gives us a rejection of the feminine. At the same time, it gives us the modernist poem's rejection of time and history for the more "indurate and strange" material of poetic work. Images sort into male/female orders: "the break / Of waters" suggests childbirth; the relationship of "suns [sons] can make" to "soil" rewrites the old "tilling the fields" metaphor for sex and, together with "land of change," connects to traditional analogies of the woman and the land. The punning seems merely witty if the poet is imagined as a man, but strong and ironic if we see her as a woman: "this youth" has had too much of childbirth and is off to look for other materials to express his/her creativity. It is important to look closely at Bogan's musicality. The rhyming words—*break/make*, *change/strange*—work the thematic chords by setting up internal contrasts. The "masculine" rhyme of *break/make* is unvoiced, the similar sound of *change/strange* voiced, but *break* and *change* both belong to the system that is being put in the past, and *make* and *strange* to the future. *Indurate* foreshadows the moral: that "nothing dares / To be enduring." It is a word with built-in irony since the verb *indurate* is to make hard, but the adjective is more than hardened—resistant, obstinate, without feeling—and implies persons as well as soils. The enduring will be implicated in rigidity and alienation.

The tale of the youth setting out for the strange land overlaps with a separation. The reversals intimated in stanza one at the level of sound become explicit in stanza two at the level of myth. The youth cuts himself away from a maternal enclosure: "What holds his days together / And shuts him in, as lock on lock." But this space, this matrix, is time itself, change, and its markers—the weather vane, the ticking clock. The rhyme (*lock/clock*) continues the unvoiced stop of stanza one, a ticking. This myth does not imagine the familiar enclosure as stasis but rather as change. The locked room of the womb, like days and weather, holds the subject immersed in time. It is a pre-Oedipal history, and it will see that the cut of the thetic establishing symbolic stasis and regulation also introduces an impossible relation of the sexes.

The hero mythos gains greater hold on the poem's narrative structure as the youth's story is defined with the word *seeking*, which transforms "goes to see" into its more spiritualized, imaginary analogue, the quest. But its "light" metaphor is rendered domestic, "still as a lamp upon a shelf," and personified: "a light that waits." Furthermore the quest turns to an object rather than the active principle of *suns*: The speaker is inserted into the middle of this quest with "I think." The speaker was, of course, from the first marked by *This* but moves into a position of judgment from which the moral will be articulated in the next stanza. The land is the desert terrain of the seeker, far from the sea—the "hills like rocky gates" seem to keep out the sea. It is a scene of denial. The sea is notably absent, and this absence is an enclosing and internalizing of the sea's change and the break of waters at the moment of denial ("no sea"), when reflexivity is structured ("leaps upon itself").

The moral of the story appears before the end of the poem as a prophecy, in future time: "he will find that nothing dares / To be enduring." This casts the narrative present of the poem into the past, relative to the speaker, and casts the whole poem as a preamble to foretell the action of the book it introduces. The moral takes the form of another denial: "Nothing dares to be enduring." The land, the light, the lamp are caught up in a figure which both personifies and splits them in a specular encounter. Both seer and seen are themselves split: "torn fire glares / On beauty with a rusted mouth." Light has become "torn fire" and the object "beauty with a rusted mouth." Both *torn* and *rusted* bring the vocabulary of the domestic wasteland to this desert. The verb *glares* personifies the "torn fire" which resonates with previous words in the poem: *suns, days, a light, lamp*. Both active and passive aspects of the light are articulated syntactically as "torn fire" and "beauty," and the object is also personified.

The couplet which ends the poem is stripped of concrete geography and reduced to the syntax of the look, where it locates the story: "Where something dreadful and another / Look quietly upon each other." The split principals of this equation are both object, *something*, and the reciprical subjects of *Look*. The reciprocity also means both are dreadful and other. The sharpest turn of the poem, however, is mounted against the equation of noise and change with strangeness, and this comes with the unaccented insertion of *quietly* in the last line. What dares to be enduring is this scene of quiet, reciprocal dread—the extemity ("south / Of hidden deserts") of strangeness.

The poem inaugurates Bogan's collections with a narrative of the uncanny. The terrible strangeness has certain parameters for Bogan that emerge in this poem, a geography which is meant to depict the irony of the cut which will install an unchanging syntax of otherness. The speaker may be a woman, but her gender is marked only by her alienation from the male heroic quest, and the mutuality of his fire and the beauty that would be feminine but is also another "something dreadful." The youth and the beauty are interchangeable in this otherness. If this is a tale about Bogan's marriage, it records the otherness which the cultural sign system imposes as she takes up the subjectivity assigned to the married, not a differentiation but a loss of heterogeneity. The poet enters into the cultural symbolic system both as youth, subject of the tale, and as wife, beauty, object. Bogan re-creates the splitting which the cut organizes as a dreadful narcissism, a repeated sameness which the voyage into marriage and Oedipal normalcy entails. What is perhaps most dreadful about these indurate others is their uncanny resemblance to the writer, their strange resonance in the writing with the subject of the text who speaks.

This poem puts into circulation the charges of resistance which will shape Bogan's work. There is the overlapping resonance and musicality which returns to undo all absolutes, to open up the breaks and locks by a poetics of affect which Bogan herself connects to women's writing. And there is the other resistance, estrangement—the "indurate" and "strange," the denial of denial which dares to endure even in uncannily monstrous forms. This symbolic resistance is connected, perhaps, to the hard demands of social will, but also to Bogan's mastery of the abstractions of a critical, judgmental discourse.

"A Tale" opens up the unexpected relationship of the artist to melancholy. The poem speaks on the other side of a love story, with ironic wisdom. It does not bring us the melancholy notice of the lover's loss but rather the loss of love itself, and the meaning of the quest. Although that loss is denied, at the same time the poem's sound restores that breaking of waters, the submersion in repetition.

Julia Kristeva writes about the "enigmatic chiasmus" of melancholy in the artist. It is a loss that propels the imaginary act and the disavowal of loss in the fetish of the word.[18] Bogan's poem moves between the object loss which can be filled by a loved/hated other and the deeper loss, essential to the very self, which makes sorrow itself its object. And, as Kristeva has it, such a loss has "the image of death as the ultimate site of desire" (111). According to Kristeva, the repetition of sounds and names can then be seen as "the anaphora that replaces the unique object: not the 'symbolic equivalent' of the mother but the deictic 'this' that, devoid of meaning, points toward the lost object" (113). As an example, Kristeva analyzes the "hysterical affect" of Dostoyevsky's suffering, "the fluid overflowing of which carries away the placid signs and quiescent compositions of 'monological' literature" (115). Does Bogan participate in this undoing of the monological? By the sound? I am inclined to sense that she does, that in her work that "fluid overflowing" works like Pollock's dripping, set within the Medusa effect, which is played out as a horror of female identity.

What is Bogan's attitude toward her own work, her poetry? Is it not the ambivalence registered here? At the same time the literary work repeats the melancholy and so restores the loss as loss but also produces an object, a fetish, an accomplished other. Thus the poem is at once land of change and "something dreadful," locus of the dreadful encounter. Both the musicality beyond symbolization which undoes and opens up language as symbolic work, and the production of the dreadful other have to do with loss and horror of the feminine maternal body. Bogan's work brings the melancholy loss into close contact with the horror and refusals of abjection, and with refusals of the death toward which desire seems to lead. The compression of her forms enforces the pain of the contradiction—the poems produce pain rather than fables of coherence.

Thus, hypocrite lecteur, we are addressed from the beginning with a tale of reading which defines reciprocal dread, a mutual look full of uncanny returns. What has always vaunted its immortality—the indurate and strange materiality of poetry—finds here a moral which both romanticizes such desire: "nothing dares / To be enduring, save where . . . torn fire glares / On beauty" and unromantically prophesies the doubly dreadful result. This intimacy of poet and reader is a love/hate relationship indeed.

Poetry precipitates the body into the cold withdrawal of beauty, into chastity and death, but also into the fire of a criminal seductiveness. Bogan believed that the poet must be a criminal. Rimbaud provided a model. But as a woman, Bogan commits the more dangerous crime, connected with the fatal lure of a maternal fertility as well as sexuality. The body of the poet becomes a bawd. Elizabeth Frank thinks images of "frozen life" are a central theme in Bogan's life and work: "Life stopped dead in its tracks, young female beauty arrested in the act of moving toward life, or away from it."[19] The problem, I want to add, is that art itself is what arrests the act, and that female beauty in Bogan, even when young, is not innocent—to the contrary, the woman is (like the poem) the locus of intemperate, dangerous, antisocial desire.

Bogan rewrites the narratology of myth into a fantasy or nightmare of loss. The hero loses the plot itself, as time becomes space, as narrative becomes antinarrative. This is, of course, part of what makes her "modernist," and also part of what makes the modernist subject seem feminized, outside history. But in Bogan's work, the other and another are without hierarchy, and gender is without a weighted marking. The fantasy may be a horror story—Bogan does not idealize this ungendering. In "A Tale," the search for the unchanging results in a terrible reciprocity. In "Medusa," the shape of the countermyth emerges as nightmare: the hero/heroine is stopped forever by looking into the eyes of the Medusa. If something terrible haunted Bogan, it was not simply a matter of personal psychology. Is this not the general nightmare, the context of Bogan's life, the fear of what will happen if the repressed woman shows her face?

In "Medusa," the temporality of a life narrative becomes the thematic foreground, as life becomes the "still life" of art and therefore becomes as well the reminder of death, like the skull in so many paintings about meditation, representing the subject's gaze into a mirror (4). The hero/heroine confronts Medusa and is turned to stone; not only the hero/heroine but the entire scene becomes "dead," unchanging. This is perhaps the moment not only of artistic seduction but also of the woman's seductive encounter with woman. The moment when the woman encounters the monster and is transfixed has been theorized within film theory. Linda Williams suggests that this is an extension of woman's condition within the gaze, so that the shared status as objects results in a moment of identification.[20] When woman sees the other woman, the monster, she is seized by an uncanny recognition. Here the alternative pleasures of beauty and feminine desire break up heroic looking and promise a horrified enchantment.

The "still" immortality of art explored by Keats depended upon a separation of artisan and urn, speaker and object, poet and poem. Here it is the speaker that must stop, so that the poem pivots on the sequence of verb tense: "I had come," "Everything moved," "This is a dead scene forever now," "Nothing will ever stir," "And I shall stand here like a shadow." While the *time* of the verbs locates the speaker in an eternal present, narration itself does not necessarily stop. The story addresses a reader with a past, present, and future. Thus the story is dissociated from the storyteller by the possibility of a reader. The separation is not between subject and object but between that specular instance and the subject of another text where life goes on, perhaps beyond horror and despair.

"Medusa" signals its entanglement with the maternal in a number of ways. The scene is womblike, an ambiguous shelter, the house itself enclosed "in a cave of trees" in contrast to a "sheer sky" that seems vaguely threatening by its very (clifflike?) height. The multiplied resonances of house-cave-trees recall both good and bad maternal figures, witches and grandmothers, rather than the abode of the Gorgons where Perseus slew the mortal one of the trio, Medusa. The other kind of medusa, the bell-shaped creature which is the sexual stage of the hydra, is here in the soundlessness: "a bell hung ready to strike," a transparent shape of silence.

Time is monumental, cyclical. Sun and reflection define a paradigm of life's mirroring. If the bell sounded it might articulate this scene with a particular moment of time; instead, it is the house—or space—which is particular. The stanza sets up strong but irregular patterns of rhythm, with all three lines after the first beginning on an accented syllable: "Facing," "Everything," "Sun," and a number of words accented as part of a spondee: "sheer sky," "bell hung ready," so that emphasis supersedes regularity. A number of sibilants—lines ending with "trees," "sky," "strike," "by" with a repetition beyond rhyme, "facing a sheer sky," "Sun" beginning the final line—reinforce the repressed menace of "strike" and the hissing of the stanza. As in "A Tale," the sounds invoke certain paradoxes of relationship between motion and stillness. The "strike" would continue life, not bring death. The spondee rhythms seem to resist the level of expression with its sibilants and its alliterative repetition of "come," "cave," "sky," "strike," "reflection," almost like a ticking. Thus "Everything moved" but is stopped at the moment of telling.

> When the bare eyes were before me
> And the hissing hair,
> Held up at a window, seen through a door.
> The stiff bald eyes, the serpents on the forehead
> Formed in the air.

The second stanza describes an instant of horror and recognition. The speaker is elided as a syntactic subject, and subjectivity transfers to the third person, the "bare eyes" and "hissing hair." According to the myth, Perseus avoided the danger of the bare eyes by using his sword as a mirror, so he was able to kill Medusa. The serpent-hair, once, perhaps, an emblem of fertility, has become the symptom of evil and terror but also, perhaps, of a lost maternal power. This vision seems to be of a decapitated Medusa, a head "Held up at the window" almost as if held by someone else, a Persean shadow, and "seen through a door" as if the gaze were illicit. The signifiers of the Medusa are repeated, and this repetition of the forbidden look enters an extra line into the stanza: "The stiff bald eyes, the serpents on the forehead," so that only this stanza has five lines. The eyes seem not only horrible but horrified, "stiff" but perhaps also dead, and "bald," as if so wide open in fear that eyelashes are not visible.

The unnaturalness of this look makes it prototypically uncanny. Is the Medusa the cause of the speaker's fear, or its strangely familiar reflection? The eyes and the serpents are "Formed in the air," disembodied, unreal, dreamlike, perhaps the construction of the observing imagination.

The figure has much to do with the Freudian traumatic fantasy. The Medusa with the horror-stricken eyes is a reflection of the traumatized psyche, a memory of the mother caught in the revelation of sexuality but also the mirror image of a stricken self. The Medusa image is glimpsed like an unrecognized image in window glass. The words seem to form themselves out of one another like anagrams: "bare eyes" and "were before me," "door," and "forehead / Formed." The word "hissing" thematizes the sibilants and sutures sound to signification to produce a kind of terrified compulsiveness, a self being spoken. This is the inscription of Medusa mythology in the subject who knows herself in language. Clair reminds us how recently—since the Renaissance—this rational terror of Medusa has decisively prevailed over the representation of her as fascinating young woman, object of desire. In the poem, the Medusa speech is accompanied by the mutation of "I" to "me," an objective agency. What does this have to do with feminine subjectivity? Does it not record the horror of another

woman? The hero of the Medusa myth cannot confront those bare eyes—
cannot look at her as the subject.

At this point the speaker of the poem emerges to pass judgment:

> This is a dead scene forever now.
> Nothing will ever stir.
> The end will never brighten it more than this,
> Nor the rain blur.

The present tense intervenes to exercise its function of making present the
subject of discourse. The peculiar effect of the statement arises from its
connecting the deictic "This is," which ought to designate a very specific
location of the subject, to "a dead scene forever now." The words resemble
a curse. The other three lines of the stanza, in future tense, likewise seem
ambiguously descriptive and prophetic. The absolute vocabulary rings out:
"forever," "nothing," "ever," "never." (Like lines out of Poe?) This decisive
negation marks the "dead scene" as the place not only of paralysis but
also of *loss*.

Bogan's poem is not quite ironic because it is not fully detached. What
is lost is motion and change, but the vocabulary suggests also emotion.
What is lost is ambiguously a quality outside the observer or an internal
perception or feeling. The power of the poem depends on its externalizing
and objectifying, so that the speaker has no agency, no imaginative will.
Religious, mythological, romantic explanations of such visionary moments
will not do, but neither will the therapeutic diagnosis. The poem may seem
to represent an experience of the individual "I" and the particularity of
this instance, yet the experience is, precisely, a catastrophic loss of particularity, a collapse of time's differentiating force, the spacing between
ever and never.

Louise Bogan's success in unsettling the imprisonment of feminine
subjectivity within the private and domestic space of personal experience
depends on this experience becoming impersonal. The narrative itself is
installed within the stasis of the scene's eternal present, "This is." Fear of
the feminine is attached to the fear of art, with its "dead scene." Thus the
rest of the poem will adumbrate what the observer, now outside the poem,
must see—the fatally charmed moment, bright with sunlight, within which
the kind of scene Keats mused about seeing on the Grecian urn seems
dangerous. The rhetoric is the "never again" trope of elegy. It has a force
which is the opposite of Keats's "happy melodist, unwearied, / For ever
piping songs for ever new," even though both contemplate the ironic immortality of art. The speaker of Bogan's poem is—unlike Keats—captured
by the otherness of the encounter.

The water will always fall, and will not fall,
And the tipped bell make no sound.
The grass will always be growing for hay
Deep on the ground.

The elements of the scene are divided from themselves by this future of never—the water from its fall, the bell from its sound, the grass from becoming hay. The subject in process is stopped. This internal separation is not like Keats; his lover will never kiss the maid, but "she cannot fade." The urn is "still," but its beauty is not dead. The speaker of "Medusa" will fade, become "like a shadow"—that is to say, she will be taken up into the system of sun and reflection, "the great balanced day." What she will see forever is not the paralyzing face of Medusa but "yellow dust." The pastoral scene is a simulacrum of the mortal human body, shadow and dust. This loss is of mortality, separating the human subject from what defines her, from her body.

This is also a loss of the maternal, at once a loss and a rejection. The bell of the womb, the "tipped bell," is stopped by that figure of maternal sexuality, Medusa. As one of the Gorgons, Medusa figures forth the remembrance of matriarchal goddesses made hideous by patriarchal mythology. What is glimpsed by the poem's speaker is a shadow of herself, a feminine subjectivity that is unspeakable and uncanny. Imaged in discourse she becomes the object, "Medusa," the *poem*, a terrible and life-threatening beauty. Bogan sees clearly how much the woman writer might fear the poem she might become.

What might becoming a poem mean? Thinking of this problem both from the point of view of the woman as the centering object, gendered image, and position which culture produces for "woman," *and* from the point of view of the woman as subject, the "other" of language and hence in a position of negativity as a subject, I want to suggest that Bogan's "Medusa" produces the effect of the uncanny because it is a narrative of feminine poetic agency, of the gendered pre-Oedipal melancholy and the word become fetish. The drift of sound is stopped and sutured. This is especially significant for Bogan's work, where the contrapuntal effects of sound figure so importantly. The rich complexity of the rhythm, the rhyme, and the play of anagrammatic punning develops usually into what she calls in "Sub Contra" "some thick chord of wonder" (5). After the break in "Medusa," however, the sounds of words ever and ever seem melancholy and unstressed, and the tone almost nostalgic. There is a thinning out of affect to pure elegy.

This kind of reduction locates the site of the sentimental, where the conventions of loss and nostalgia begin to supersede the poetic gesture and turn sensibility into meaning. In order to resist meaning, like other

American modernists, Bogan uses the imagist image to undo the hold of the familial imaginary. "The grass will always be growing for hay / Deep on the ground." In spite of the symbolic resonance of "grass" with the Biblical image of mortal flesh, or with Whitman, the image appeals rhetorically to the reality of the objective, empirical world and the dramatic impossibility of its stasis.

In the first poem she published, "Betrothed," her disillusionment about the "lost delights" promised by love and domesticity depends on the last stanza's assertion of a realism: "But there is only the evening here" (7). Focusing on the limits established by "the sound of willows / Now and again dipping their long oval leaves in the water," Bogan installs the antidomestic appeal to perceptual experience advocated by modernists from Pound to Williams to Hemingway. For instance, Pound's narrative of Agassiz's method of learning natural history, which involved looking closely at the fish until everything is observed, relies on the ideology of perceptual empiricism, science, and objectivity.[21] With respect to the genteel literary tradition, such objectivity seems nonverbal, lodged in the image rather than conventional language.[22] A certain renewal of a realism is involved. So Bogan's poem cites "the sound of willows" as if that, and not the sound of the poem, were the material base of it, its body. Thus the poem distances its own making (perhaps, because it is in free verse, more than later poems whose formal qualities exaggerate the intensity of the affect which plows up the orders of the imaginary). Similarly, the image of the other glimpsed in both "A Tale" and "Medusa" cites the visual perception as if the trauma were in the real world. At the same time, the image, the trauma, and the poem as fetish or art object do not quite obey the symbolic objectivity and the system of impersonality endorsed by modernism.

III

This is not to say that Louise Bogan is not a modernist poet. I want to say, instead, that she endangers the modernist cover-up. By showing the dependence of modernism on the maternal sentimental and its language, she shows the way out of the modernist apolitical impasse. Even T. S. Eliot's attempt to define the necessity of an "objective correlative" for emotion in poetry is a fudging and a denial of the complicity between gendering and objectivity. It is the problem Hamlet produces at the inauguration of modern gendering and *The Waste Land* produces at its crisis: because the poet works at the borders of the sign, the poet also works in the margins of gendered identity. The abject—not the object—prevails. Emotion exceeds representation. Otherness encroaches on the borders. The sublime and the spiritual are very close to the disgusting and the repugnant, in Eliot as in Bogan. Body and soul are not separated. The status of the image itself becomes questionable. Does the objective image escape abjection or enforce it? Because there are to be "no ideas but in things," as Williams had it, the objects of modernist poetry, of Bogan's as well as Williams's, Eliot's, Yeats's, are saturated with the fantasy of resisting the mother tongue which speaks them. Bogan's poetry is at once modernist and countermodernist.

What did Marianne Moore come to learn from Bogan when she attended her poetry class at the YMHA in 1956, filling her notebook and asking numerous questions?[23] Of the two women, Moore from the beginning wrote with that ironic precision that modernism identified with maturity, seeming to eschew the sentimental. Let me cite a couple of reminders: the lure of marriage in particular had attracted the force of Moore's poetic resistance in "Marriage," together with other forms of the ideal, and her definition of poetry, beginning with "I, too, dislike it," resisted sentimental claims for verse. Advanced in her career, illustrious, Moore seemed not to need anything from Bogan. It was almost a case of the mimetic, objective, empirical spirit coming at last to seat herself before the romantic. Bogan had spent her life mastering a wilderness of passionate response, the wilderness her poem said women did not have in them—enforcing the limits and restraint that seemed to come so naturally to Moore.

In that class, both women were half-immortal already, even though their books were, for the moment, out of print. They were figures of greatness in the legends of poetry, and they were literary mothers with influence that already flowed into the next generation of greatness—into, for example, the work of Elizabeth Bishop and May Sarton. Their achievement is similar in one respect: in the extraordinary concentration of their effects, which fuse the words into form. What they demand of a reader is extreme, and what they have contributed to literature is likewise extreme. But Moore's poems have a more realistic surface, seem less painful and melancholy. Bogan's poems are more hermetic and mysterious by contrast, for Moore's allusiveness seems to refer to things in the world (Persian velvet, bulbul, the Chili pine) and the authority of other texts ("Compression is the first grace of style," from Demetrius) which she documents in her notes.[24] She extends the aesthetic attention one might give a Chippendale chair foot to the jerboa's claw or a Ming vase to the ordinary animal. Bogan says Moore "applies a naturalist's eye to objects of art and of nature."[25] This resembles in one respect the principle of Freud's reading: an empirical attitude to language. Moore's great success with Williams, Eliot, and Stevens may reflect, in part, the overlapping of modernist precision of description with realistic and scientific prose.

Bogan, however, sees something else in Moore, a premodern sensibility, a "passion for miscellany" that is seventeenth-century, "unmarked by the flattening pressures of an industrial age" and poems that make morals, that function like fables or like sermons.[26] In her review of Moore's translations of La Fontaine, Bogan calls their differences "superficial divergences"—"the fact that La Fontaine's moral sense is more materialist and pragmatic than Miss Moore's and that while Miss Moore in her own work observes animals in detail as part of nature, La Fontaine uses them as symbols illustrating the foibles of mankind" (305). Bogan calls attention to Moore's Protestant vigor. "She stands at the confluence of two great traditions, as they once existed, and as they no longer exist"—the one that of the High Renaissance connoisseur, of Francis Bacon, and the other that of the moralist (306–307). Moore stands, in other words, as a recuperation of that sensibility which had not yet worked to create the ideal image of the middle class, and had not yet become sentimental. But how, thus delineating her debts to tradition, can Bogan think of Moore as particularly American? Bogan emphasizes the peculiarly American nature of this confluence, this overlapping of disparate traditions—as Kay Boyle emphasized the American innovation in modernism. This recuperation of the past signals a kind of free association that forecasts the emergence of postmodernism.

The American speaker is not so firmly installed by history in one discourse or another. Bogan's own work also demonstrates the principle of confluence, put under the pressure of condensation by form. As a form of resistance to the purifying forces of modernity acting upon language, this multiplicity enforces a negativity at the place of the writer's identity and offers not only a particularly American way out but a way out for the woman writer, who will become the avatar of postmodernism. When Moore came to Bogan's poetry classes, she was acknowledging the new authority of woman, an authority that Bogan argued but never seemed quite to believe.

Louise Bogan is a connection between the premodernist Emma Goldman and the postmodern Julia Kristeva. Like Goldman, she endorses passion. But Bogan "defamilializes" it by the antinarrative, her antinarcissism. Does she defeminize it as well? And, worse, does she depoliticize it? Her distrust of politics remained intransigent throughout the thirties when other literary figures and friends were deeply involved in John Reed clubs, in the *Partisan Review*. She takes an anarchic posture toward all institutional authority, wanting to avoid the master/slave relations inherent in institutionalizing codes, including the regularities of the left, but she does not even advocate anarchic politics.

What is the complicity of art—including the avant-garde, the experimental—with the conventions and ideology of imprisonment? Bogan seems to think it is great, and she is as critical of the left as of the right. This

complicity is delineated not only in extreme politics but in the commodification of the intellectuals who are caught up in the middle class like
Flaubert's Bouvard et Pecuchet, the literary marketplace where "the commodity books are being dealt with by the commodity critics."[27]

This complicity of the intellectual extends within literary discourse,
within the operations of what Frank Kermode called the "romantic image,"
an image of the woman which both defines the ideality of the image itself
and imprisons women in order to define beauty, love, art. According to
Kermode, the image which dominated modernist poetics was continuous
with romanticism because of its association with artistic estrangement.[28]
Thus Bogan's poem "The Romantic" demands: "Admit the ruse to fix and
name her chaste," and accuses: "In her obedient breast, all that ran free /
You thought to bind" (12). But this romantic is within, in the ruses of
romantic language itself. And since it is the romanticism of the avant-garde
which frees as well as imprisons, the struggle is within the language which
cannot be separated from the self. The romantics opened, Bogan said, "the
difficult and unpopular battle against the eighteenth-century's cold logic
and mechanical point of view."[29] The field of battle for Bogan, as for Goldman and Kristeva in their own senses, must be internal. For better or for
worse, this location of the struggle in the subject may also locate it within
the private, psychological (and so domestic) space which separates it from
the public and the political and associates it with the space that is gendered
feminine.

One might infer Bogan's sense of the poet's task by the greatness she
describes in Emily Dickinson: "she advances into the terror and anguish
of her destiny; she is frightened, but she holds fast and describes her fright.
She is driven to the verge of sanity, but manages to remain, in some fashion,
the observer and recorder of her extremity. . . . the inmost self can be
haunted" (100). Bogan locates Dickinson as a precursor of Rimbaud and
Mallarmé. Dickinson, she says, "begins to cast forward toward the future"
in the *voyant* quality of her work: "This power to say the unsayable—to
hint at the unknowable—is the power of the seer, in this woman equipped
with an ironic intelligence and great courage of spirit" (102). But Dickinson
is also a precursor to the precision of Marianne Moore: "How exactly she
renders the creatures of this earth. She gives them to us, not as symbols
of this or that, but as themselves" (102).

What distinguishes this womanly symbolist tradition for Bogan is its
exploratory trajectory, its struggle to "say the unsayable." But that is also
what makes Bogan want to separate poetry from political attachment. She
criticizes Archibald MacLeish for "the dangers of appealing to the People"
even though he, as she says,

has heard of the sentimental come-ons and exhortations of demagogues and
evidently does not wish to ally himself with such persons. The difficulty is

that he is writing political poetry, even a kind of official poetry, and therefore
the strict checks and disciplines of poetry written for itself (as a result of
reality making a direct emotional impact upon the unique temperament of
a trained and exacting writer) do not hold. (292–93)

Her attack forecasts more virulent attacks by many on Millay for her an-
tifascist and pro-American war poetry. Bogan's use of the word *sentimental*
exposes the modernist bias against appeals to the people clearly as her
own.

Her notion of the womanly in modernism is decidedly antirhetorical,
and so antifeminist in any political argument. In her review of Paul Eluard,
she seems to see poetry preferably as a kind of knowing hysteria. Rimbaud
was a "symptom" of the scientific revolution of relativism that was to come
(114). At the same time that she takes up symbolism as the most important
and exemplary movement for the development of literature, Bogan very
much dislikes surrealism with its commitments to the Russian Revolution.
Such commitments seem to Bogan to prevent exploring the subconscious.
She thinks Dada was "a far more vigorous assault against logic and the
weight of bourgeois ideals than Surrealism." Dada "resembled the forms
of hysteria, but it was the hysteria of an intelligent living entity suffering
from shock. It never developed the paranoid symptoms of Surrealism"
(115).

The connection of poetry with the spiritual, and the poet with the
mystic, a connection she makes again and again in her criticism, makes
the great tradition coherent for Bogan. What she means by the spiritual
has little to do with belief in a religious mythology and nothing to do with
an opposition to the body. Rather, she opposes the secular personality.
Maturity, she believes, is the taking on of spiritual issues, and that means
not ease but suffering and dissonance and confronting the fear of death.
This is a necessity which creates a bitter irony. She writes in 1939 to criticize
Edna St. Vincent Millay for her failure to come to terms with necessity:

It is difficult to say what a woman poet should concern herself with as she
grows older. . . . But is there any reason to believe that a woman's spiritual
fibre is less sturdy than a man's? Is it not possible for a woman to come to
terms with herself, if not with the world; to withdraw more and more, as
time goes on, her own personality from her productions; to stop childish
fears of death and eschew charming rebellions against facts? (299)

When she turned to psychoanalysis for help with the emotional extremities
that came upon her, she was in serious trouble. She saw psychoanalysis
as in some respect occupying the place of religious structures. With the
decline of religion into individualism, she wrote, there is no external ritual

of release, and "the individual conscience . . . is asked to bear the full weight of the individual's transgression" (313). The encounter between "something dreadful and another" cannot be escaped: "Dread, in literature, has now shifted from the outer to the inner scene" (318).

Bogan's way of conceptualizing the spiritual connects it with the problematic developmental models of maturity favored not only by psychoanalysis and John Crowe Ransom but by modernism's view of history as tragedy. She praises Roethke for his theme: "the journey from the child's primordial subconscious world, through the regions of adult terror, guilt, and despair, toward a final release into the freedom of conscious being" (302). What she thinks of as the enduring success of modern poetry, as she puts it in her 1959 review of Robert Lowell, is "the ability to face up to, and record, the raw contemporaneous fact" (287). What she means by that toughness, what she writes, shows the cathartic value of art as "release into the freedom of conscious being" for the melancholy subject. In her relationship to women, this facing up to the facts may sound like betrayal: the poem titled "Women" begins "Women have no wilderness in them" and closes with "As like as not, when they take life over their door-sills / They should let it go by" (19). It is not surprising that women have read Bogan's work as unfeminist. As a modernist poet and critic, Louise Bogan takes up the very conventions which cast the "fact" in the shape of a woman who is the dreadful other.

These conventions also appear in psychoanalytic theory: the first "fact" in Freud is the separation from the mother. The rejection of the maternal characterizes the struggles of the pre-Oedipal stages. Behind the rejection is the melancholy at her loss, and the necessity of mourning. Since Melanie Klein, psychoanalysis has seen a number of theorists who raise questions about this Oedipal sequence. What is the necessity of separation, and its character? What Bogan gradually came to admire as maturity is accepting separation from the mother, the Oedipal crisis, and the advent into symbolic normalcy. That is, she seemed to accept the American reading of Freud which emphasized the desirability of being socialized, and failed to sustain the critique of culture and its conventions which post-Lacanian psychoanalysis has made more visible, and more possible.

Nevertheless, what she writes about women resists Oedipal normalcy. The cut is what leads to "something dreadful." She reworks the modernist tragic fact by her strict accountability. The fact in Bogan's work is that she can never finish with separating or with sorrow, with the fury or with the pain. She is never *not* a woman, her mother, her daughter; never past love, never beyond the issue. In "The Sleeping Fury" she addresses "my scourge, my sister," whose hair is "no longer in the semblance of serpents." In this poem the dreadful figure is asleep, and the speaker acknowledges the female power of her violence:

> You who know what we love, but drive us to know it;
> You with your whips and shrieks, bearer of truth and of solitude;
> You who give, unlike men, to expiation your mercy. (79)

Practicing a poetry of expiation, Bogan surely hopes to thereby secure mercy for the tormented woman who is both herself and, in the "ignoble dream" of the twentieth century, her reader.

It is the family romance which situates the woman, genders and regulates her identity. When she writes about the "facts" (as in "facing facts"), Bogan also produces the whole structure in the shadow of the imaginary. Does she simply reproduce once again the imprisonment of the woman in the romantic image? If so, Bogan is captured in the gendering of the personal; at worst one could fear that her poetry marks nothing more than the crankiness of American individualism.

If Bogan's work resists the recuperative gesture of such a reading, it is not by avoiding the sentimental but by restoring the feminine pain which doubles its expression. So strong is the hold of an objectifying move to distance the sentimental that the very notion of feminine pain may sound itself objectionable. When Roethke congratulated Bogan for avoiding the "caterwaul" usual to the love poet, he recognized the strength of her success. If talking about the pain directly is a "caterwaul," it is also too easily recognized, reduced to personal experiences (that is, the usual complaint of women), and dismissed as sentimental. Bogan allows the rending conflict of the woman to emerge, as conflict. She is caught/positions herself between the dreadful and the sublime in an antinarcissism which both recognizes the fact of the woman's terrifying strangeness to language and recognizes the impossibility for the woman ever to gain sufficient distance from that strangeness. She is caught/positions herself between the love of men and the love of women. She turns down May Sarton's offer of a woman's love ("So far as desire is concerned, I must wait") and confesses her extremity with her husband ("I was a *demon* of jealousy . . . and a sort of *demon* of fidelity. . . . A slave-maker, really, while remaining a sort of slave. Dreadful!"), but the letter confesses: "With a great price bought I this freedom."[30] Her work inevitably confronts the impossibilities of love, for man or woman.

Is this estrangement in her or in the crisis of modernity around her? In Bogan's work, the crisis is (sentimentally?) within. By that I mean no part of the usual pejorative sense of *sentimental*. Bogan, however, exported estrangement in the form of tough critical judgment, writing rather cruelly about May Sarton to Ruth Limmer: "If she would only stop writing sentimental poems! I had her take out two mentions of 'kittens,' from one poem. 'Cats,' yes, 'kittens,' no . . . " (325). Forty years earlier in the opening years of modernism, in 1921, Hart Crane had noted the sentimentality of Charlie Chaplin's humor and defended him as the poet in "Chaplin-esque": "For we can still love the world, who find / A famished kitten on the step, and know / Recesses for it from the fury of the street."[31] Crane had been called a failure and suffered for his romanticism too—as Bogan knew, kittens are as impossible for a modernist poet as love. If Bogan herself avoided the sentimentality of kittens, she did not avoid love.

The poem which ends *The Blue Estuaries* triangulates the conflict in three voices, "Three Songs": "Little Lobelia's Song," "Psychiatrist's Song," and "Masked Woman's Song." The voice of the child as little Lobelia is Blakean. This is no song of innocence; the irony of experience here speaks to the modern exclusion of the personal from poetry.

> I was once a part
> Of your blood and bone.
> Now no longer—
> I'm alone, I'm alone. (132)

It also speaks to the exclusion of the woman from language:

> I know nothing.
> I can barely speak.
> But these are my tears
> Upon your cheek. (132)

The poem seems to be about the unconscious, and Lobelia seems to be a dream remnant who has emerged in symptom. Lobelia, that is, represents a figure of hysteria. The poem suggests that the female "caterwaul" has its origins in repression:

> Give me back your sleep
> Until you die,
> Else I weep, weep,
> Else I cry, cry. (133)

By contrast, the "Psychiatrist's Song" is in a kind of Marianne Moore free verse, which wants to lead toward a Marianne Moore perspective, a natural historian's interest in the world. Nevertheless the poem is neither sermon nor miscellany but rather an uneasiness with the sound which haunts it (134). The poem ends with the vision of an object-grounded "firm dry land" which could provide respite from "hours when murderous wounds are made," "phantoms of flesh and of ocean." The speaker—the one who must listen—finds silence. This self as psychiatrist knows what to invoke: "Vision of earth / Heal and receive me." It is an escape from persons and voices, a vision of objectivity that turns into a pleading. And the final poem, "Masked Woman's Song," restores the gothic fantasy which overturns the beautiful and installs the sublime—or, perhaps, simply, romantic mystery (136). The woman is masked, the man, whom "Few women should see," is "tall," with a "worn face" and "roped arms." If Lobelia poses the sound of hysteria with her weeping, the psychiatrist represents a desire to escape that pain, and the masked woman asserts the sexual/ spiritual criminality of the speaker's vision beyond good and evil. Emotion is nowhere sublimated, but it is surrounded and contained by excessive silence. The abandonment, the scene of terror, the alarm of evil—all are condensed into small space with much surrounding whiteness.

What Louise Bogan said about women writers we should argue for her. It is women who have continued the line of emotion in poetry. At the same time, her willingness to see her work and the work of women as "minor" reflects her perhaps unwilling acquiescence to the intensity of the conflicts she engaged. The intensity, the condensation, the overdetermination of her poems keep the alarming news confined and may even allow the resistant reader to leave them behind as beautiful objects. But Bogan's poems are also symptoms of a melancholy hysteria which, she must have thought, would be dismissed only if it were written out at greater length, if it became recognizably the seductive madness of woman. The story that they do not turn into narrative is a nightmare. The compensation that they leave is the body of song.

Revolution, the Woman, and the Word
Kay Boyle

I

Women's experimental writing had an especially problematic relationship to modernist experiments with poetic language because the women were part of the culture of modernism, representing attachments to everyday life that were not literary. Even though it may now seem that modernist men and women were inventing a kind of *écriture féminine*, challenging paternal conventions by a maternal authority, the men and women of modernism repressed the specific innovations of women writers because they denied these feminine connections. Kay Boyle's early work put the old categories into motion and marked out a new literary space of intense descriptive prose. Yet her impact on literary history has not seemed so powerful as her writing would warrant. In 1928, Boyle signed the manifesto for *transition* calling for "The Revolution of the Poetic Word."[1] Other signers included Hart Crane, Harry and Caresse Crosby, and Eugene Jolas. The "Proclamation" asserted, among other things, that "the literary creator has the right to disintegrate the primal matter of words" and that "we are not concerned with the propagation of sociological ideas except to emancipate the creative elements from the present ideology."

It must be admitted that Boyle's rewriting of the new word was a different matter from the poetics of someone such as Hart Crane, a difference she in fact had signaled herself in a critique of his obsession with the primacy of words, in "Mr. Crane and His Grandmother."[2] Although she shows herself to be in the tradition of Baudelaire and Rimbaud as well, Boyle prefers the American renewals of William Carlos Williams and Marianne Moore. Her innovations in prose style qualify her as a revolutionary of lyric language.[3] In her early works, such as "Episode in the Life of an Ancestor," "Wedding Day," or "On the Run," she swerves her narratives into a language of illumination and intensity that disorders story sequence and the familiar forms of remembering.[4] She experiments in a way that recalls the hallucinatory surrealism of Rimbaud's prose and fulfills the aspiration of the poetic revolution for "the projection of a metamorphosis of reality." But what does this powerful disintegration of conventional writing have to do with writing as a woman?

The strong old forms of the sentimental novel were part of what this modernist poetics—and she too—rejected. And yet, for the modernists, the cultural image of women and writing was deeply involved with that past. A shattering of language seemed to be at odds with writing like a woman, and challenging the image of woman seemed itself feminist and sentimental. Like other modernist women who felt they had to separate themselves from that conventional past, Boyle herself has taken pains to dissociate her work from the older tradition of women's writing and from the politics of feminism. Nevertheless, her reworking of the relationship between time and place, narration and description, also makes the connection between the time of poetic revolution and the place of the woman. I am going to suggest that Boyle shows us how the transition was made, from a representation of woman as the author of conventional romance to the function of woman as a disruptive, disturbing—and so revolutionary— difference in the rhetoric of fiction.

Julia Kristeva, herself a woman who has complicated relationships with revolution and women's writing, may help us to see how time operates in Boyle's work. In her essay "Women's Time," Kristeva redefined Nietzsche's idea of monumental or mythic time, a kind of temporality that is left out of rational discursive history.[5] Kristeva defines "women's time" as "repetition" and "eternity," in contrast with the linear movements of history. Women's time is characterized by

> the eternal recurrence of a biological rhythm which conforms to that of nature and imposes a temporality whose sterotyping may shock, but whose regularity and unison with what is experienced as extrasubjective time, cosmic time, occasion vertiginous visions and unnameable jouissance. (191)

If the order of production defines the time of history, it is the order of reproduction which seems to define this other kind of time, time which is so bound to the monumental, and the regional, that it is almost a kind of space. The cyclic and monumental forms of time associated with female subjectivity are far from the linear times of progress and project. But we must proceed very carefully, with Kristeva as with Boyle, for it would be wrong to suggest that either of them advocates a splitting away of a woman's order from human history.

In her *Revolution in Poetic Language*, when Kristeva associates certain innovations in avant-garde poetics inaugurated by writers in the tradition after Mallarmé with a breaking open of the possibilities of language, she is ambiguous about how women writers might participate in that fracturing.[6] If language itself oppresses, the language itself must be broken in order that marginal subjects, such as women, may be able to speak. And the woman, as marginal subject, is in a position of privilege to do this. But Kristeva's theoretical practice, like Boyle's prose, has been at odds with the discourse of feminism. Let us be careful not to see her antifeminism or Boyle's as simply old-fashioned modernism (let the paradoxical vocabulary resonate for us), for it is attached to some of the most unsettling and promising aspects of modernist experiments with subjectivity.

Boyle, in her practice, resists the binary coding of opposites which would make clear gendered structures for her stories, working instead at multiple and complex borders. Her early work practices this resistance to extremism in the midst of the 1920s modernist extremism about gender. She defies the ideological either/or which would either deny the existence of gender difference in the name of equality or, in a move which Catharine Stimpson calls the "modern counterreformation in support of patriarchal law," claim gender difference, as D. H. Lawrence does, for example, to be the final truth.[7]

If Boyle refuses to write polemically, in behalf of an alternative woman's reality, she also refuses to omit gendered, female elements from her writing. Working within a culture of gendered extremism, she softly moves to put the contradictions into motion. The word *soft* has a certain significance; in an age which favored the tough over the tender, Boyle uses it so frequently it is almost a stylistic marker. A certain radical fluidity characterizes the forward movement of her narration. Hers is not a strikingly avant-garde text, not even at its most experimental, in the sense that such a text by its mode of presentation challenges the reader's ability to read, or breaks flagrantly with the bourgeois norms of realistic prose. But she makes visible the movement of what is left unspoken by the controlling enigmas of realism. So the luminous otherness of her work might well pass unremarked, since it is "soft," since it is neither an embrace nor a refusal of modernism's radical gendered Other.

Boyle's work resists certain categories, traps of ideology, and this includes the categorical oppositions of male and female. It would be too easy to imagine that time could be divided and separated into the two orders: the male order of linear plots, the female order of cycle and reproduction. But, as Julia Kristeva has argued, women's time cannot escape history, and the question for women today is, "What can be our place in the symbolic contract?"[8] Given that our language sacrifices the specific moment as it sacrifices the individual's bodied, material relations to others, Boyle like Kristeva is interested in an aesthetic practice which would make the excluded felt and known. The attention to structures based on linear time and productivity has left us separated from reproduction, from the maternal, from the moral and ethical representations once provided by religion—that is, from cyclical and monumental forms of time. Radical feminists of the seventies, recognizing this, began to talk about a separate female utopia, as if women's time and space could be wholly separated and alternative to the linear forms which organize modern culture. Language does not bridge the gap between individuals because they are identical or identically subjected, inscribed within it, but makes the connection across difference, metaphorically.

II

Kay Boyle's work might be thought of as revolutionary, then, not only because of the shattering of syntax which connects her experimental writing to the avant-garde. She makes the metaphorical connection between individuals, across difference. Her writing subverts the male plot, linear time, by a recursive, anaphoric temporality. And perceptions flow with the voice of the speaker across the boundaries of subject-object, rewriting the romantic identifications with exterior images which Ruskin criticized as the "pathetic fallacy." Boyle uses the fluidity of poetic forms to wash out the one-track temporality of male discourse and to undermine the singularity of gender ideology by a multiple sympathy. She unsettles the stabilities of identity. Women's time enters into history, making it less singular, undoing its regularities.

Three of her early stories will serve as examples of how Boyle's writing might participate in such a project. What kind of narrative time is operating in the story called "Episode in the Life of an Ancestor"? What kind of story is an "episode"? Is it singular or plural? A kind of turning point, or a repeated event?

In the story, a young woman defies her father's conventional desires for her to act like a submissive woman. The masterful way she treats their horses is like the mastery she exercises over her father and a would-be suitor, the schoolmaster. But the conflict between the father and daughter is framed by the long view of history. This is the story of an ancestor, very close to that of Boyle's own grandmother as a young woman.[9] The whole shimmers ambiguously between the backward long vision of memory and the immediacy of a present moment: "But at a time when the Indian fires made a wall that blossomed and withered at night on three sides of the sky, this grandmother was known as one of the best horsewomen in Kansas" (17–18).

The point of view also shifts to produce discontinuities in the linear structure of the plot. It is her father's egoistic will to dominate which provides the conflict in the story: "Her father was proud of the feminine ways there were in her. . . . It was no pride to him to hear [her voice] turned hard and thin in her mouth to quiet a horse's ears when some fright had set them to fluttering on the beak of its head" (17). The daughter/grandmother, however, is not drawn into the conflict. Her perceptions involve the repeated, habitual, physical world, and her mode is exclamatory, even joyful: "What a feast of splatters when she would come out from a long time in the kitchen and walk in upon the beasts who were stamping and sick with impatience for her in the barn" (19). From the daughter's point of view, sympathy is a strong recognition of difference, and her "way with horses" is mastery without egotism. Her point of view flows into the animal sensations of the horse:

> This was tame idle sport, suited to ladies, this romping in the milkweed cotton across the miles of pie-crust. Suddenly he felt this anger in the grandmother's knees that caught and swung him about in the wind. Without any regard for him at all, so that he was in a quiver of admiration and love for her, she jerked him up and back, rearing his wild head high, his front hoofs left clawing at the space that yapped under them. (23)

The wildness of the horse seems to represent some kind of primeval vigor and sexuality that might remind us of D. H. Lawrence. It is, however, an energy both shared and directed by the woman. Against this energy, the father's will appears as unreal imaginings: he longs for "the streams of gentleness and love that cooled the blood of true women" (18). He doesn't know what is going on inside her or outside her. As he sees it, she goes off into the unknown for her ride into a night "black as a pocket." The ironic folds in the fabric of their relationship turn about the schoolmaster, a "quiet enough thought" by comparison to the woman and the horses until the father imagines him in the sexualized landscape of her midnight ride. Then his rage produces a paranoid close-up of the schoolmaster's face in his mind's eye—the detail of hairs and pores—in a failure of sympathy which wildly reverses itself again at the end with his unspoken cry: "What have you done with the schoolmaster?" (14). The father's fantasies are chairbound and disconnected from life. In the end, he cannot even put them into words.

The grandmother has hot blood, a heat that spreads and permeates the vocabulary of the story in a membranous action. The woman is woven into the fabric of the moment as she is into the words of the text, part of the whole cloth of experience. This displacement of human energy onto the surrounding objects of perception makes the descriptions seem luminous, surreal—not imaginary but strongly imagined. The grandmother's intensity spreads into the landscape with its contrasts of soft and hard, white and red, domestic flax and wild fire: "soft white flowering goldenrod," "Indian fires burning hard and bright as peonies" (20). The deep valleys and gulfs and the blossoming prairies form a topology of pocketing and hollows. The father registers how the daughter is a very figure of thereness: "When she came into the room she was there in front of him in the same way that the roses on the floor were woven straight across the rug" (23). He, on the other hand, is the very figure of absence, speechless, longing nostalgically for someone "of his own time to talk to" (23). On the recommendation, apparently, of the schoolmaster, the woman has been reading the passage from *Paradise Lost* about the creation of Eve. Milton's lines expose Boyle's poetic figure, the mutuality of flesh and landscape, and the spousal emotion. But this revelation of poetic influence offends the father, perhaps as much as the sexuality implied in the passage.

Like Milton, her father takes an accusatory stance toward the woman's sexuality. However, the daughter's refusal to be feminine his way, "the cooking and the sewing ways that would be a comfort to him" (20), undoes his ego-centered plot, an undoing which opens possibilities for the woman to be heroic in more multiple ways. Instead of a single hero dominating a single plot in time, Boyle produces the double figure of the daughter/ grandmother and a narrative which circles back from a lifetime to an episode. Instead of a hero who would make the woman over in his own image, she produces a heroine who moves through mastery—of the horses, the schoolmaster, even her father—to a sympathy which is not identification with a male voice. The story is contained by long-distance temporality, as if written on a tapestry, a legendary mode which mimics the male heroic modes only to name them "episode." Female desire reshapes the forms of narrative as well as the forms of description: the woman is a hero who changes the forms of the heroic.

But in "Wedding Day," Boyle does not shrink from showing us female power of a less attractive kind, allied with the bourgeois projects of family and possessions, and the literary mode of "realistic" representation. In this story, it is the mother who works to dominate, through organizing the details of the daughter's wedding day which will initiate her all-too-energetic children, the too-loving brother and sister, into the empty exchanges of proper social relations. The wedding will initiate—and separate—them. It is the mother who makes the violent cut that institutes order—as if she were founding the very system of culture by preventing the incest of brother and sister—but the gesture is also absurd and grotesque. So it finds its image in the "roast of beef" that "made them kin again" as "she sliced the thin scarlet ribbons of it into the platter" (26).

Not that the mother has, exactly, forced this marriage; she says it was not her idea, and her son defends his sister's choice—whose choice it was is confused. The issue is more primitive; the mother's negativity is on the side of the cut, the ceremonial structure, against any outbursts of trouble or love. She opposes her son with a prayer for "dignity," but they find her, returning from a last excursion together, on her knees tying "white satin bows under the chins of the potted plants" (28).

She must maintain the objects of family life as intact mirrors—so it is that she counts the wedding "a real success, . . . a *real* success" when "no glass had yet been broken." Of course, it is the bride at the wedding who is "broken," but that happens beyond the precincts of the "real" which the mother so carefully maintains. Thus, from the point of view of the mother, the story has a happy ending; if she were the author of it, the incestuous energy of the brother and sister's love would be repressed.

Just as the brother and sister threaten the social order and its objects with their desire, the descriptive intensity of Boyle's style violates the decorum of the ceremony with a contradiction and violence that threatens to flood out the containing devices of concrete objects. What are these images doing at a wedding? The red carpet was to "spurt like a hemorrhage." "No one paid any attention" to the wedding cake, "with its beard lying white as hoar frost on its bosom." What is this negativity? There is the "thunderous NO" of the mother, who refuses to give the copper pans to her daughter as the spirit of a family inheritance might suggest. The mother must keep the pans orderly and unused, the "pride of the kitchen," "six bulls—eyes reflecting her thin face." She wishes, indeed, for the orderly household objects to serve as mirrors for the son and daughter as well, representations of the selves she would have them take on.

The young people challenge the civilizing project. These two are Nietzschean creatures, with "yellow manes," "shaggy as lions," "like another race." Like a refrain, the brother keeps repeating, "It isn't too late." But what else might they do except enter into the schemes laid out for them? Something, this story suggests, as it exceeds and overwhelms the bourgeois "real" of the mother: "in their young days they should have been saddled and strapped with necessity so that they could not have escaped. . . . With their yellow heads back they were stamping a new trail, but in such ignorance, for they had no idea of it" (27).

The necessity of youth, of freedom, of a new race encounters the violence of April, like Eliot's April the "cruelest month," bringing the death, here, of childhood. "Here then was April holding them up, stabbing their hearts with hawthorne, scalping them with a flexible blade of wind" (26).

"Over them was the sky set like a tomb, the strange unearthly sky that might at any moment crack into spring" (28). The brother and sister take a ride in a boat together. If the boat ride were solitary, it would be an easy allegory; the wedding would represent the shackling of the poetic spirit. However, they are two; what is between them we are less likely to see as a visitation of the romantic imagination than as incestuous desire. Neither they nor we know if they should act on what they feel. "And who was there to tell them, for the trees they had come to in the woods gave them no sign" (27).

The signs of the story produce not a judgment about how the plot should have gone but a negativity that opens up the forms of the wedding and the story to something else, something which like the sister and brother does not wholly fit in the bourgeois "real," something full of energy, destructive and exuberant. At the end the daughter's "feet were fleeing in a hundred ways throughout the rooms, . . . like white butterflies escaping by a miracle the destructive feet of whatever partner held her in his arms" (29). The wedding, far from locking her exclusively to one person, has propelled her into an anonymity of social exchange. The brother's antagonism scatters the calling cards around the rooms. An exotic, almost romantic, energy inhabits the mother's performance as she dances, undermining her decorum, and destroying the very syntax of the sentence: "Over the Oriental prayer rugs, through the Persia forests of hemp, away and away" (30).

In "Wedding Day," Boyle reveals the hidden violence of the social contract and releases the energy of exposure to work on the forms of prose. At the same time, she does not wholly cast the mother as executioner, the daughter as victim. Rather, she exposes the sacrificial violence of the wedding itself, and the relentless secularity of its bourgeois forms. Boyle resists a "women's writing" which would trap her in an oppositional category identified with the bourgeoisie; she neither endorses nor combats but rather eludes capture in the mother's forms.

Boyle's elusiveness produces an unsettling. She is always in favor of something which illuminates the landscape with significance—call it love— something which bends the narrative plot away from its resolutions, which turns the eye inescapably to the detail, apparently decorative, but now repeating anaphorically the interestedness of the subject who writes. These are stories not about isolated selves but about the mutual imbrications of relationships among people, and so they do not disguise the complexity of perspectives which our feelings for each other are likely to generate.

Even a story as purely focused as "On the Run" shows the contrary motions of resolution coming up against one another and that language of significance breaking closures, keeping the time itself open. The situation is close to autobiography: two lovers, like Boyle herself with Ernest Walsh, are wandering across the south of Europe, unable to find a place for the sick man to rest—thrown out of hotels because he is dying. In "On the Run," memory is left permeable—fragile, undecided, unpunctuated, determined only by the universal timelessness of death that thus seems everywhere. David Daiches says that Boyle's stories are like parables, with "a special kind of permanence" about them.[10] In our culture, this sense of permanence may be identified with women's time, appearing as a contrary narrative that works across the linear, historical plot. This is especially visible in "On the Run," where the history is known, and the story exists nevertheless not in a past but in a recurring present, like a parable.

The young couple must deal with a woman who orders them to leave rather than helping them. It is not just a person but social convention itself which opposes them. The proprietress of the hotel is, in fact, in mourning. She seems to know all about death:

> Bereaved in the full sallow of her cheeks bereaved and the tombstones rising politely polished with discreet sorrow bereaved and remembered with bubbles of jet frosted on her bosoms and mourned under waves of hemmed watered crepe. I have mourned people for years and years this is the way it is done. (105)

She seems also to possess a kind of knowledge about religious conventions of sacrifice: there was her "rosary hanging like false teeth," and "the Christ bled with artistry" on her crucifix. But her knowledge has all been projected onto the objects, reduced and transformed to fetishes. So what she says is: "Your husband cannot die here. . . . we are not prepared for death" (106). Here is the terrible irony, that the sick man must keep on going. Like the mother in "Wedding Day," the proprietress does not seem to know what women are supposed to hold in custody: the value of relationship, the cycles of time, of the generations, of biological time. And like the mother, she has translated all of it into the social symbolic.

Thus women's time must return through the narrative of the story. Boyle's writing stops the forward pressing of historical time, like the train stopped at "Saint-Andre-les-Alpes," and sidetracks it into sensuous, loaded detail: "As the train stopped a soft pink tide of pigs rose out of the station-yard and ran in under the wheels of the wagon. The crest of little alps was burning across the roofs of the town, with the dry crumbling finger of the church lifted and the sky gaping white and hot upon decay" (103). She strips the sick man's words of their history to let them fly out as if prophetic, repeated, stripping them even of punctuation: "Get her out of here he said I am going to cough Christ is this where the death will get me take the cigaret and when I cough walk around the room and sing or something so they won't hear me" (104). There is no period after his words.

The conflict with the proprietress does not appear as a single plot with a conclusion but as the anaphoric structure of enduring betrayal. The message of betrayal is repeated three times, each introduced by the phrase "The bonne came back to say." It is a sacramental structure. At the end, too, the man's words seem to escape the symbolic conventions of the story and sound in the mind like stream of consciousness, recurring. This is anamnesis, a resurrection of the past and not just memory: "Keep on keep on keep on he said maybe I'm going to bleed" (107). Such a resurrection takes place in the process of a narrative dialectic between the linear time of history that is past and the personal time of remembrance, anamnesis. Anamnesis is the form of recollection which Plato associated with eros—and with access to eternal truth. It is the word for the "remembrance" of Christian communion. And it is the unforgetting of the past which Freud advocated, the healing memory of pain which psychoanalysis could effect. This time which Boyle produces is associated, as well, with what Julia Kristeva calls "women's time."

This resurrection—and not just recollection—of a moment of pain and love inserts difference into the history. The position of difference which we may associate with women's time here is different from the polarized opposition which some of Boyle's characters, like the mother and the proprietress, seem to inhabit. This alternate version of narrative, with its descriptive intensity overwhelming the forward movement of plot, opens language up to the surreal, the hallucinatory. Narrative time gives way to descriptive space.

The energy is not in the story, or the forward movement of plot, but rather in the metaphorical connections among people and places—in relationship. Even though these connections shift and develop through time, so that it looks as though there is an elaboration of plot, the motive force of the story is not erotic in the masculine mode. That is, the displacement of desire does not take the form of an adventure. The energy here is moral, even if the situations are unconventional.

Let us look a little more closely at this descriptive language which so many of Boyle's readers have noted—which Margaret Atwood cites as one of her most striking attributes.[11] Sandra Whipple Spanier associates it on the one hand with a Joycean project and on the other with the romantic perspective in Boyle: she "depicts the external world as a reflection or projection of the perceiver's consciousness."[12] Like Joyce, Boyle writes a "lyric" novel, which decenters the lyric subjectivity, the image of an ego. Boyle opens language to the pressure of the unspeakable; her words are saturated with the residues of what cannot be said but can be mutually felt. In doing this, she changes the way we might think about the so-called pathetic fallacy.

Boyle rewrites the romantic reflexivity, shattering the mirror relationship of self and nature under the pressure of a point of view that flows everywhere and comes from no single or stationary ego, or subjectivity. In this, she eludes the very categories of romantic, unified selfhood, of the "true and false appearances" with which Ruskin had thought through his influential critique of the "pathetic fallacy."[13] Ruskin, let us recall, had argued that it is "only the second order of poets" who delight in the kind of description produced by violent feeling, a "falseness in all our impressions of external things" which "fancies a life" in foam or leaf instead of maintaining distinctions. Ruskin's "great poet" masters feeling:

> But it is still a grander condition when the intellect also rises, till it is strong enough to assert its rule against, or together with, the utmost efforts of the passions; and the whole man stands in an iron glow, white hot, perhaps, but still strong, and in no wise evaporating; even if he melts, losing none of his weight.[14]

The whole man arises in the imaginary as if forged in the steel mills, the image of reason. This nineteenth-century vision of the strong ego, the rational individual, has retained its heavy influence in twentieth-century criticism, visible in the work of critics such as John Crowe Ransom and Yvor Winters, and visible in the great fear of a "sentimental" softening which permeates criticism.

Boyle's practice, like Joyce's, breaks open this paranoid logic of the subject. In the place of individual heroic figures, she has the multiple connections of relationships; against the center of a linear plot she brings a counternarrative to bear. Words do not simply mirror subjects; the luminosity of her language tracks the energy of a freed desire to make connections. Hers is the logic of a poetic revolution which makes room for the woman, as for others. In this it is not simply experimental, and indeed, the chief characteristics I have observed here are to be found, in slightly different forms, in her later, apparently more conventional work.

Boyle works to rewrite the extreme imagination of reason which erases woman from the place of the subject or installs her as the singular Other of male discourse. Hers is instead a lyric refiguring of the story which produces more multiple possibilities. It might simply be called the logic of sympathy.

Freud introduces the sentimental into the heart of rational discourse, and that is the formula of modernism, but he also strengthens the rhetoric of countersentimentality, which forbade not only happy endings but also love stories. Boyle's fiction allows this anamnesis of the sentimental to overwhelm the tragic plot, so that her insistent interruption of forgetting produces a certain politics of solidarity not with family ideology but with women's lives.

The struggle of narratives appears in fiction by men and by women. Ernest Hemingway's *A Farewell to Arms* is like much fiction written in the painful aftermath of World War I, seized by the desire for some kind of return to human relationships. As Sandra Spanier has convincingly argued, critics have lost sight of the context of Hemingway's work. Catherine has the qualities Hemingway most admired, attributes usually associated with his male heroes.[15] Her death because of childbirth in the novel should not, then, be attributed to a cynicism about love on the part of Hemingway. The novel is an example not of countersentimentality but of the increasing impossibility felt by writers of producing an anamnesis of love and of maternal themes which would not be contained by a more tragic plot: it is an example of Hemingway's sentimentality. And it is an example of the deep longing to escape the tragic plot which would permeate modernism from Proust's *madeleine* to Eliot's rose garden, and emerge as the dominant chord of postmodernism, whether as carnival or as nostalgia.

This struggle with love and desire appears in literature at the time when the efficiency of the machinery for regulating and organizing human labor had been ratcheted up several notches, first by the military in the war, and then by the Taylorization of industry and the invention of the assembly line. As the forces of work become more and more demanding, it becomes increasingly important that work contradicts the domestic plot which it pretends to support—work drives the family underground. That is, the separation from the maternal leads to not a *paternal* role but a rejection of the whole enterprise—the father absents himself, and the family, not just the woman, is repressed. The military attitude was surely no more antifemale than the industrial, though the military has been more forthright about its stance: "If we wanted you to have a wife, we'd have issued you one" was a Marine Corps commonplace as late as the war in Vietnam.

The important place of irony in modernist literature is related to this repression of the domestic. The wife that used to make it all possible is now a hindrance; technology takes over the wifely work, as Barbara Ehrenreich and Deirdre English have detailed in *For Her Own Good*.[16] Sandra Gilbert has argued that women's culture and men's culture separated dramatically before the 1920s because of the First World War, when women found themselves newly powerful and men found themselves disillusioned.[17] Paul Fussell's *The Great War and Modern Memory* greatly influenced Gilbert's notion of the war's impact.[18] He argues that the horror-filled and nightmarish experience of the infantryman grounds a sense of reality which patriotic optimism denied. Irony is the only possible point of view. Gilbert goes on to conclude that women's experience was excluded from a literature with such assumptions. But our ability to read even Hemingway is severely affected as well.

The dialectic of love and tragedy, the personal and the public which generated male modernism hardened into a critical party line which excluded not only women but attitudes that seemed feminine, or sentimental. Fussell, says Ian Hamilton in a 1989 review of his book on World War II, is so driven by his own terrible years as an infantryman in World War II that he rejects all but the ironic stance and "his hostility to America's 'unironic' temper, to its earnestness and sentimentality, is of such depth and ferocity that it leads him to over-value almost any piece of writing that is not actively soporific or mendacious."[19] This suggests that, while Fussell has helped us to interpret modernism, it is because he represents the modernist attitude, and the obsession with the repetition of military horror which reproduces it. The ironic stance is thus more than irony; in the form of this horror it has seized the imaginary and come to seem the only credible stance for the whole of this century's literature.

Yet neither Freud's sense of tragedy nor the postwar bitterness of disillusionment provides an alternative to the overdetermination of a single narrative plot and the domination of an image of separation and loss extended as linear time. And even though the story seems to entail growing up to face reality, it involves denial of the human bonds which situate the maternal real. It is a plot writers have struggled to rewrite, and the struggle between irony and American sentimentality does not belong to women writers alone. The dominance of a thematized irony has meant exploring alternatives to the alienated individual who spins off into war and into the free-market economy, free as well from any complicated or novel-length human connections. The pain of these explorations surfaces as the recollection of feeling in style. In that respect, Kay Boyle is both innovative and paradigmatic in her writing. Her attention to the issues of women places her closer to the borders of the problem. Far from giving us the sentimental as an escapism, she makes us recognize how a love story might be closest to the real problem.

III

The "revolution of the word" appears to precipitate a crisis of the family by rejecting domestic claims along with domestic, genteel fiction. Thus the themes of free love appear and reappear, and challenges to the old codes of a social Puritanism make up an important part of what seems revolutionary, from Emma Goldman through Henry Miller. D. H. Lawrence and James Joyce both celebrate sexuality at the same time that they open up family structures to intensities of disequilibrium, so that the carnivalesque of style which undermines conventional prose also undermines conventions of sexuality and family relations. The family order of mothers, fathers, daughters, sons seems not the origin of emotional freedom but the very structure which oppresses. Freud's narrative sequence dominates narrative form, directing plot toward separation. At the same time, the family romance provides the fictional matrix, so that the more the discourse is about escaping the maternal, the more it is contained by the maternality thus conjured, which operates as an unconscious eternal return of the same. The conflicts generated by this internalizing of narrative mark modernist fiction and modernist life with extreme violence.

Writing inside this extremity, Kay Boyle nonetheless seems to discover a style which opens up the crises of the family. That is, she puts the sentimental narrative back into play, not as a mode of mastering the plot and rescuing it for family values but as a discourse which softens and disputes the forms of revolution. Nothing, at the end, could be more like having it all than the multiplicity of loves for which she manages to find a place. Yet this protean inventiveness is not quite comic; it has, in fact, its own irony. She does not deny violence and pain, and she resists the narrative closures which might provide a contemplative or satirical distance.

The first pair of novels she published operate like a counterpoint opening up the impossibilities of love in a culture dominated by bourgeois manipulations. The descriptive voice—speaking the American speech as Williams heard it, as an empirical, democratic voice which believes in perception—establishes a strangeness relative to its setting in European bourgeois culture. This descriptive empiricism separates patriarchy from the ordinary American observer. In *Plagued by the Nightingale* and *Year before Last*, Boyle writes the kind of closely observed love story that a French sensibility might recognize, but this does not mean that the style is European, not at all. The negativity and questioning evoked by the revolution of the word are directed against the European patriarchal orthodoxy instead of the middle-class gentility of American culture, where, Boyle claims, it is merely derivative and translated.[20] Thus Boyle's modernist critique of the domestic and the genteel is very different from that of Eliot or Pound, who are critical of American culture but, like James as well, identify with European conservative attitudes.

Furthermore, the narrator representing the ordinary American free individual is a woman. Such a point of view is already well connected to themes of feminism, independence, and even free love in American literary traditions, and after Daisy Miller and Edna St. Vincent Millay, readers may have almost expected Boyle to present such a female narrator. But Boyle separates her critique of the bourgeois family from the conventions of free love, with its rebellions against the connectedness of individuals and its unholy alliance with Mill's rationalistic feminism. This sensuous narrative voice lodges its critique in the body, the figure, the symptom—not accepting the family romance in any of its formulas. The narrator rebels against the bourgeois family's manipulative economy, for example, by deciding to do exactly what the family apparently desires: have a baby. There is no retreat from the sexuality of the maternal.

In *Plagued by the Nightingale* Boyle critiques a classic French bourgeois family. Two newlyweds arrive for a summer with the family and find themselves trapped, Nicolas the victim of the family's disease, and both without escape from its "safe" imprisonment. Family imperatives are diseased, crippling in themselves, and parallel the crippling illness imposed by the family genes on the young husband. The new American wife, Bridget, who tries to learn both French and the family language, finds herself at odds even with her husband, who fights and is ever more entangled.

European patriarchy constructs domesticity as a feminine world, "a world of women who lived without avarice or despise . . . a woman's world built strongly about the men's fortune and the men's fortitude" (69), and Maman's forceful management extends to the village, where she organizes the people to fight a fire. It is the men who have the disease, who act like children—Jean, with his fortune, is forever dissolving in tears—but it is the men, too, who police the bourgeois standards: there is "Papa's intense feeling about immoral literature" and Oncle Robert, who presses past Maman's defenses to discover the glass ring left on her cabinet, and leaves a judgmental remark with the others about Bridget's earrings. Nicolas feels the disease is the family's, that they never should have had him knowing the crippling heritage, that they are responsible for him now. His rage is murderous—"imagine the joy of slowly killing Maman . . . ripping Papa up the middle!" (50)—but the family's desire is always for more children, for babies, and the family desire is inexorable.

The story is told from the point of view of Bridget, who does not speak French and who comes from an American family which let its members go off as individuals. Thus the book is written as if outside language and culture, in objects and gestures and places, without judgments. The bourgeois feminine world is "strange." Bridget enters it first to last as a body, as the object of the family gaze and the design for more babies. When she goes for a swim, her legs are bare, but the others cover themselves in bathing dresses, and Bridget sees Annick, the daughter who would be a nun, look at her with "half-revulsion for her exposed legs and arms" (13). She is a female body, the object of reproductive desire but also of revulsion.

The family plots revolve around the family's own reproduction. Charlotte has married the first cousin, Jean, brought his fortune next door, and produced five children. The three girls—Annick, Marthe, Julie—are in long-term pursuit of the young doctor, Luc, who visits each year and seems ready to be ensnared by the family. And Nicolas has brought home the American bride, who must now produce a child. The men's control of the fortune is all directed toward managing the family's reproductive will. Papa promises fifty thousand francs to the couple if they have a child, while

Jean and Oncle Robert refuse to lend them any money to make an escape. If it is a feminine world, the women's only power rests in maintaining themselves in this time of reproduction, apart from history and change. When Charlotte's body becomes repulsive in her last pregnancy, as she grows more horribly sick, her breath foul, her tongue white and swollen, her revolting body confined to her dark bedroom, the family's ruthlessness becomes more apparent: they delay the necessary surgery too long and she dies. The woman is the sacrificial body, and woman's work is having children.

What Bridget's American point of view brings to this family plot is not a male alternative—not escape, not adventure. Instead she finds some mutual attraction and encourages Luc's resistance until he decides not to marry into the family: "What was the nightingale's small liberty to the deep wide exemption she had given Luc, she thought" (334). She agrees with Nicolas, that she brought him back to "the heart of his family and now it is up to me to get him out" (211). She listens without denial to his proposals that she have a child with another man, to avoid the disease. At last she resolves to have a child. Whether Nicolas will be the father is left decidedly open. Thus the reproductive realm of "women's time" comes to operate not as the defining center of the bourgeois family but as a maternal irony that recognizes the family's deadly exploitation of Charlotte's body—and Bridget's enduring ability to escape family regulation altogether by the freedom to make love with someone else. This maternal, female irony is not the utopian vision of total escape associated with advocates of free love—it is the irony always available to the oppressed, to colonized, domesticated peoples (including America) as to women.

As the novels work out the implications of sensuous style on an external scale, on the level of culture as well as experience, one of the chief consequences is that style works to elaborate a borderline individuality, not isolated but rather metaphorically related to others, to place, and to context, woven into the tapestry. The experimentalism in linguistic point of view that crosses boundaries and denies isolation works not only in Boyle's early stories, where condensation and stream of consciousness make the form private, intense, and lyrical. Comparing the short story "On the Run" with her second novel, *Year before Last*—written after the death of Ernest Walsh—may suggest how the shift from internal to external focus operates.

The scene represented in "On the Run" appears again in *Year before Last*, greatly changed. Instead of concentrating all the times when hotels rejected the dying man into a single, symbolic moment, the scene is one added chapter in a painful series. The novel externalizes the private experience, extending it across many spaces: the northern town, the southern chateau, the restaurants, train stations, hotels, Saint-André, St. Jean-les-

Pins. The question is not whether Hannah and Martin will love each other—there is no courtship, only consequences. Nor is it whether or not he will die: he is living on a pension, on externally funded time. He has, in a sense, already been killed in the war:

> There's nothing to me, said Martin. I'm not here at all. My boots were found on a tree-top, sticking up to scare the crows from their direction. My clothes, he said, and he touched his cloak, are now hung on a peg and stuffed with straw to make them human. Touch me, Lady Vanta, said Martin softly leaning forward. Touch me. That was the night I died. (182)

What changes as the story develops is, instead, the relationship with the other woman, the relationship between Hannah and Eve (was she always already other?). It is not allegorically simple; the two women are like sisters, rivals, and like mother-daughter. Eve is a difficult, strong—and "virginal"—woman who owns the magazine which Martin is at work editing. "But there was Eve as well, between them there on their first morning together: the woman who could go to prison for a thing. . . . She was a brave woman, thought Hannah" (5).

The question between the women is whether the erotic young love of Hannah and Martin has any moral force. Hannah has left her husband, Dilly, to be with Martin, and Martin's alliance with Hannah has caused Eve to leave him, withdrawing not only her financial support but also her magazine.

> Now if I were a brave and a simple woman, thought Hannah . . . I would see sin and virtue and be able to distinguish between them. I only believe in sin when I see the fury on Eve's face, and I must be the sinner. When I see the look she has now with him I know there can be no virtue in having come between these two. (67)

The two women are reconciled at the end, at the scene of Martin's death: "Hannah, Hannah, my darling, Eve cried out like a woman gone mad. Hannah, will you save him! Can you save him, Hannah, Hannah, my lamb?" (219). The women seem to occupy two points of a Freudian family triangle. This is not to argue, however, that Eve represents the maternal and Hannah the erotic in a straightforward psychological allegory: Hannah cares for Martin as she did for her husband in a motherly way, starching the collars of his shirts, administering his medicines. Eve, on the other hand, is cruel and jealous and flirtatious.

Nonetheless, the elements of plot are a familiar triangle: they are the endlessly recombining elements of the family drama, and like the soap opera, they have no necessary conclusion but death. That is, the forms that structure this work are continuous with the forms that structure the texts of mass culture—the best sellers and romances for women as well as the soaps.

That does not mean that we should be critical of such forms. Like the experimental structure of the short stories, the relational plot lets Boyle overthrow the hero-centered formula of fiction. Tania Modleski's argument in *Loving with a Vengeance* for the interest of women's mass culture texts will perhaps help us to carry on this discussion in a way that continues to take these forms seriously.[21] That women's plots are easy to recognize should not make them any more trivial than masculine plots with more action and less moral agonizing. Modleski suggests that the pleasure women take in the soap opera might be something feminists would want to build on rather than reject, because the apparent limitlessness of the text has the effect of "decentering" the classic (masculine) heroic self or ego: "soap operas may not be an entirely negative influence on the viewer; they may also have the force of a *negation*, a negation of the typical (and masculine) modes of pleasure in our society" (105).

I am arguing as well that another kind of plot needs to be put into dialectical relationship with the linear plot of action and adventure. In *Year before Last*, Boyle writes a love story, refusing to make it carry some other significance about the tragedy of desire. Words, almost a good in themselves like the colors aroused by paint or the light of perception, take up the energy of a desire for connection. Another kind of temporality is installed. Boyle's style performs the drama, making precise the metaphorical nature of subjectivity. Thus objects—like words—become acts: they dramatize not only the self but the way the self connects to others, to the world. Take, for example, Eve's dresses:

> She had taken a room on the other side of the hall. And there were her frocks shaking out on their hangers. Five pairs of elegant shoes were out of her bags already and set along the wall, waiting, with their toes turned in. Waiting for tangoes, waiting for rhumbas, waiting till Martin could go stepping out again. I've been taking dancing lessons to fill in the time.
> The time, said Eve and the word gaped wide before them. (209)

It is as if the motive force for action were not lodged in a singular "I" but rather was dispersed into all the environment. The point is to resist "the time" of inexorable death. The law of cause and effect seems beside the point, and morality is not a matter of rules and consequences. But the acts of individuals are not wholly irrational either; they take place as a function of context, as a matter of what can be described rather than analyzed. *Year before Last* coheres around the intensity of lost love, and the tragedy that not heroism but the loss of a connectedness brings. The metaphor of relationship proves to be the figure of a moral law.

Boyle's early fiction seems experimental but not political, and as her later fiction becomes less experimental, it also seems more involved in the context of history, more firmly embedded in historical time. Superficially, her career seems to follow an evolution of writing away from the personal and toward more public forms. But this is misleading. Contrary to this appearance, her early work already establishes the basic moral principle, the metaphor of intersubjectivity. Furthermore, I believe that her later work becomes more difficult and less accessible in a way that is significant for feminism. As the novels become "clearer," and more clearly lodged in a sense of political history that defies dominant positions, they also become more rhetorically challenging to familiar (family) ideologies of human relationship and more clearly *different* from familiar male narratives.

Boyle's soft revolution defies convention by describing the intensity of relationships that should not be "interesting," like the relationships of women to one another, or that should not be seen sympathetically, like the love of an American woman for a Nazi doctor in *Death of a Man*, or the pain of a prisoner of war returning to Germany in *Generation without Farewell*. She does not give us predictable American attitudes or relationships. Jaeger, the protagonist of *Generation without Farewell*, is a man who identifies with women. But more than that, couldn't we say that the narrator, winking at us over the heads of these characters, is a woman? Nancy Miller's *The Heroine's Text* explored how male narrators looked at the reader through the texts of their heroines, so that the story is still governed by a male exchange.[22] It would be interesting if we could show that Boyle institutes a female narrator who does the same. But if so, how do we explain this femininity in a narrator looking into a phallogocentric culture? Isn't this move out of the hands of the author?

Boyle works this by identifying her female narrators with other oppressed subjects and subjects of colonization. Jaeger, displaced, is a returned German prisoner of war, working in ersatz-wool clothes and secondhand shoes, identifying with the Jews and with the resistance. And is the female narrator, looking past him at her readers, not in a similar position? The character who at once represents his German culture and yet resists it resembles the American Kay Boyle, and the resistance of women. Thus there is an exploration of the complexities of complicity, of loss of power, of subversion. But this figure—Jaeger—is a difficult hero. Who is to identify with him? What reader will be able to read such a point of view? When Boyle lodges subversion in this kind of resistance, a negativity which depends upon the response of readers, and does not direct it, she makes her text vulnerable to the other readings of history which surround her. And indeed, she has suffered.

Boyle is a modernist writer, but not in the mainstream of American modernism. Description in her work is different from both journalistic reporting of historical events and a certain line of modernist metafiction. In her work description is infused by an ideology of democratic appeal— call it sentimentality—which *represents* the problem of the feminine, thematizes it. Yet her description also problematizes the woman in language at the level of the signifier, forcing language back upon itself into internal reflection and disrupting its paternal functioning. Alice Jardine's comparison of American and French writers can perhaps help to clarify Boyle's position. In *Gynesis*, Jardine argues that modernity operates differently for the two traditions.

> The American interpretive response to twentieth-century crises in legitimation has not been one of exploding paternal identity, concepts, and narrative to get at their feminine core, through a rearrangement of *techne* and *physis*, a radical rearrangement of gender. . . . The writing subject and his sentence both remain integral unto themselves—and very male—by shoring up textual barriers against the "Nature" that threatens them (Burrough's "virus") or by deriding and dismembering that body, which, if explored, would disturb their satire as technique (Barthelme's Mother and Julie). . . . [The American version of *gynesis*] seems to exist here only at the level of *representation*. (236)[23]

But, as Jardine points out, the insertion of female voices into this dichotomy reveals new possibilities for feminists to take advantage of the interrogations modernity has inaugurated. Boyle's work identifies the narrator with other suppressed voices—challenging male modernity at the level of representation—and at the same time puts the gendered subject under question at the level of the signifier, a practice which differentiates her work from American modern and postmodern texts. What Jardine means by "modernity" begins with the period which includes American modernism but is really most of all what we call postmodern. Boyle needs to be seen within this cosmopolitan modernity, as a writer who has written after modernism from the beginning, and a writer who has directed European sensibilities and American speech to a practice American interpreters cannot quite recognize, inserting the question of the woman into *style*. Nonetheless, the confusion or even the disregard of Boyle's readers may signal for us how difficult such work must be, and how the revolution of modernism has not finished.

In a speech titled "Writers in Metaphysical Revolt," Boyle tries to specify the nature of the literary revolution of which she was a part. It is democratic. It involves putting the voice of the people into writing. She sees herself, like William Carlos Williams, like William Faulkner, as part of a particularly American project: "There was . . . before the twenties, no lively, wholly American, grandly experimental, and furiously disrespectful school of writing, so we had to invent that school" (3). American culture, however, is not necessarily receptive to the disrespectful, especially when the woman furiously subverts the panaceas of family respectability. What Boyle submits to the experimental cauldron of her prose is the most threatening of cultural forms, the very plot of the family romance.

Forty years after those novels of the late twenties and early thirties, Boyle wrote a closely autobiographical novel from inside the events of the late sixties in San Francisco: the protests against the Vietnam War, the jailing of protesters, the concurrent struggle for civil rights engaging black Americans, and the darkness of the Hell's Angels and the cult of Charlie Manson. *The Underground Woman* thematizes a politics grounded in personal attachments and confronts the pain of a family order which comes apart on the level of representation. Boyle might well remind us here of Emma Goldman's voice telling of the same descent into the other world of prisons, outrage fueled by the same maternal sympathy. The political is personal. "Believe that our separate lives are of no importance? . . . Is anybody ever prepared for that? Isn't that the thing they always forgot to make convincing in church or school or whenever we asked for advice?" (55). And the fiction is rhetorical, filled with argument for a moral stance. By its overt advocacy it is kin to Harriet Beecher Stowe and the old traditions of women's prose. Its appeals are sentimental. It is hard to read, and for different reasons than *The Waste Land* was hard.

In *The Underground Woman*, Boyle tells the horror story of a mother whose daughter is taken away by a cult, juxtaposed with the more public story of the woman's protests against Vietnam. Athena, the Kay Boyle character in the book, is a professor of mythology—an interpreter of ideologies, not a writer. The members of the cult invade Athena's house, propelled by the fury of "Pete the Redeemer" who had declared, "I hate the world, and I'll hate it until it's completely destroyed" (119). There are different orders of destruction in the book: the cancer that killed Athena's husband, the cult that takes her daughter, the government that goes on with the war. But Athena is not propelled by hate. The mother's solidarity with another protesting mother, Calliope (Joan Baez's mother was the model), is absolutely dependent on their moral commitments. When they go for a climb up Angel Island on a free day, they find disengagement from the antiwar effort very difficult, almost immoral.

> "This is the one day in our lives we can have away from everyone!"
> "We can start by rejoicing that we're free" and at once the shadow of guilt fell on their hearts. (257)

The guilty freedom seems escapist. Deer follow them, and Boyle turns to one of the most conventional of sentimental emblems to express the commitments that mobilize their fellow feeling. In spite of the two women's shared experiences in jail, in the free pleasures of the hike there is a veil between them. "Yet if one of these deer, just one, should be felled by an illicit hunter, Athena pictured how she and Calliope would turn as one person, inseparable in its passionate defense" (259).

Is this use of sentimental rhetoric something we should criticize in Boyle? A sort of need for irony may be generated in us by these emotional appeals, even though they ground the argument through history for all humanitarian appeals. As readers, we are well trained in modernism. It is extremely difficult to talk about a feminine rhetorical *tradition* as "senti-mental" which connects the political fiction of Boyle to the political autobiography of Emma Goldman without seeming to denigrate both writers. The tradition comes into view always already discounted. And yet Boyle's appeal is to a convention so familiar that postwar Americans would think of it as the "Bambi" appeal—this is public rhetoric, not a less accessible literary imagery. Boyle extends the pain and love of experiences between mother and daughter, man and wife, woman and woman, across the limits of family into the politics of protest against the war. This fiction is rhetorical. We have great difficulty reading this kind of work. Boyle herself thought it had problems. We have been brainwashed by antifeminist constraints to think of it in literary terms that narrow and reduce literature itself.

And what appears strongly in *The Underground Woman* is the solidarity of women in the very scene of oppression. In the jail they learn to question the isolation of individuals: "they were learning that night that they were not, and had never been, a hundred women lying on their cots in the dark, isolated, and thus lost, in their own identities, women now who were neither black nor white nor Chicano, but all with interchangeable skins. The attack upon one girl in the darkness of her cell was an attack on their flesh . . . " (113). At the same time, no social form can be adequate to the revolution, and the potential for evil influence is great. In spite of Pete the Redeemer's promises, "the commune was not for an instant a revolutionary place," and "the redemption he offers is fame and fortune, these words of promise given his followers like a Bank of America card or a Master-Charge plate" (116). Freedom finds its act in resistance to the story, "there isn't any *story*" (184).

The plot of the book moves from one form of imprisonment—the jailing of protesters—to another—the malign influence of the commune—and returns to another jailing. There is no progress. Martha, an alcoholic prisoner who hoped to reform, returns at the same time as the protesters, with her eye black, her face a "wreck." The conclusion is a return, not only to the "barren walls" of jail but to the recognitions of personal loves and personal losses: "Sybil and Paula would write, but Melanie and Rory were gone forever, somewhere far, far away. *Oh, reality, hold me close, hold me close* the underground woman asked in silence of the barren walls" (264).

The "reality" which Boyle as underground woman here faces is configured as the bare walls of jail. This "reality" is metaphorically connected to the reality of oppressive state societies addressed by a literature of subversion since Dostoyevsky's *Notes from the Underground*. The prison metaphor is also a fact of life, a part of contemporary history which Boyle recalls in her essay on her imprisonment, "Report from Lock-up." She sees a connection between the unfortunate women she finds in prison and twentieth-century history, from the prison memoirs of Emma Goldman's old friend Alexander Berkman, to the Birdman of Alcatraz, the Chinese once imprisoned on Angel Island, and the Native Americans who took Alcatraz back for a time. Imprisonment is a feminist tradition: she cites Alice Paul (whom her mother had brought home to lunch) and Doris Stevens's report of the force-feeding of Paul in a psychiatric ward.[24] The prison metaphor is a modern matrix, calling up a kind of new mythology. The new commonplaces of twentieth-century literature are these scenes of violence and despair, in prisons, in confrontations with the police. In *The Underground Woman*, Boyle invokes these images and at the same time she juxtaposes them to the other set of commonplaces, the interior scenes of family relations, the domestic, the sentimental. She finds the violence at home. *Home*. The horror stories of European culture are relocated inside American institutions and inside the experience of the ordinary American individual—that is, of course, inside the woman.

IV

The solidarity of women in Kay Boyle comes out of family feeling but also defies the family romance. Boyle makes us see the alternatives within canonical modernism—she is, or ought to be, part of the modernist canon. She practices the revolution of the word in a way that should be visible from a postmodern point of view. She writes, that is, in full recognition of both the possibilities of style and a need to recuperate love as the final metaphor, the best subversion. She allows the antiplot to emerge into rhetoric only in later works, particularly in *The Underground Woman* and then explicitly in essays. But she maintains the political commitments that the modernist revolution seemed to imply in the beginning. Her childhood experience with feminism joins with a perspective about the place of the intellectual that most American modernists shared with Europeans in the time of the expatriates:

> It is *always* the intellectuals, however we may shrink from the chilling sound of that word, and, above all, it is *always* the writers who must bear the full weight of moral responsibility. Frenchmen will tell you that the decision to speak out is the vocation and life-long peril by which the intellectual must

live. . . . American intellectuals . . . prepared and oriented our revolution: the only revolution in history . . . which did not destroy the intellectuals who had prepared it, but which carried them to power. (190)

This resistance to the fatalities of irony is not an antimodernism. It is inherent in modernism as part of the struggle—the sentimental *within* modernism: what, in fact, makes the literature so powerful. Boyle's relationship to modernism is that of a second generation which has really absorbed the implications of the first. Like young women growing up right now, seventy years later, Boyle heard *Tender Buttons* from her feminist mother. The family in Boyle is divided into a patriarchal order of violence and oppression— or failure—and a maternal order of subversive pleasure and morality. In her essay "The Family," Boyle describes her extraordinary mother, who was responsible for her most important education and introduced her not only to the words of Stein but to a virtual honor roll of the revolution:

> George Moore, Dreiser, Shaw, Isadora Duncan, Caruso, Roman Rolland, George Santayana, Oswald Garrison Villard, Mary Garden, James Joyce, John Cooper Powys, Alice Paul, Alfred Stieglitz, Norman Angell, Susan B. Anthony, Mozart, Upton Sinclair, Margaret Anderson, Jane Heap, Bach, Eugene Debs, Jules Massenet, Cezanne, Monet, Picasso. . . . (6)

Her mother was in fact friends with some: Alice Paul, Alfred Stieglitz, Mary Garden, John Cooper Powys. Boyle attributes her mother's involvements to simple human motives such as "her wish to help a beautiful and talented young woman," Marie Lawall, on whose behalf her mother contacted Mary Garden. But the mother's knowledge is mysterious.

> I do not know how . . . she realized it was important to take me to the Armory Show in New York in 1913 to see Marcel Duchamps' "Nude Descending a Staircase" and Brancusi's "Mlle. Pogany" and his "Bird in Space." . . . Isolated as Mother was from the literary scene, I also cannot explain her understanding of the urgent need to send word of support to Margaret Anderson, who was threatened with arrest for publishing in the *Little Review* chapters of Joyce's banned *Ulysses*. (8)

But it was probably the very isolation of women that propelled her, "an unending loneliness."

The first experience Boyle had of the solidarity of women was with the alliance of her mother and herself against the men in the family, an alliance connected specifically with the modernist revolution:

> It was difficult to speak at the dinner table at night of the acts of moral courage achieved by total strangers, inasmuch as the men of the family spoke

of more familiar things. It was because of instances such as these that Mother and I became part of a conspiracy of silence and discretion, one that involved a great many people, some of whom lived in other countries, a conspiracy to bring to life another reality in which one could put one's faith and it would never be betrayed. (8)

The "moral courage" to present "another reality" is joined to social action: "There was another complicity in her life, and that was her covert alliance with the underprivileged, the lost, the poor" (8). In Boyle's mother, as in Boyle's fiction, the revolution of the word is joined to a moral revolution, a conspiracy on behalf of "another reality."

Boyle's modernism implies a political practice. In her 1947 essay "Farewell to New York," she remains critical of writers who failed to support the Spanish struggle against Franco in 1939: "if I feel guilt . . . it is because there are writers and poets to whom the invitation to speak was given, a long time ago, and they gave their answers" (76). She cites Pound, Evelyn Waugh, and T. S. Eliot. In 1953, she wrote "Farewell to Europe," juxtaposing the voices of Europeans who counseled staying away from an America transfixed by McCarthyism, and her decision to return: "This is one of the times in history when one must go back and speak out with those of the other America clearly and loudly enough so that even Europe will hear" (98). This reflects her conviction that it is an American voice, an American speech, which is revolutionary. Nothing about the disillusionment of the twenties challenged that assumption so violently as the McCarthyism of the fifties must have done. Boyle and her husband, Joseph Franckenstein, were victims, the subjects of a loyalty hearing. The *New Yorker* dropped Boyle as a writer. Her writing was blacklisted—for a decade she could not publish anywhere. If she spoke for the "other America," that voice was indeed not to be allowed.

If we read Boyle as a daughter of feminism and modernism, we will begin to understand the particularly contemporary complexity of her project. At the same time that she rejects patriarchy, she asserts continuity with women; at the same time that she destroys narrative continuities, she softly moves to enlarge the province of sensuous perception so that the perception itself is imbued with emotion and the experience of commitment. These are texts like a body of pleasure but also an embodiment of moral perspective, texts like Emma Goldman.

Boyle is one modernist who does not revolt against the maternal tradition, whose maternal tradition *is* modernism and the promise of moral progress. She is in the lineage of strong women such as Emma Goldman and Gertrude Stein. She reminds us that there is such a lineage. She is decidedly not in the lineage of submissive women who subsume their own moral certitudes to the "realities" of jails and Mastercards or to the masters of the house. Boyle's work upsets the hierarchical order and reminds us again and again of women's time as a space of freedom and love.

In *The Underground Woman*, Boyle violates the sense of direction implied by Freudian narratives. She deplores the isolation of individuals, she sees the loss of her daughter as tragic, and she claims that bonds of compassion are the foundation of political action. The book is not about justice, or violations of law or even of principle. It advocates a return to the maternal enclosure of human relationship—even though this solidarity has to be located within the barren walls of prison. This is not, in other words, the substitution of a woman's story leading to togetherness instead of the male story leading to separation; it is a recollection of another order which ruptures the story and stops the movement of separation, which drives language itself to turn aside. That opening up of language to the pressure of emotion is both modernist and womanly.

Whether or not a writing which practices this kind of revolution may be powerful enough to work larger changes in literary culture remains, however, an open question. This writer offers us an artistic practice which can say things that could not be said otherwise. As her readers, it is up to us now to find ways to speak about Kay Boyle's words and the revolution of the woman.

WOMEN AFTER MODERNISM

The Woman in Nature
and the Subject of Nonfiction
Annie Dillard

I

Who is speaking? Who is looking at this place, this Tinker Creek or Puget Sound or Galapagos or Ecuadorian village, or Pittsburgh, which seems to be a place we all inhabit, a real world, a nonfiction? Annie Dillard is the author, but who seems to discover the nature which we as readers find in the text; who is the seer, and who the teller? Does her work produce the figure of a woman as its subject? But women—like nature—have seemed in the conventions of natural history the object of knowing, not the author.[1]

When we read Dillard, we don't know who is writing.[2] There is a silence in the place where there might be an image of the social self—of personality, character, or ego. There is little mention of her sex or her work or her success, or even—until later works—of the color of her hair. The style of realistic fiction and the objective style of fact are commonly anonymous and faceless in the service of giving us the illusion of nonbias. But this lack of self in Dillard is not a lack of subjective bias. Indeed, her prose style enacts a stylistics of bias, writing out the very gesture of perception as a kind of poetics. This "poetics" makes perception and self-identity figurative. At the very place of lack, there appears a figure of self-consciousness. Women writers have not been admitted to the status of the disinterested, the transparent knower—gendering has always subsumed the woman under the separate sphere of personal interest and ultimately denied that she could author the representation of nature: rather, woman's body represents the natural object.[3] But Dillard says that even in her autobiographical *An American Childhood*, "I left out, as far as I could, . . . myself" (67). Is it possible that Dillard has produced the figure of woman not as an object but as an author of knowing? That would violate (or productively refigure) the long-standing distinctions of subjectivity and objectivity. Such a figure seems contradictory, hard to imagine.

The difficulties with calling Dillard's voice a woman's voice have not, in truth, seemed especially visible to other readers. In spite of the fact that Dillard's narrator does not call attention to her gender, and in spite of the striking absence of female detail, Dillard's writing has already drawn attention as woman's writing. But is this because we know Dillard to be a woman writer, or because she writes like a woman in some ways we can specify?[4] Vera Norwood believes that Dillard represents a woman's point of view, and that her celebration of wildness has specific, liberating implications for women, emphasizing nature over culture.[5] Norwood's suggestive observations are extremely attractive. They seem, however, to leave unanswered questions. If Dillard is self-conscious, does that mean she creates an individual identity in her speaker? How do we know her? If nature wins over culture, that must silence the writer altogether—who, after all, practices a version of culture. The problem is that the speaker in Dillard's work, to be "she," must be problematic, producing a perspective which will make us question our knowing and evade our oppositional categories: male/female, nature/culture.

Dillard herself has called attention to the epistemological consequences of questioning the speaking subject. Although she has not connected her criticism to the problem of the woman writer, Dillard has advocated the problematic speaker as it appears in modern literature. In an essay called "Is Art All There Is?" she argues that when you begin to wonder about the perspective of the witness, you are being drawn into the important debate about knowing itself:

> Related to the theme of art, but actually grounded in metaphysics, is the modernist attention to the relationship between a tale and its teller. . . . Clearly fictions that have a biased narrator, or many biased narrators, deal in part with perceptual bias as a theme. . . . But perceptual bias is not limited to cranky characters. It is every artist's stock in trade. It is every perceiver's stock in trade.[6]

Perhaps Dillard is writing about her own practice here. Her work gives us a multiple answer to the question of who is writing, and the vulnerability of her narrator to changing contexts introduces a kind of bias into her observations, a bias like the fictional bias she is calling modernist. Furthermore, what she does not acknowledge is that this subject of *literature*, as opposed to natural history, the place of the writer, has seemed "feminine" to a long history of observers, up to the present.

But Dillard is not writing fiction. She is writing nonfiction. When the speaker of her prose seems as problematic as a fictional speaker, she crosses the boundaries between fiction and nonfiction, raising questions about the status of both. Her liminality has implications for the way we might read text into context, context into text, for border crossings of gender as well. Discovering figure within perception, Dillard extends the postmodern reversal of empiricism. Knowledge comes from learning, from art, from metaphoricity—from culture, then, and not from the immediacy, or intensity, of natural experience alone. The writer reads other writers. At the same time, Dillard refuses to call this metaphysical theme "postmodern": "modernism is not over" (61). In "Is Art All There Is?", written in the seventies (later she will emphasize the importance of nonfiction), she argues that contemporary art continues the discoveries of Kafka, Proust, Joyce, Faulkner, that "the techniques they developed and the wider capacities for meaning they explored are the basis and origin of the radical direction of some of our most interesting contemporary fiction"—she cites Borges, Nabokov, Beckett, Coover, Barth, Hawkes, Barthelme, Pynchon, Worlitzer, Disch, Lem, Robbe-Grillet, Sukenick, Baumbach, Hjorstberg, O'Brien, Calvino, Landolfi, Cortazar, Puig, Fuentes. This roll call of the *nouveau roman* avant-garde is notably male. One could say that Dillard also extends the modernist exclusion of the female subject, even more severely than Louise Bogan. Like Julia Kristeva, Dillard participates in the avant-garde at the expense—apparently—of feminism. And yet she is at work to unsettle the old constructions of author and authority. She invents a stylistic tool of enormous power for feminists.

Dillard argues that the modernist interest in persona and point of view has implications beyond the boundaries of art, because the unstable, limited subject is all we have—we are all decentered, uncertain.[7] In *Living by Fiction*, Dillard talks about the special status of the mystic, the poet, the madman, the child. These are figures whose perceptions are not reduced to the expected normal, who see a tree of light when the rest of us just see a tree. And, indeed, the observer in Dillard seems at times to see things like a mystic or poet or child or even like a madman. She oscillates between the writer of conventional exposition and the writer of a more singular text, in a repeated gesture of ordinary perception swerving to the extraordinary. Her writing seems itself to exemplify the paradox of living by fiction, for her style reworks a conventional reporting of what she experiences into something new and strange. The ordinary becomes metaphorical; the un-questioned observer becomes figurative, a figure of bias and difference.

Again and again she gives us what appears to be the natural, real world of experience and breaks it open, to expose its forgotten figurativeness. Take, for example, this passage from *Pilgrim at Tinker Creek*:

> Now the blackness is in the east; everything is half in shadow, half in sun, every clod, tree, mountain, and hedge. I can't see Tinker Mountain through the line of hemlock, till it comes on like a streetlight, ping, *ex nihilo*. Its sandstone cliffs pink and swell. Suddenly the light goes; the cliffs recede as if pushed. The sun hits a clump of sycamores between me and the moun-tains; the sycamore arms light up, and *I can't see the cliffs*. They're gone. (21)

This interference with our habitual ways of looking at the world makes us question the perceiver, makes the artist visible, and marks the world as a modernist text, resistant to reading.

This figure-making style which turns life into literature has much to do with the aspect of the speaker which Dillard does not talk about, the woman. "She" is the unspoken subject. By that I don't mean to suggest that Dillard is writing as a feminist or an advocate of women in any straight-forward way. I mean that what subverts the coherent character presented as a speaker, what undoes the convention and makes the nonfiction literary, is the unspoken "she," a recurring strangeness, or estrangement, which acts as a counterpoint to the traditional and literal authority of the (male) observer—the naturalists, adventurers, and other writers whom Dillard cites. Dillard is/is not an author among them; she does/does not participate in the authority and mastery over nature of scientific discourse. Her prose is not transparent; it is metaphorical. The speaker is in question, and, as Dillard suggests, that raises the question of knowledge itself.

Dillard does not represent herself as a woman narrator; she does not, as a speaker, solidify into any figure of certain identity, not even female identity. Instead, the female undermines the very principle of identity, elaborating an antihumanism. Dillard does not let us off the hook by giving us herself as a cranky character, the artist, either, whose subjectivity is responsible for the distortions in "nature." Identity itself is a metaphor. Nature also writes on her, through her, making a sometimes bloody in-scription.

This speaker's voice admits the painful sacrifice of self involved in the pursuit of knowing: "I am an explorer, then, and I am also a stalker, or the instrument of the hunt itself. . . . I am the arrow shaft, carved along my length by unexpected lights and gashes from the very sky, and this book is the straying trail of blood" (PTC 13).

II

If we look at the cover of *Pilgrim at Tinker Creek*, we now find the restraint of the classic: print and abstract forms decorate it. But the earlier edition, the one that defined Annie Dillard as a classic in the first place and won her the Pulitzer Prize, was quite different. Pictured there is a very blond young woman, dressed in brown outdoor gear with sturdy shoes for walking, who is nonetheless somewhat ethereal, her build slight, the light making a halo of her long, fair hair. She is sitting at her ease in a rocky place filled with twisting tree roots and twiggy, rough tree trunks, also illuminated by the play of light. It could be winter; the tops of the trees are cut out of the picture. There is no green, no sign of other life; everything is brown shadow and luminous gold, dark and light. She is at the center of the picture. She looks directly at the camera, or at the reader. Even though her clothing is functional, ungendered, she is most definitely a she. It is a photograph. Therefore, though its play of light and dark seems almost symbolic, an appeal to imagination, we take the image as "real."

Dillard represents herself, the image of her proper person, as, presumably, she does in the voice of the text. The conventions of "real perception," not verisimilitude, will govern our reading of both photograph and text: this will seem to be a book about the experience of a real person, looking by herself, speaking for herself. As "natural" readers, we are not expected to think critically about the narrator; we will not read her as a character, a fictive creation who constructs her own subjectivity by the point of view she takes as she speaks. Rather, we will try to read her world as if it were a photograph. We will read according to certain conventions of realism.

However, this cover of *Pilgrim at Tinker Creek* also promised, in words written under the title, "a mystical excursion into the natural world." And on the back: "Mystery, Death, Beauty, Violence." If the photograph on the front seemed to promise a faithful and objective transcription of someone's real experience, its play of bright and shadow, dark and light suggests the symbolism of good and evil associated with another kind of knowing, with mysticism. In Dillard, the special, unreasonable knowledge of the lover, the child, the poet, and the mystic is spoken by the voice of a female subject. A differing from rational order thus comes to be represented by the figure of a woman. She is not so much the subject of knowing as subjected to it.

A nature that she later calls necessity—powerful, animal, sensual— overwhelms each of Dillard's beginnings. And each of them violates ideas of the self in nature that the reader might expect to find. "Mystery, Death, Beauty, Violence" make the moment ambiguously like rape—or rapture. *Pilgrim* opens with the scene of a repeated awakening: her "old fighting tom" cat, "stinking of urine and blood," would leave her "body covered with paw prints in blood." These stains, signs, markings write on her flesh messages which she cannot decipher: "What blood was this, and what roses? It could have been the rose of union, the blood of murder, or the rose of beauty bare and the blood of some unspeakable sacrifice or birth. The sign on my body could have been an emblem or a stain, the keys to the kingdom or the mark of Cain. I never knew" (PTC 2).

The writer begins, in other words, with a sense of strangeness, not a knowing but "mystery." What is mysterious is the self's encounter with signs of otherness—a violation, known only by its bloody traces. The meaning is untranslatable. This scene brings together two codes which violate each other: if this writing is about brute nature, the facts are what we're after, and it's shocking for her to describe these details and conclude, "I never knew." But if the writing is about the mystery of good and evil, heaven and hell, the bloody messages and the suggestive scene are an animal intrusion into spirituality, bestial grounds for meditation. The metaphor of identity resembles the site of erotic violation, the scene of a rape. The only signs of gender suggest the abject, a fascination with and a horror of feminine sexuality—the passive body of the speaking subject is "kneaded" by the tom cat, "as if sharpening his claws, or pummeling a mother for milk."

Here there is no trace in the narrator of the post-Enlightenment man of reason, no sense of mastery over nature, or of the world as body, and self as knowing mind. In this scene of blood roses, this writer speaks from unknowing, not momentary but a condition of existence ("I never knew"); here she is no more authoritative than the common people whose lack of mastery is signaled by their grammatical lapses: " 'Seem like we're just set down here,' a woman said to me recently, 'and don't nobody know why' " (2). At this beginning, quoting the folk in their anonymity, the writer speaks as one of them, also anonymous, without ego. She records on her flesh, unresisting, the tracks of the old fighting tom, like film taking the print of the photographed image. The writer is defined—she is written by something else, something strange.

Dillard's voice in this beginning signals difference—but is it the difference of the woman, or of the poet? The madman or the mystic? Are they mutually overlapping? Dillard associates the poet with the madman, the mystic, and the child in *Living by Fiction*, but not with woman. Jacques Derrida, on the other hand, has suggested that the place of woman in language *is* displacement, difference.[8] And Susan Griffin, who says she was influenced by Dillard, has presented a record of the displacement of woman and nature in *Woman and Nature: The Roaring inside Her*.[9] A sacrificial and alienated identity, from the point of view of literary traditions, might remind us of the poet—victim, at least since Rimbaud, of the visionary illumination in which "je est un autre"; witness, especially since Hopkins, to a beauty which is flawed and even violent.

On the other hand, this receptivity—this abjection—might remind us, from the point of view of a nonliterary tradition, of the passivity Freud associated both with the feminine and with the religious, the position Julia Kristeva explores in *Powers of Horror*.[10] This sacrificial posture of a self which is neither subject nor object is the *abject*. For Kristeva, it is a subjective position associated with the woman and the mystic. As in Dillard, the abject opens to both horror and ecstasy. But there are other kinds of voices in *Pilgrim*, other moments when Dillard does not take on the attitudes of the abject. Dillard again and again speaks, in fact, with the cumulative voice of mankind: she quotes the natural historian, such as Teale; the scientist, such as Jeans; the explorer, such as Scott, Peary, Byrd; Pascal, Einstein, Thoreau, Xerxes, King David, Rimbaud—a citing of the male subject to provide the facts of expertise and the context of culture.

Again and again Dillard evokes this male culture, these male conventions, and then works them at a bias, calling up and altering their cumulative hold.[11] Marius von Senden, for example, provides Dillard with the histories of sight restored to cataract patients. Then, in a sort of dialectic, Dillard provides the estrangement, adopting a falling away from the familiarity of the seeing culture into the metaphor of new sight—the world as patches of color and shadows, the contradictions of death and revolting fecundity:

> So shadows define the real. If I no longer see shadows as "dark marks," as do the newly sighted, then I see them as making some sort of sense of the light. . . . This is the blue strip running through creation, the icy roadside stream on whose banks the mantis mates, in whose unweighed waters the giant water bug sips frogs. Shadow Creek is the blue subterranean stream. . . . (PTC 64)

The perceiving teller of Dillard's narrations moves again and again from the realistic detail provided by observation and citation, what we might associate with the cultural mastery of the natural world, to a being overwhelmed, rape as rapture—the female version of the fortunate fall.

On the idea of being surrounded by locusts, she writes: "I cannot ask for more than to be so wholly acted upon, flown at, and lighted on in throngs, probed, knocked, even bitten. . . . being so in the clustering thick of things, rapt and enwrapped in the rising and falling real world" (PTC 226). The "I" is grammatical subject here, but the very syntax is a passive construction. The subject is the object of the "real world," and we are far from the powerful speaker of Western discourse about nature, and far from the objective style of scientific prose. Perception itself is nothing but receptivity: "For that forty minutes last night I was purely sensitive and mute as a photographic plate" (PTC 201). Her observations are on the margins of what we can take without being appalled—her words close to the appalling natural fecundity she sees in the mantis laying eggs, clothes moths, rock barnacles, parasites: "the world as an intricate texture of a bizarre variety of forms" (PTC 183). What can she get away with? She works the mixing of texts, risking the moment when the reader drops away with revulsion at the uncanny recall of the female:

> You are an ichneumon. You mated and your eggs are fertile. If you can't find a caterpillar on which to lay your eggs, your young will starve. When the eggs hatch, the young will eat any body in which they find themselves, so if you don't kill them by emitting them broadcast over the landscape, they'll eat you alive. . . . Not that the ichneumon is making any conscious choice. If she were, her dilemma would be truly the stuff of tragedy; Aeschylus need have looked no further than the ichneumon. (PTC 174)

The strangeness comes from a speaking subject which is vulnerable to being overwhelmed by a loss of borders, and the catastrophe of a violated self. But the strangeness is mixed with another perspective, the absurdity of regarding the ichneumon as the stuff of tragedy. Dillard's postmodernism shows itself by the parodic element. Tragedy is absurd when the ichneumon is our model of the heroine; art inscribes the catastrophe as the punch line of a joke. The joke is not at the expense of nature but at the expense of the posturing humanity whose lives do not exceed the ichneumon.

These moments need the context of the cultural citing to keep the dialectic of voices. The male tradition gives distance, authority, a framework of conventions that mediate abjection and make female creativity less physical, more metaphorical, and a matter of art. But Dillard takes the bodily powers of metaphor seriously. For example, she gives us an image of the wind as impregnating her:

> A wind like this does my breathing for me; it engenders something quick and kicking in my lungs. Pliny believed the mares of the Portuguese used to raise their tails to the wind, "and turn them full against it, and so conceive that genital air instead of natural seed. . . . " Soon something perfect is born. Something wholly new rides the wind, something fleet and fleeting I'm likely to miss. (54)

She can understand Pliny's assumptions. The conceit is a concept, conceived in the brain like a child in the body. Dillard's conceit is also epistemologically ambitious—she is talking about herself, real experience, the perceiver's metaphor being all we have of knowledge. And the knowledge

she is talking about is physical, of the flesh, not from imaginings or cog-
nitions or spiritual insights or textual conventions alone. In the paradox of
living by fiction, emphasis is on the living as well as the fiction. She sees
by Pliny, and conventions of the maternal are written into perception, into
the flesh.

Interestingly enough, the dialectic of male and female subjectivity
seems most pronounced in *Pilgrim*, where it is also most metaphorical. The
author there never appears in her own proper person, as a woman—never
reveals her gender by any detail of appearance or activity. There is no
cultural feminine in the book. The later works, in contrast, portray the
speaker as a woman in certain ways, and yet they give us portrayals of her
that are much less attached to images of female sexuality, to reproduction
and physicality. The shattering of codes works on a different level.

Furthermore, even though Dillard's work opens again and again on a
scene of abjection, there are important differences in these inaugural
scenes. The beginning of *Holy the Firm* seems much more clearly in the
tradition of religious meditation than *Pilgrim*. What seizes her is not the
cat but the holy. At the same time, the erotic quality of the scene is strong
enough that we can't be sure if the god is a metaphor for human lovemaking
or the flesh a metaphor for the god:

> I wake in a god. I wake in arms holding my quilt, holding me as best they
> can inside my quilt. Someone is kissing me—already. . . . Today's god rises,
> his long eyes flecked in clouds. He flings his arms, spreading colors; he
> arches, cupping sky in his belly; he vaults, vaulting and spread, holding all
> and spread on me like skin. (HF 11–12)

What can she mean? This is not fantasy: "The day is real." Yet it seems
that the things of the world are of a more manageable demeanor than they
were in *Pilgrim*: this cat is "a gold cat, who sleeps on my legs, named
Small." As it turns out, the metaphors of identity here, too, will connect
both to femininity and to writing, but somehow in a more controlled way.
Here, too, there is violence and sacrifice. "There is a spider, too, in the
bathroom, with whom I keep a sort of company. Her little outfit always
reminds me of a certain moth I helped to kill" (HF 13). Here, too, there
will be an alienation of the writer from herself, made vivid by the flaming
death of the moth, emblem of the writer. Then the story of "Julie Norwich,"
a young girl whose face is burned in a plane crash, evokes the image of
Julian of Norwich—woman, and mystic.

Even without Frederich Buechner's note on the back cover of *Holy the
Firm*, many readers would think of Virginia Woolf as we read Dillard's
narrative of the moth flying into the candle. Here the literary and mystical
connections are made out loud:

> She burned for two hours without changing, without bending or leaning—
> only glowing within, like a building fire glimpsed through silhouetted walls,
> like a hollow saint, like a flame-face virgin gone to God, while I read by her
> light, kindled, while Rimbaud in Paris burnt out his brains in a thousand
> poems, while night pooled wetly at my feet. (HF 17)

And here the ambition becomes quite visible: to overlap differences associated with male and female subjectivity, to make the analogy of the
artist and the mystic extend into the "natural" experience of a real woman,
who was camping out in the world of the moment when this happened.
To colonize natural history for art. The most everyday ordinary perceiver
of our common lives could see and say the same things, she implies. Gender
seems not really intrinsically related—though the moth is a "she," and so
is the camper, and so is the writer, and so is the other writer about the
figure of the moth as the artist, Woolf. Rimbaud was a male poet, but he
was deeply implicated in the history of symbolism and *gynesis*, or the
woman effect. (Furthermore, Dillard got her Rimbaud from Enid Starkie.)
And behind all stands the female figure of Julian of Norwich.

But is it possible that a woman needs to stand at this place, to draw
together the artist, the saint, and the overwhelmed witness out in the
woods? For literature and nonliterature have been strictly segregated, and
this is the rhetorical issue: can the speaker of a writing about the nonliterary
universe allow himself to be unknowing, passive, overwhelmed, or consumed? Can the unconscious or the not-conscious appear? Can nonfiction
have any authority without the mastery of understanding, since Bacon?
Dillard's mind refuses to exercise authority over the nature of things. Her
witnessing offers testimony to the powers of horror as well as to the powers
of awe, in the tradition of Emily Dickinson. Thus she violates the codes of
understanding itself.

One might ordinarily think that *Teaching a Stone to Talk* should not be
considered a third book in a series but rather another genre, a looser collection of essays. But Dillard urges us to think again, and she further
provokes the question of herself as speaker (conventionally male? writing
as a woman?) in an author's note which refers to a writer with a male
pronoun: "this is not a collection of occasional pieces, such as a writer
brings out to supplement his real work; instead this is my real work, such
as it is" (TS 8). Is she distinguishing herself from a writer (in the male
tradition) whose "real work" has some kind of centrality? Is her "real
work," resembling the supplement, to be distinguished as some other (non-
male) kind of genre, marked by the quality of the "occasional" (a trait
sometimes associated with women writers)? But the words have a postmodern resonance: *occasional, supplement*.

The first essay, "Living Like Weasels," does not open with any "I" represented but with a questioning "who." The question is: "A weasel is wild. Who knows what he thinks?" (TS 11). It is several pages before Dillard as narrator enters the picture with a narrative of her own experience, the encounter with the weasel. But that meeting represents wildness that exceeds language and a mutual gaze that eliminates separate selfhood altogether:

> Our eyes locked, and someone threw away the key. Our look was as if two lovers, or deadly enemies, met unexpectedly on an overgrown path when each had been thinking of something else: a clearing blow to the gut. It was also a bright blow to the brain, or a sudden beating of brains, with all the charge and intimate grate of rubbed balloons. It emptied our lungs. It felled the forest, moved the fields, and drained the pond; the world dismantled and tumbled into that black hole of eyes. (TS 14)

When Rilke wrote, in the Eighth of the *Duino Elegies*, of the exchange with an animal gaze, he thought that we never see purely like the animal does:

> With full gaze the animal sees the open.
> Only our eyes, as if reversed, are like snares
> set around it, block the freedom of its going.
> Only from the face of the beast do we know
> what *is* outside. . . . [12]

Dillard writes within this symbolist tradition, but she is not writing poetry; she is carrying the tradition into the postmodern in nonfiction. Look at her diction—it's parodic, hyperbolic, comic: "Our eyes locked, and someone threw away the key." The vernacular is good enough for the mystic; it is not the work after all that represents necessity. What she is talking about in the scene with the weasel, this "bright blow to the brain," defines the power that seizes the writer again and again—something not visionary or utopian or of the imagination, not the poet's power, but radically other: something other than subjectivity and prior to it, Rilke's "what *is* outside," to which the writer becomes abject. What the weasel's gaze teaches is before words:

> I might learn something of mindlessness, something of the purity of living in the physical senses and the dignity of living without bias or motive. The weasel lives in necessity and we live in choice, hating necessity and dying at the last ignoble in its talons. I would like to live as I should, as the weasel lives as he should. (TS 15)

That is, she gives us not freedom but necessity—not mastery but submission. Although their gaze is like "two lovers," she and the weasel are not about human love or desire but about the intimacy with necessity that determines the animal self. She is looking at a subject that is undivided into speech, at "mindlessness," unknowing. The word from nature is silence.

The experience of the speaker that in *Pilgrim* seemed almost like the scene of a rape has lost most of its extreme physicality—its urine and blood. Nevertheless, Dillard's metaphor here has her abandoning the tame and human self to mate with the weasel: "I could very calmly go wild. I could live two days in the den, curled, leaning on mouse fur, sniffing bird bones, blinking, licking, breathing musk, my hair tangled in the roots of grasses. Down is out, out of your ever-loving mind and back to your careless senses" (TS 15). This Dillard, a bit fantastic, like the heroine of a children's story or Alice in Wonderland, does not quite threaten our imaginations with the horror of bestiality—but the scene is lined and edged with the bones and musk of an animal experience. And she connects this encounter with the weasel both to the descent into the animal senses and to a mystical path, the "way down and out."

There is something, a little, of the romantic and Gothic about this tale: the woman runs away with her demon lover, the weasel. But there is also something of the sardonic, the joke. This story takes place outside the conventions of serious (or adolescent?) sexuality. The speaker is at once wild like the weasel and overtaken by its mindlessness. Could the speaker here as easily be a man? Perhaps—this loss of ego and cultural identity is where the female subject intersects with the poet and the mystic; with Rilke, for example. The boundaries of the speaker are in flux, the identity of the self is neither human nor animal, male nor female. When she solidifies into an "I," the subject of a spoken word, it is with a sense of regret and belatedness and separation: "I remember muteness as a prolonged and giddy fast, where every moment is a feast of utterance received. Time and events are merely poured, unremarked, and ingested directly, like blood pulsed into my gut through a jugular vein" (TS 16).

Language mediates; the writer breaks silence and stops the flow of lifeblood. Like what Geoffrey Hartman once called the "unmediated vision" of poets such as Wordsworth, Hopkins, Yeats, Rilke, and Valéry, Dillard's is the paradoxical subject explored by symbolist and modernist poetics: the one who breaks the cultural traditions coded by language, who opens up imprisoning conventionality. What kind of utterance might break the hold of the expected phrase? How can wildness and the reader, mute, encounter one another's look?

The obvious metaphoricity of Dillard's work could seem *merely* figurative and not "real," not saying anything about nature or the world beyond the purview of creative writing. If the persona who speaks seems to be literary, she may cease being dangerous—or interesting—for the power of nonfiction is that language is *not* just appealing for its own sake, that style functions to make an argument, as Chris Anderson has put it.[13] Dillard carries wildness out in a work that disregards the cultured boundaries of the literary; her nonfiction carries fiction into living, poetics into the wild, invention into natural history, female subjectivity into language. She thematizes form. The traditions of tragedy become parodic. In this, I want to designate her (in spite of her resistance) as postmodern.

The techniques of discovery are at work on the medium of language, but Dillard violates the well-guarded modernist barrier between literature and ordinary language. If her style takes up the impersonal stance of the modernist poet, it also opens up to the multiple voices of ordinary people. The logic of the two discourses is at odds, and so the poetic itself is violated by the unpoetic. For example, in "An Expedition to the Pole," a counterpoint of texts juxtaposes information about Arctic expeditions with a very commonplace church service. The codes collide, opening the text to the nonsacred, the general chorus, to words that are unpoetic and unlovely, to the general public. This is a loss of control like the abandonment of modernist high seriousness: "There is a singing group in this Catholic church today, a singing group which calls itself 'Wildflowers.' . . . They straggle out in front of the altar and teach us a brand-new hymn" (17). But she advocates this loss:

> Must I join this song? . . . We are singing the Sanctus, it seems, and they are passing the plate. I would rather, I think, undergo the famous dark night of the soul than encounter in church the dread hootenanny—but these purely personal preferences are of no account, and maladaptive to boot. . . . Unaccountably, the enormous teen-aged soprano catches my eye, exultant. A low shudder or shock crosses our floe. We have split from the pack; we have crossed the Arctic Circle and the current has us. (33–34)

The exchange is electric with *sympathy*, but if this is sentimental, it is not personal. In "The Deer at Providencia," there is a specific rejection of personal sentimentality. The emblem is a deer tied to a tree for future slaughter. The North Americans in this Ecuadorian jungle setting are expected to have certain attitudes: "They had looked to see how I, the only woman, and the youngest, was taking the sight of the deer's struggles" (64). "When we walked by the deer at Providencia for the last time, I said to Pepe, with a pitying glance at the deer, 'Pobrecito'—'poor little thing.' But I was trying out Spanish. I knew at the time it was a ridiculous thing to say" (66). She is not talking about a realm of freedom here but a realm of a necessity where she, like the deer, is condemned to be killed. Her work produces, that is, the effect of "fact," a tough ecology: she is subject to the law of death the weasel knows. Theology in Dillard is no comfort.

But the social context—friends, lovers, enemies, politics—can't save her either, nor can history, any more than poetry or nonfiction. Her stylistic modernism dismantles the humanist subject, leaving only the joking of the condemned.

III

Since the advent of postmodern criticism, it has become impossible to pretend that figurativeness and undecidability characterize only the literary: all discourse may be seen as having a fictive relationship to the real. Literary nonfiction does not occupy a place that is epistemologically anomalous: we can't say in simplicity that it is distinguished by being a literature of fact. Nonetheless, calling a work "nonfiction" suggests that there is some kind of resistance at work, a resistance to the creative autonomy of the romantic writer at the least. It is like the difference—not easy to specify—between imagination and memory. Even autobiography, long acknowledged to be a creative endeavor, is not the same as autobiographical fiction. Something resists the fictional, and if to call it the truth doesn't help us, nevertheless that tug toward rhetoricity has much to do with what the genre of nonfiction might mean. Even the autobiographer must cross the boundaries of private inventiveness and make peace with—or refuse—the public record, with public memory as well as memory made public. William Zinsser's fascinating collection of essays on the memoir is titled *Inventing the Truth*, and perhaps the part that should attract our attention is not just the old news that the memoir is invented but the renewal of the old claim to tell the truth.[14] The idea that truth could be the understanding of how one invents the self gives a newly privileged attention to the tradition of the cultured self, the traditional place of the Emersonian individual, the literary, the feminine.

The subject of nonfiction is what interests me here. Annie Dillard's essay in Zinsser's collection, "To Fashion a Text," tells us that she wrote her memoir, *An American Childhood*, because she was interested in consciousness, and "for a private, interior life, I've picked—almost at random—my own." As for her first book of nonfiction, *Pilgrim at Tinker Creek*, she says, "I knew I wasn't the subject." Furthermore, she tells us, she first wrote the beginning chapter of *Pilgrim* "in the first person, as a man," and then changed to herself as speaker (57). She is the subject of language, the "I" who speaks, but not the object, not the self who appears as the writer (67). Not only the story but also the heroine of the drama is *impersonal*, so much so that she could begin by writing as a man. She represents the impersonality of experience. Her subject is experience, and it is selected, crafted, and not autobiography. But the question of the impersonal subject of this experience is made acute by the question of gender. When Dillard quit writing *Pilgrim at Tinker Creek* in the persona of a fifty-year-old man, did she then begin to write as a woman?

How does gender appear in the text? Does Dillard escape domestication by gender when she makes the subject disappear? Let me return to the poststructuralist argument that there is no female subject of language, that the subjective pronoun *I* is always male. The centered selfhood is, after all, imaginary—deconstructing the subject also deconstructs the domination of male logos. What that might mean depends on how we think cultural history is inscribed in language. When Luce Irigaray and Hélène Cixous attacked the "phallogocentrism" of language, they went on to try to create a woman's writing, an *écriture féminine*. Dillard is claiming no such thing, and yet her disruption of conventions by her style could be compared to an *écriture féminine*. Julia Kristeva says that the idea of a feminine writing is too positive, and so it simply re-creates the old categories of binary gendering, and I think that Dillard would similarly resist our seeing her innovations as gendered. At the same time she similarly sees both avant-garde style and the place of the woman as sources of subversion. But the avant-garde and the feminine both impose limitations.

The vernacular culture that Dillard loves so much is coded for gender, and Dillard in general prefers the active life, what boys get to do—the baseball over the softball. Even if, like Louise Bogan and Kay Boyle, Dillard makes significant contributions to a woman's literary history, wouldn't she resist the very idea of modern literature as a war of male and female traditions, male and female writers? When we construct such a history, Dillard might prefer to show up on the wrong side.

Dillard is an advocate of literary nonfiction. She argues that "other literary genres are shrinking" but that nonfiction offers the writer a chance to exploit forms and structures. When she stopped writing poetry and turned to nonfiction, Dillard says, "I felt as though I had switched from a single reed instrument to a full orchestra" (75). The point is not that nonfiction tells the truth better than fiction but that right now, in this postmodern era, nonfiction offers the greater place to art. Like fiction, like everything made of the material of words, nonfiction creates artistic structures and forms. Nonfiction replaces nonverbal memory with the forms of words. Nonfiction responds to the question of subjectivity with the text. In other words, the subject of literary nonfiction is the verbal form of experience. And is verbal form itself gendered?

By writing about the private life, Dillard chooses a domain which is the purview of the feminine in our culture. But so did James Joyce, so did T. S. Eliot and Wallace Stevens. The impersonal (and oppressed) subject of modernist literature *is* feminine, a kind of *gynesis*, as contrasted with the economic masculinity of nonliterary discourse. Annie Dillard writes like a woman *and* like a literary modernist when she writes about the private life or about experience. The impersonal subject of such a text may be absent from the polemics of the historical patriarchal struggle, but it is already by this very withdrawal and receptivity a feminized form.

I wonder if literary nonfiction does not gain considerable power from not only the intersections of the genre, lying at the crossing of fiction and fact, but also the intersection of gender, of public discourse identified with the masculine, and the other discourse, the literary—defined as separate, not expedient or instrumental or utilitarian, and so located in the domain of private experience, the domestic space allocated by the history of culture to the feminine. Its very refusal to serve persuasive and utilitarian ends makes literary nonfiction resistant, as modernism was resistant, to the patriarchal imperatives. That these intersections work for Dillard to give her power and authority suggests that the modernist separation of the literary from the nonliterary has given way under postmodernism to an accessibility, a literary culture more open to women's writing.

IV

Thus Dillard extends the discovery of modernism into the postmodern literature of fact, advancing the feminine ecstatic impersonality as a mode of authority which also refuses to assert authority. The undoing of a reasonable will by the painful, the catastrophic, or the unexpected sublime does not take the form of a feminine masochism. Nor does Dillard sound quite like the speaker of an Emersonian essay, or even of Thoreau, in the pursuit of discovery. Her optimistic note emerges from a humorous, vernacular irony and not transcendence. The painful fact of human mastery is the inevitable flaw in it: the teacher who keeps a polyphemus moth in a jar too small, until its wings are crippled; the airplane crash that burns the child's face; the airplane crash that kills the stunt pilot. Life is a line of words probing the unexpected, inside the fact that the one thing we ought to expect is death, the final reversal.

The catastrophic and the sublime take form in Dillard's work within the effects of sympathy and of a melodrama of pathos, but as the unexpected turn in a democratic form: the joke is always on us. Female authority in Dillard has to do with an appeal to her reader's participation, a version of pathos that includes irony and humor. Thus she renews the sentimental within modernism by enclosing modernism within an extraliterary appeal. The form of that rhetoric is important because it includes a kind of subversion without a politics.

A joke is a verbal catastrophe because it suddenly rearranges a whole pattern organizing thought, revealing a subversive underside. The plea-sure, Freud says, comes from a momentary lifting of repression. Dillard's joking often gives us what reason has repressed, which is, among other things, a kind of magical thinking, a welcome childishness. She begins her essay "Teaching a Stone to Talk" with a short narrative about a person—"Larry"—"who lives alone with a stone he is trying to teach to talk." Perspective by incongruity is part of the style, which retains its air of reasonableness: "I do not think he expects the stone to speak as we do, and describe for us its long life and many, or few, sensations. I think instead that he is trying to teach it a single word, such as 'cup,' or 'uncle' " (68).

The ridiculous *is* the sublime in this formulation. Not only does Larry's project make a good story, but the story has a moral, or a punch line: "Nature's silence is its one remark, and every flake of world is a chip off that old and immutable block" (69). While we are groaning at the tour de force of puns, we also understand that this is as serious and metaphysical as any statement about writing nonfiction could be, a reinvention for nonf-iction of the place enjoyed by *wit* in the history of poetics. Serious wit challenges the Ramist notion that style does not participate in the discourse of knowledge. What the cascade of verbal play enforces with its final turn on the reader, who is flooded with the unexpected, is not always the joke's laughter but the joke's replacement of tragedy by art. This is a kind of irony (a distancing and an impersonality), but it is an irony which separates the speaker from power over anything but her audience, and so it is rhetorical. It is a rhetorical metaphysics.

Dillard lets us in on the importance of jokes in *An American Childhood*. Her parents were avid practitioners of the art of the joke, from the long story to the wisecrack. "Telling a good joke well—successfully, perfectly—was the highest art. It was an art because it was up to you: if you did not get the laugh, you had told it wrong." The children were apprentices of the craft. They learned "every technical, theoretical, and moral aspect of the art," experimented with narrative structure, and "polished the word-ing" (50). For Dillard, jokes are the literature of American vernacular cul-ture. "We were brought up on the classics. Our parents told us all the great old American jokes, practically by number" (52). And a running joke or a good story connects the teller to the listener with a payoff of pleasure which depends on a finely drawn-out balancing act of timing and feints: "how long could you lead them to think you were stupid, a dumb blonde, to enhance their surprise at the punch line, and heighten their pleasure in the good story you had controlled all along?" (54). In the same way "a brick" reappears after long delay in a shaggy dog story, words and phrases reappear in Dillard's prose, each time with a little or large surprise, with the pleasure of a new connectedness and the surprise of a certain incongruity. It's the return of the signifier, cut loose from the signified—indeed, from reference and systems of meaning—as if the only coherence were in the material of language, its sounds and images.

An American Childhood concludes with "would the music be loud enough?" a phrase from Jack Kerouac cited by her father, who had once headed down to New Orleans himself in search of something (255). It is the moment of adolescence when Annie Dillard is about to separate from family and home: "I was approaching escape velocity" (254). The last word is not insistently funny, but it is a comic recuperation of separation itself and the romantic agony of the young writer. If she goes off to find "music loud enough," she after all follows a familiar refrain. However great the influence of Rimbaud, the influence of the eternal return of "a brick" supersedes it. Impersonality in Dillard is not alienation; the way her language reaches out again and again to hook the reader, to keep us going, to give us at last the drawn-out pleasure of a verbal closure—this is comic, and the establishment of this kind of community happens at the level of *style*.

If the narrator of Dillard's prose—including her memoir—is not herself, this lack of a well-defined presence is not a verbal absence but an excess; her writing is in excess of the critical and romantic visionaries she admires, sometimes almost in a parodic relationship to Emerson, to Thoreau. Everything happens as if she were a twentieth-century transcendentalist, except that she also writes within the rhetoric of the popular joke, a comic citation that punctually invokes the family and the ordinary person as an audience around her, and refuses the authority of transcendence. Juxtaposed to the strangeness and mystery she addresses is the astonishing *familiarity* of her style.

Locating otherness within the familiar, Dillard gives us a twist on modernist narratives about the subject. Maturity does not arrive with the adolescent longing for escape, not with separation from family and community, not with the poet as egotist. The adolescent Dillard "loved Rimbaud, who ran away . . . and his poems' confusion and vagueness, their overwritten longing, their hatred, their sky-shot lyricism, and their oracular fragmentation" (AC 232). The adult Dillard clearly loves Rimbaud still, in spite of her disavowals, but she rejects the tragic vision that inhabits modernist irony and the Oedipal narrative. Maturity, she implies, is not resignation but a return of childhood, pleasure, joy: "I thought that joy was a childish condition that had forever departed; I had no glimpse then of its return the minute I got to college. I couldn't foresee the pleasure—or the possibility—of shedding sophistication, walking away from rage, and renouncing French poets" (235).

Maturity seems to be a return to childhood which is neither rage nor dissolution but within reason, somehow. As she talks about the books which she read during those teenage years, Dillard says, "I read Freud's standard works, which interested me at first, but they denied reason. Denying reason had gotten Rimbaud nowhere" (AC 238). If Dillard's work can be approached from a psychoanalytic perspective, it must be with this dismissal in mind.

The point is not to deny reason but to remember the joke. Emerson "was a thinker, full time, as Pasteur and Salk were full-time biologists" (238). She liked him because, if Emerson was metaphysical, he also was in favor of rebellion. His transcendent importance to Dillard is signaled by the appearance of her comic style: "I wrote a paper on Emerson's notion of the soul—the oversoul, which, if I could banish from my mind the thought of galoshes (one big galosh, in which we have our being), was grand stuff" (238). Here is the Annie Dillard sublime, "one big galosh." Her ecstatic impersonality is at one with the sublimely familiar seen anew. It is a knowing and grateful return to childhood and the mother, from the other side of escape—from, in reality, an irrecuperably distant setting.

V

Dillard knows that her careful delimitation of attention to consciousness alone leaves her vulnerable to the charge that she has willfully disregarded the problem of history and economic oppression. Does she write from a perspective that is, finally, the luxury of the privileged? Simply a perpetuation of bourgeois ideology? The pastoral has always, as a genre, been implicated in both the impulse to escape the culture of city life and the painful discovery that suffering and death inhabit the country as well ("et in Arcadia ego"). Dillard's passionate attention seems to function as a counternostalgia, focusing not only on the abjection of the insect world but also on the ubiquitous presence of industrial civilization.[15] The weasel is wild, nature is silent, but this wilderness is not a setting; it is the resistance by which we know necessity. Thus, in a sense, the pastoral in Dillard does not seem to operate as an escapism but rather as a confrontation. Pleasure does not come by avoiding pain but by the joke which formalizes a sense of humor beyond irony. The form (momentarily) relieves pain through catharsis, in the classic role of literature.

Nevertheless, this enclosure of consciousness seems to leave out the social and political world and the suffering caused by human differences of gender, class, and race. *Encounters with Chinese Writers* makes visible Dillard's refusal to take sides or to take political issues seriously, as if, that is, they were "fact." Instead her text redistributes ideological detail so that the sketches are dislocated and estranged from social context. The photographic vignettes of the Chinese writers on their visit to America resist

ideological closures, but their turn to the American vernacular seems to
suggest a claim for the powers of popular culture. The Chinese assert that
"American songs have no feeling, no depth. . . . They are too bouncy—
not subtle" (102). Allen Ginsberg and Dillard find themselves in the bus
with the Chinese writers, trapped in a traffic jam on the L. A. freeway, on
the way from Disneyland. They start jamming the blues, improvising.

> When the Chinese writers grasped that we were winging it—singing almost
> faster than Ginsberg was pulling the lyrics out of thin air, out of the very
> highway billboards as they appeared—then, slapping their knees, they all
> began to sing, any old words or la la la to those blues progressions known
> in the bones of almost every adult on earth. They were laughing, I say, and
> by god they were belting it, all those solemn old Chinese Communist Party
> members; they were belting, and rocking their shoulders, and opening wide
> their jaws. (105)

American entertainment culture may lack depth, but American blues
give us a mutual voice, communist and capitalist, as we are lost in traffic
on our way from Disneyland, lost in relentless secularity. Bias here is the
bias of the powerless modern, victim, subject of the blues. The differences
of woman, mystic, poet, homosexual, communist, Chinese intersect with
the otherness of American blacks: the blues are the music of the oppressed.
But they are laughing. Am I arguing that Dillard writes on behalf of the
oppressed, then? No, for in her work, the abject is felt not as oppression
but as *jouissance*. The power of writing as of the blues is in dissolving the
conviction of clichéd oppositions. At the same time, this is a subversiveness
that may be easy to approve.

She addresses this problem in *An American Childhood*. Dillard's family
and the family business, American Standard, were part of the great capitalist industrialist class of Pittsburgh—her genealogy entwined with the
history of the Carnegies and the Mellons. Her representation of difference
seems in many respects compatible with the contradictory stances of nineteenth-century liberalism, which takes otherness into account and makes
prejudice against difference not acceptable at the same time that the very
image of the free individual casts out gender, race, and class. The disturbing
way that modernism recuperates difference reappears in Dillard at the level
of personal history.

Everything that Dillard as a child found that was subversive, in fact,
also seemed to be approved of by the adults. The vice-president of Jones
and Laughlin taught her the "scandalous document" of the Bible in Sunday
school class. "They didn't recognize the vivid danger that we would,
through repeated exposure, catch a case of its wild opposition to their

world" (134). Similarly, books—and especially the European books after World War II that brought knowledge of concentration camps, ghettos, prison camps, bombs, survivors—conveyed "the actual, historical, moral world—in which somehow I felt I was not living." This, too, was subversive knowledge: "There is a life worth living where history is still taking place; there are ideas worth dying for, and circumstances where courage is still prized. This life could be found and joined, like the Resistance" (183). She also discovered the British war poets, Asian and Middle Eastern poetry in translation, and Rimbaud. Here it was pure lyricism, stripped of history, that was subversive. "I wanted beauty bare of import; I liked language in strips like pennants" (236). And still the interior life was confined within the Ellis School which the small group of Pittsburgh girls on the same social list attended together. "It galled me that adults, as a class, approved the writing and memorization of poetry" (236).[16]

Dillard's rage provoked her high-school teacher to write in her appraisal, "Here, alas, is a child of the twentieth century" (239). She rejected her family, her familiar social context. "I approved almost nothing. That is, I liked, I adored, I longed for, everyone on earth, especially India and Africa and particularly everyone on the streets of Pittsburgh—all those friendly, democratic, openhearted, sensible people. . . . excepting only the people I knew, none of whom was up to snuff" (191). Thus Dillard locates the postwar critique of American middle-class life in the (more childish) past, in the adolescent rage of the twentieth-century child.

Dillard is, then, writing within some kind of return to American life, some kind of recuperation not only of the family but of the American culture that the Pittsburgh of her childhood, from the alley to the big rock house on the hill, represents. Anarchy and conventionality are rewritten together. The anarchism of her style ruptures the masculine subject and the hierarchies established around the unified individual. Her negativity operates like her rejection of her father's defense of capitalism, in sympathy with her anticonformist mother. Her father argued that money worked like the water system in a house, "the way water flowed from high water towers into our attic bathroom," and rivers flowed to the Gulf of New Orleans. "The money, once you got enough of it high enough, would flow by gravitation, all over everybody" (204). But her mother replied, " 'Remember those shacks we see in Georgia? Those barefoot little children who have to quit school to work in the fields, their poor mothers not able to feed them enough'—we could all hear in her voice that she was beginning to cry—'not even able to keep them dressed?' " (204). Here, the narrator says assertively, "Father, who knew the real world so well, got some of it wrong" (204). The terms of his mistake are significant. The father is not being sentimental here, and the scene of mother's tears is as old as Sterne's

Sentimental Traveler and as vulnerable as the whole tradition to dismissal. The joking and anarchic mother is also sentimental and embodies a certain resistance.

Dillard's sublime is related to the child's experience of her mother. From the pine shed where she writes *An American Childhood*, she sees a movement in the trees outside:

> concentrating, lost in the past, I see the pale leaves wag and think as my blood leaps: Is someone coming? Is it Mother coming for me, to carry me home? Could it be my own young, my own glorious Mother, coming across the grass for me, the morning light on her skin, to get me and bring me back? Back to where I last knew all I needed, the way to her two strong arms? (250)

Is it fair to see the earlier Annie Dillard of *Pilgrim* and *Holy the Firm* in the framework of this more clearly drawn nostalgia? Here, the language is seized by the echoes of black folk expression and white renditions of black music, by the tragic longing of the oppressed, and the colonizing appropriation of that emotion as nostalgia ("coming for to carry me home"). This use of language does not make distinctions about the loss of *home* but rather takes it as a personal experience common to us all. From this point of view, the recollection of emotion in language, of childhood, seems perhaps questionable, sentimental in the bad sense, a contribution to the ideology of individualism which works to obscure social realities. Not that Dillard claims to write about any but her own experience, but that the radical claim of her style, to embody the vernacular, might be vitiated by such a retreat to individualism and subjectivity.

How can she get away with this? What protects Dillard against the reader's irony? Isn't she asserting everything modernism has been ironic about: religious belief, joy, love of family, and even (embedded in the landscape as well as the wisecracking vernacular) love of country? Isn't she, furthermore, showing how modernist style itself is locked into this assumption about personal experience?

This problem, that personal experience seems at some point to cease being subversive and to act as a conflation of differences, is the issue that haunts women's writing. Some might say, indeed, that here is the evidence for Dillard's speaking as a woman—representing, in fact, the most conservative and sentimental view possible. The conjuncture of family, religion, and country situates the patriarchal woman, a figure who strongly represents the gendered ideal of the nineteenth-century bourgeoisie, as translated into twentieth-century American populism. But this womanly figure is doubtless an image Dillard has been at some pains to avoid. Doesn't she, like so many women of the avant-garde, take up a variety of male voices, male styles, from the reason of natural history to the irrationality of Rimbaud, precisely to dissociate from this sentimental? And yet here she is risking it three ways at once, layering the landscape that moves us and the remembrance of Mother and the sounds of a cultural longing for home.

We know Dillard is postmodern because we know as readers that this writer is not going to stop here. The writing goes on, letting memory fall into its discontinuous pieces, its sudden rapprochements, following what Dillard characterizes as awakenings, remembering oneself. But "you must take on faith that those apparently discrete dots of you were contiguous. . . . that those severed places cohered, too. . . . that the multiform and variously lighted latitudes and longitudes were part of one world . . . " (249).

This history of a consciousness is like women's history because it is not held together in a continuous whole by a public self, a subject in history. And this is why women's history is subversive. It is made up of those moments when the other life (the interior life, often) realizes itself, coming into contact with history (writ small or large) and working to remember itself in vain. This loss of continuity is, for Dillard, the primordial experience of loss repeated: "probably all children feel this way, as adults do; they mourn this absence or loss of someone, and sense that unnameable loss as a hole or hollow moving beside them in the air" (172). Psychoanalysis would name the loss separation from the mother. But for Dillard the loss continues as compensation, translated into change itself, and more particularly into the gaps articulating the sense of self and the self's remembering. Change makes the loves and hates of childhood comic. "I had vowed to love Walter Milligan forever; now I could recall neither his face nor my feeling, but only this quondam urgent vow. . . . I had vowed to keep hating Amy in order to defy Mother, who kept prophesying I would someday not hate Amy" (AC 172–73).

The childish impotence of all our attempts to be consistent about our most impassioned experiences marks the fragility of that interiority. If the private experience is gendered feminine, it is, in Dillard's representation, also severed from the realm of public memory, and characterized by inevitable loss. Recalling this becomes the child Annie's impossible vocation. "As a life's work, I would remember everything—everything, against loss. . . . who would remember any of it, any of this our time, and the wind thrashing the buckeye trees outside?" (173). The task of the writer is remembrance, but the narrative of personal history is impersonal, cut and fragmented and elusive to the vows of will. The inevitable loss of "this our time" is both good and bad news.

Freud argues that the structure of the joke depends upon the psychic economy of repression and release. A joke allows repressed contents of the unconscious to appear momentarily. Wit provides the model of all art, which acts like Mona Lisa's smile as the anamnesis of the lost maternal smile, a kind of mastery over loss. And the joke, by its sudden release of repression, may turn pain into pleasure, just as the classic tragedies do. But it does not provide a permanent release; repression returns. Dillard says, on the one hand, that art—or the *bias* of the subject—is all we have. On the other hand, if writing is "an epistemological tool," the writing life is characterized by "unfinished business"—you leave out what it was you meant to say, the resolution to the "sore spot" that functions as source (WL 3, 5, 20). The pleasure principle is superseded, Freud says, by another principle, a compulsion to repeat which is more primitive than pleasure, a mental function which reveals the limited mastery of consciousness. Dillard moves the line of words close to the borders between a mastery which would establish the pleasure of consciousness itself, and the *jouissance* of contact and submersion in which the self and the ego is submerged: "I break up through the skin of awareness a thousand times a day, as dolphins burst through seas, and dive again, and rise, and dive" (250).

This bias of style at the ongoing edge of perception raises the question of the writer's—and the reader's—*pleasure*. What does art produce? Is pleasure subversive? In Freud, the instinctual economy of the death drive, with its pressure toward repetition, its conservatism, is associated with childishness and the child's love of the repeated story.[17] Adults, on the other hand, insist on the pleasure of novelty—a pleasure associated with the life instincts, with sexuality. But Dillard rewrites childishness into adulthood as the surprise of repetition. She gives us the pleasures of the obsessive, who Barthes says "would experience the voluptuous release of the letter" like "all those for whom language *returns*," but also of the obsessive's opposite, the hysterical reader, who "joins in the bottomless, truthless comedy of language, who is no longer the subject of any critical scrutiny and *throws himself* across the text" (63).[18] The pleasure principle and the reality principle overlap in Dillard's work, change positions, as does the ecstatic and the critic. This is not exactly contrary to Freud; in fact it mimics the Freudian dialectic. However, Dillard's "necessity" may not quite function like the reality principle which, in Freud, comes finally to dominate and subsume pleasure, because she does not ever cease to undermine the discourse of reason by her style, the "truthless comedy of language."

Choosing to write nonfiction, Dillard is nonetheless not taking up the logocentric ideal of coherent histories. She does not construct an ego, look for meaning. What she writes seems closer in many respects to the unconscious, the "censored chapter" of personal history, written down in the monument of the body as the hysterical symptom, in the archival documents of childhood memories, in the "stock of words and . . . particular vocabulary," in the traditions and legends of personal history—and in the distortions which result from connecting the conscious to the repressed.[19] This is not to say that she expresses her own unconscious but that she traces the subjective bias embedded in this setting, of Tinker Creek, of Puget Sound, of an American childhood in Pittsburgh. The release at the punch line tells us the repressed is collective. Far from giving us the solitary individual imagination, Dillard gives us something much more communal, its popular elements associated with the pleasure of the forgotten familiar. It is a pleasure associated with the punch line, or the cut which introduces both discontinuity and release.

Writing is, she says in *The Writing Life*, like chopping wood. "If you aim for the wood, you will have nothing. Aim past the wood, aim through the wood; aim for the chopping block" (59). Clearly, the cut is relocated— it is not the Oedipal cut—the cut no longer separates the present from a maternal loss. She recuperates the sentimental. But this loving enchantment is cut away from familiar continuities, as from any hope of escaping death and destruction. Like Barthes's *A Lover's Discourse*, it is modernist, cut away from history, except as an intertextuality. Instead it appears with all the nostalgia that parody can evoke, its theatricality inscribed in the metaphorical and evocative style. The sentimental discourse appears as a fragment cut off from serious humanism. It is a remedy to Rimbaud and to the egotism which Dillard associates with irrational despair. This move away from Oedipus marks Dillard's negativity, and the parodic, highly staged style which she takes up is thus feminized in relationship to the stability of a technology of the self—the self produced as ego—just as popular culture is feminized in relationship to serious culture.

In Dillard's metaphysical joke, the discourses of the other—the carnivalesque and the sentimental—overlap. Figures of centrality—God, science, the individual imagination—all reappear in their most metaphorical extremity. Knowledge is only the love of knowledge—"There was no one here but us fanatics"—and so knowledge is the effect of passionate attention and a precipitate of pathos (AC 159).

Locating pathos and the interior life as the starting point of epistemology as of metaphysics, Dillard gives us a mode of inquiry compatible with feminist traditions of the personal. But it is also a reprise of Emerson, a post-Nietzschean Emerson, a gay science whose perspectivism juxtaposes rapture and learning to pitch a baseball. Dillard sees science and art not as opposite faculties but as similar consequences of passionate *attention*. The mystical joy which dares to violate conventions of dignity—like St. Teresa—is, Dillard proposes, like the child's joy and the child's act of faith. From the point of view of French feminism, it is also, let us add, the public spectacle of feminine *jouissance*. In Dillard's version of this spectacle, she was running down the street testing whether or not she could, with sufficient energy and belief, fly:

> I knew I was too old really to believe in this as a child would, out of ignorance; instead I was experimenting as a scientist would, testing both the thing itself and the limits of my own courage in trying it miserably self-conscious in full view of the whole world. You can't test courage cautiously, so I ran hard and waved my arms, hard, happy. (108)

Although other adults looked away, embarrassed, she met a young woman who exchanged a sympathetic glance: "So Teresa of Avila checked her unseemly joy and hung on to the altar rail to hold herself down. . . . we passed on the sidewalk with the look of accomplices who share a humor just beyond irony. What's a heart for?" (109). Here is Dillard's paradigm for science, for art, for religion—all effects of acts of faith, joy, the complicity of humor—all flying in the face of absurdity. And the child's affront to pedestrian dignity is nothing compared to the affront of the writer against civilized irony. Dillard's *jouissance* is as unacceptable to literary decorum as running down the street trying to fly, and "in full view of the whole world." Nevertheless it is the impossible experiment of flight that discovers accomplices. Thus modernism joins the vernacular as "a humor just beyond irony" that the very impossibility of a woman's writing may locate—not in isolation but in the exchange of a sympathetic glance.

Who is speaking? In a masterful disguise like the dumb blonde of the joke, is it not literature? The paradox of a literary inquiry into nonfiction style arises from its longing to prove that the genre is a sleight of hand; that all writing, and the reality that appears in its traces, is domestic, is fiction-making. In Dillard, the symbolist revolution of poetic language extends into nonfiction. Dillard gives us a poetics which shapes not only the seen but also the seer. She gives us perception—Tinker Creek, Puget Sound—as a form of reading. And thus she defines by her style not the weasel but the gaze that seizes it, the persona of an ecological knowing. She reveals, on the one hand, its debt to the spiritual exercises that helped define the poetics of the lyric from Donne to Stevens, and its place in the pastoral conventions. On the other hand, even more important as a qualification of perception and the discontinuities of popular history is the vernacular joke.

Dillard traces the ecstatic impersonality of a female subject. This female self is impersonal because without power. The speaker is not the ego, not created by conquering the body of nature. If the object of her pilgrimage is the real world, still it is an object which is known by its action upon the subject—we read together with the gesture of her responsiveness the signs of an otherwise blank mystery, of an untranslatable real. And Dillard's real world makes itself known by messages violently counter to our desires, against even our desire for life itself. The messages come like the bloody tracks of her cat on her flesh. The world limits and refutes the experience of will, enforces abjection. It takes a poetics, or a joke, the subversion of language, to define what we know. And yet ecstasy comes with the recognition of powerlessness: that she neither wills nor creates the creek, the bay, the cat, the crash, the weasel, Pittsburgh. Although she may write the terms of her encounter, her writing itself turns to the inscription of otherness, with the receptivity of an author-ity that is, in this strangeness, feminine.

The Sentimental and the Critical
Maternal Irony, Alice Walker,
and a Feminist Conclusion

Reader, my story ends with freedom;
not in the usual way, with marriage.

>   —*Incidents in the Life*
>   *of a Slave Girl*

And us so happy.

>   —*The Color Purple*[1]

I

Women's postmodernist writing
does not necessarily evoke the forms
of modernism: indeed, Alice Walker
reaches back to recuperate the female
past and reaches boldly across the
boundaries between the serious and
the popular. Like Harriet Jacobs's nineteenth-century autobiography, Celie's plot ends not in marriage but in
freedom. *The Color Purple* can be seen as a rewriting of nineteenth-century
slave narratives, but also of sentimental love narratives and the epistolary
mode. The book cites a familiar feminine plot, with its trajectory toward
the domestic. But here domesticity allows the stories of women and children to be separated from the fatal sequences of erotic romance. This serious
fiction is implicated in the "popular," I shall argue, not because it moves
to a popular happy ending but because rather than working by the literary
subversion of conventional language, it exploits a crossing of literary conventions and the vernacular to recall both the desire for freedom and the
lost maternal enclosure.

In spite of the horrors Celie has endured, her story closes on so optimistic a note that it violates the irony usually required of modernist narratives. Is this a flaw, a lapse into sentimentality? According to the
conventions of ironic discourse, such hopefulness is hopelessly uncon-

vincing. This kind of violation, in fact, is part of what has earned a bad reputation for women's popular novels. But is it possible to reconcile irony with narratives of possibility, like the mother's story or the slave's pursuit of freedom? Or like the utopian narratives of feminism itself? Are Walker's "womanist" fictions, as she calls them, falling back into new versions of the old liberalism, patriarchy for females? Walker cites *Jane Eyre*: "I am not speaking here of the most famous short line of that book, 'Reader, I married him,' as the triumph, but, rather, of the triumph of Jane Eyre's control over her own sense of morality and her own stout will."[2] The message Walker brought to the graduates of Sarah Lawrence was: "your job, when you leave here—as it was the job of educated women before you—is to change the world."[3]

Celie's story begins with her being raped by the man she thinks is her father and having two children who are taken from her. She is given to Mr._____, who marries her, separates her from her beloved sister Nettie, beats her, and treats her like a slave. She cleans for him, cooks for him, works in his fields, and takes care of his neglected, ungrateful children, who also mistreat her. Mr._____ cuts her off from even knowing about another life, or the possibility of rescue by an alliance with other women, intercepting Nettie's faithful letters. So brainwashed is Celie that she tells her stepson to beat Sofia, his dangerously self-confident wife.

Celie, in other words, has a life like a slave's. She occupies a cultural position where the woman as wife and daughter overlaps the history of the slave, with its economic and psychic dependency and its degradation of the self. Celie is also like a prisoner, her life not much freer than Sofia's when Sofia is jailed and then sentenced to serve the white family of the mayor. The narrative defines desire as a struggle for freedom.

But love enters into the plot, not as its purpose but, ironically, as a complement of the desire for an independent self, and a complication of gender positions. Walker calls her prose "womanist," which she defines as "feminist of color," "usually referring to outrageous, audacious, courageous or *willful* behavior," "*Also*: A woman who loves other women, sexually and/or nonsexually" (xi).[4] Mr._____'s erotic love for his beautiful mistress, Shug, provides the opening for Celie's escape, first psychological, then literal. Celie discovers that she loves Shug too, erotically, "like a man," she thinks. Celie tells Mr._____ because of their shared love for Shug that "this the closest us ever felt," and his eventual redemption through love is underway. Toward the end of the story, long after she has left him, Celie and Mr._____ learn a moral discipline together as both wait painfully for the absent Shug. Mr._____ shows his conversion to the domestic order not only by keeping his own house clean but by turning to sewing with Celie on the pants she sells. The fabric of domesticity shapes the tale, but love appears in different forms, in and out of marriage, across the barriers of heterosexuality, in spite of violence and suffering. Love is not complicit with oppressive power.

A feminine heroic constructs the subjects, offering even Mr.＿＿＿ a good ending defined by refusals of slavery and oppression and a return to the loving community. Shug and Sofia are the extreme models of this heroic, rewriting figures that were once identified with masculinity. Mr.＿＿＿ argues that Shug "act more manly than most men. I mean she upright, honest. Speak her mind and the devil take the hindmost, he say. You know Shug will fight, he say. Just like Sofia. She bound to live her life and be herself no matter what." But Celie does what the novel as a whole does, redefining heroic virtue as womanly: "Mr.＿＿＿ think all this is stuff men do. But Harpo not like this, I tell him. You not like this. What Shug got is womanly it seem like to me. Specially since she and Sofia the ones got it" (228). Mr.＿＿＿ throws off the tyranny of his own manhood when he opens himself to admitting he is a "fool." From the point of view of the patriarchal reader, the effect is antiheroic. From the point of view of the feminist reader, the effect is to precipitate both irony and pleasure. The desire for freedom moves from producing male adventure stories to resisting domination, and producing the small victories of everyday women's lives.

The overlapping of freedom and domesticity generates a rereading of desire; in this book it includes erotic love, but also maternal and spiritual love and community. And it also includes economic success, education, and self-sufficiency. The things that the women in this book want are multiple and different. The women do not add up to Woman. What they have in common is a form of liberal feminism: that they free themselves from depending on Man for their definition. But perhaps they also erode the figure of the liberal individual, whose will always depended upon a white male economic logic. Because Nettie and Shug have an erotic relationship, they unsettle the automatic heterosexuality of woman and man. Because they are black women, they also unsettle the automatic whiteness of women's narratives. One of Nettie's letters explicitly makes the analogy of slave narratives and women's narratives, finding repressive the African Olinka's attitudes that women should not be educated. The Africans say, "A girl is nothing to herself; only to her husband can she become something" (132). Nettie's daughter, Olivia, comments: "They're like white people at home who don't want colored people to learn."

The Color Purple both asserts and unsettles; it is at once an affirmation of the possibility that women, blacks, lesbians who have been oppressed can be free—and happy—and a critique of the oppressors, all those who identify with the place of mastery, who thought they knew how to read the sentimental story and the happy ending, or thought they could safely ignore it in pursuit of power and adventure. Ironically, the longing for happiness returns, just as the children are returned to their mothers. This novel solicits the popular desire for ordinary pleasure, and the woman is hero of the ordinary. Walker records what W. E. B. Du Bois called the "double consciousness" of the black American, which is a split between self-awareness and awareness of the oppressor. From the point of view of liberal subjectivity, this split is an unfortunate rending, a contradiction of loyalties that causes pain. But from the point of view of the crisis of modernity, with the appearance of a postmodern subject, this split becomes an asset, a privileged position, because the contradiction and struggle is at once played out internally (psychologically) and externally, in cultural politics.

Celie comes close to representing the ordinary American *because* she is black and female and poor—because the alienation of every person within the logic of capitalism seems both real and symbolic in her person. Conflating the real and the symbolic, the novel is sensational, in the sense Jane Tompkins used for Harriet Beecher Stowe. Furthermore, writing in Black English, Walker gives the speech of a folk to her heroine. Celie as heroine renews modernity because her voice brings the resonance of difference and the repressed body into the cultural consciousness. Celie's refusal to remain a victim represents both the hope for change of progressive politics and the recuperation of progressive politics into the entrepreneur logic of capitalism, a doubleness of defiance and complicity that cannot be foreclosed as one or the other.

The complicity makes some black critics uneasy, and it poses problems that ought to be familiar to feminists. Is *The Color Purple* popular because it is accessible and true for many women or because it does not really challenge dominant ideology, does not make it difficult for readers to imagine they understand? Trudier Harris argues that *The Color Purple* has been detrimental to the black community; that because it creates "spectator readers" who are not like the characters and "do not feel the intensity of their pain," it reinforces stereotypes, and its popularity has discouraged criticism.[5] White feminists should be careful about their own "spectatorship" as readers. Still, what Walker means when she addresses her work to her own people is to have a popular audience, and she means to have as readers those who previously would not have thought the poor farmer's daughter could be a poet as well; she means to let others profit by her people's success, if they will:

> it is narrow thinking, indeed, to believe that a Keats is the only kind of poet one would want to grow up to be. One wants to write poetry that is understood by one's people, not by the Queen of England. Of course, should she be able to profit by it too, so much the better, but since that is not likely, catering to her tastes would be a waste of time.[6]

This democratic ambition defines an American point of view and a lack of paranoia which Walker attributes to her ancestors. She thinks most white Southern writers will have their work dated by racism. "Our parents seemed to know that an extreme negative emotion held against other human beings for reasons they do not control can be blinding. Blindness about other human beings, especially for a writer, is equivalent to death" (19). Still, the question remains whether love can also be blind, whether *The Color Purple* silences complaint by its success and promotes an imaginary understanding among white readers that is not based on a common history and may obscure the most terrible differences. This is a question generally raised about sentimental fiction, and it remains an issue. Walker says that the book was written as a kind of counterhistory, with an ironic chuckle for a black male critic who thinks of history in more heroic terms. "The chuckle was because, womanlike (he would say), my 'history' starts not with the taking of lands, or the births, battles, and deaths of Great Men, but with one woman asking another for her underwear. Oh, well, I thought, one function of critics is to be appalled by such behavior."[7]

The idea that "womanist" bonding can help women to assert defiance against the victimizers cuts across histories of race and class. Thus *The Color Purple* suffers from the doubleness of feminism itself, and exemplifies the problematic status of our embodied arguments. This popular work is as vulnerable to criticism as *Uncle Tom's Cabin*. The irony of its chuckle, of its counterhistory, is easily lost.

Walker's violation of the codes of realistic fiction and the resistance of serious literature to anything that resembles a happy ending has bothered some reviewers, who seem unconscious of the extent to which their standards have been formed by an ideology they would reject. Robert Towers wrote: "Alice Walker still has a lot to learn about plotting and structuring what is clearly intended to be a realistic novel. The revelations involving the fate of Celie's lost babies and the identity of her real father seem crudely contrived—the stuff of melodrama or fairy tales."[8] Dinitia Smith worried about "the note of tendentiousness": "Walker's politics are not the problem—*of course* sexism and racism are terrible, *of course* women should band together to help each other. But the politics have to be incarnated in complex, contradictory characters—characters to whom the novelist grants the freedom to act, as it were, on their own."[9]

In other words, Walker should not violate the realistic conventions which make characters appear as free individuals, humanist subjects, no matter what her politics. But Walker gives us the logic of womanist transformation: it happens at the moment when the dependent woman realizes her solidarity is not with the slavery enforced upon her but with the other women. This is a kind of assertion that requires the help of a feminist discourse, a communal speaking out, not "the freedom to act, as it were, on their own." Dinitia Smith insists, in the last analysis, on an individual autonomy which promotes separation from that collective speaking out.

In serious twentieth-century fiction, as I have argued, irony functions not only as what Kenneth Burke calls a "master trope" or dialectic itself but also more narrowly, as the requirement for literature to maintain its borders against assertion, as the ground of the aesthetic.[10] On the other hand, as Hayden White has suggested in *Metahistory*, irony is implicated in the possibility of writing convincing history.[11] A certain skepticism about the truths of any narrative, separating the hero from ideology, seems to protect narrative affirmation. Irony keeps readers from the dangers of identification and uncritical absorption: the works ordinary readers identify with—American best sellers—are segregated from "literature" by their seeming lack of irony. In other words, novelistic and historical discourse uses irony to portray the drama of self-critical skepticism. Irony in this sense also protects the modernist narrative from external attacks on its enclosure. Popular works seem to have nothing new to say because difference is already taken into account.

In spite of the important critical work which has made the case for their significance to cultural studies, women's popular narratives have remained an unwarranted discourse, stories that are "escapist" almost by definition. Critics such as Janice Radway, Tania Modleski, and Leslie Rabine have taken the romance seriously.[12] None, however, claims that the sentimental escapes the patriarchal frame. In what sense can such stories be called escapist? One of the critical commonplaces about the sentimental is that, as Ann Douglas claims in *The Feminization of America*, the feminine, the sentimental, and American consumerism are connected.[13] Madonne Miner's studies of women's best sellers show how one kind of consuming might be connected to the woman's place in psychoanalytic narrative: the novels represent a never-satisfied fantasy of a nurturance which a lost or diminished mother failed to provide.[14] The woman's desire differs from the Oedipal plot.

By contrast, the Oedipal economy of consumerism is a mode of reification, a way of mastering the world by fragmenting it into things that can be possessed, with even women as a dismembered assortment of parts—eyes, hair, mouth—images like objects to be bought, sold, and exchanged. There is a difference in the position of the desiring subject which might help open up the question of the sentimental. If the story of life from the point of view of the Oedipal hero means leaving the maternal enclosure and becoming a separate self, ready for adventure, an important component is thus the desire for freedom. Irony enters as a recognition of limits but also as a resistance to the recognition, taking the form of a resistance to the domestic, to the private, to identification, and to the psychoanalytic itself. This male irony thus recuperates the liberal position of

John Stuart Mill. Irony for the male hero is different from the doubleness of the female, who (silently) desires not separation but a remedy to loss.

However, the desire for freedom is countermagisterial. The feminist desire for freedom is anarchic—is anarchy—without the linear direction away from maternal authority. Once the anarchic impulse is engaged, it may undermine even the governing tropes of irony. The master's freedom is different from the slave's, and that irony can be spoken from the slave's point of view.

Thus in *The Color Purple*, there is no universal maternal love but rather a maternal irony. Sofia encounters Reynolds Stanley, the baby of the white girl she was forced to care for, and tells the young mother, Eleanor Jane, "I don't feel nothing about him at all. I don't love him, I don't hate him" (224). "I got my own troubles . . . and when Reynolds Stanley grow up, he's gon be one of them" (225). Sofia is no politician, and her maternal circle does not extend to include the universal Baby.

Woman in *The Color Purple* is the subject of a mimicry, giving back the language imposed on us in subverted form, recalling alternatives to the domestic stereotypes of the Oedipal adventure. Irony is in what makes Celie so happy, the discovery that the eternal return is to everyday life. This "maternal ironic" is not limited to texts written by women writers: the domestic appears as the destination of many male adventure plots, like the western, and when the hero has resisted domestication, that return is ironic. For example, Faulkner's *Light in August* ends with Lena, a woman with a baby and no particular destination, who will just go on after the heroic extremists fail. But in Faulkner's hands, we are not encouraged to identify with Lena, or to see her overtaking the place of the hero. The stolid reproductive endurance Lena represents seems the ironic response of natural life to human struggle.

In women's popular fiction, the woman is the ordinary hero. What happens when a woman is the ordinary hero, the everyday underdog? Is the unsettling of narrative orders I have been claiming possible? The heroine appears under the *ideologème* of patriarchy, as I have used Julia Kristeva's concept. That is, under patriarchy, instead of describing gender *differences*, the opposition of male/female is reduced to a single difference, a binary which is, in fact, an identity. The female other inevitably reflects the male. All stories then would have a male hero: the tale would be the same no matter how the plot might cleverly displace it. And in fact that is the difficult situation of post-Freudian narrative, with its framework seeming inevitably to return to the Oedipal, male, drama.

But when it is a tale told from the position of the feminine, there is a difference which resonates in the very sound of imitation: it may be a maddening difference; it is obviously a despised difference, and it may be both a means to power and a dangerous trap for women. This difference which is like the gap between what the male subject posits and what the female voice repeats appears sometimes as ineptitude, or as the inevitable decline of heroic speech into the ordinary, into mimicry. Or it appears as the escape from reasoned language into pure pathos, the bold invitation to silence of the Longinian sublime. In *The Color Purple*, it is the sublime decline/ascent into black speech. This sublime pathos also appears as the political aphasia of literature itself. But I want to look at that gap from another point of view, not heroic—from the point of view of maternal irony.

Celie earns her success, in part, by the bourgeois virtues of hard work and orderliness, and not so much by her submission to being a kind of patient Griselda, but by her willingness, prompted by Shug, to assert herself. She resembles in this respect the kind of American hero we have learned to admire from reading Emerson's "Self-Reliance" in school, or from the echoes of the American success story formula made conventional fiction by Horatio Alger and convincing fantasy by Ronald Reagan. But Walker—who saw herself as a medium rather than as an author—tells us Celie's assertive turn was inspired by Walker's daughter: "My characters adored her. They saw she spoke her mind in no uncertain terms and would fight back when attacked. When she came home from school one day with bruises but said, You should see the other guy, Celie . . . began to reappraise her own condition. Rebecca gave her courage."[15] When self-reliance is spoken by a woman's voice, does it change its ideological function? Celie's success is in women's time, not in an economy of progress. Her children, taken from her, return at the end. Her victory, witnessed by the very Albert who treated her cruelly, is an instance of the maternal ironic. It is a calling down of mythic, monumental time into the orders of linear deeds. From the point of view of a patriarchal realism, such closure may seem contrived. Like the nineteenth-century melodrama, this novel takes no account of the feelings or ambitions of the hapless villain if he mutters "curses, foiled again" or "I've been a fool" in the wings.

The Color Purple invites the reader's identification with the oppressed Celie and uses the "heroine's text" against the patriarchy which produced it. Walker uses familiar literary forms: the epistolary novel associated with the rise of the feminine since *Clarissa*, and the slave narrative, like those long ago inserted into the sentimental text of *Uncle Tom's Cabin* to powerful effect. In the end, Celie witnesses a return which outrages and frustrates the economy of motives which it once served: the sentimental narrative ironically (in spite of all that would enslave it to tragedy) reasserts itself. After multiple arbitrary disasters, this kind of return makes no claims about life and no promises to the vulnerable individual. We could call it the "maternal ironic" because what the failure of the erotic hero produces is the return of another, mythic, time: the cyclic order of reproduction. It also appears as the material reminder of a haunting, bodied otherness which is everywhere being left out as all of us (male and female), speechless in everyday life, are being left out. This is a reminder of the irony which undermines the heroic, Hegel's eternal irony of the community, the reproductive irony that ordinary death but also ordinary life simply keeps going on: the domestic, the minimal, the maternal, the sentimental.

The Color Purple condenses social issues into the personal quest for freedom, but in Celie's person, the enactment of individualism—her training in self-assertion—leads to a communal resolution. When she achieves the status of a free individual, it leads to not separation from the mother but a return to her, as Celie becomes both child and mother. The children return. Like *Clarissa*, this novel has placed the woman in the position of the oppressed, as the feminine unconscious of the male ego, and in this sense Walker continues the production of gendering. But like Emma Goldman, Walker challenges the stabilities of gendered individualism. It is not by opposing the sentimental structures that Walker gives us a woman heroine. Rather, she speaks them differently, unsettling narrative orders so we hear the ironic resonance of the maternal return. Walker undermines individualism from within, because Celie is at once an individual and a representative heroine of her people. Her language is the very voice of the rural black, a communal voice of a folk. This extraordinary rupture of the conventions of stereotyping and the representation of personal experience calls attention to the gap between serious fiction and formulaic romances. Walker recuperates the didactic element of women's writing. In so doing, she also exposes the forbidden ideological content of all writing, in particular the allegedly realistic history. The bond of sisterhood which finally empowers Celie and Shug and Sofia and Nettie is extended to the reader. But the reader may not wish to shake off the doctrines of modernist alienation and pessimism enough to respond.

II

Feminism is perhaps our last religion. . . .

—JULIA KRISTEVA[16]

If we change language, do we also change the world? The relations of feminism, rhetoric, and postmodernism are contentious. When we speak from the point of view of feminism, we are speaking from a position which is already unsettled and unsettling, from within a discourse with a rich and combative history and from within generative narratives, stories with a future, often but not always oriented to change. Because its reproductive narratives are not necessarily utopian or historical but may call down the monumental time which establishes a maternal irony in dialectic with history, escaping the necessary repression of social reproduction, feminism can overlap with Marxist struggles for political change without being as vulnerable to historical discontinuity. Speaking as feminists, women most of all do not speak alone, as solitary, inventive individuals, but we also do not speak from a well-defined collectivity. The feminist position is multiple, filled with disagreement and difference, and nonetheless collaborative. And the feminist position is capable of generating discursive change. Although poststructuralist critics—including Kristeva—have taken feminism narrowly, generally calling it uncritically humanistic, as Toril Moi points out, "Kristeva's view of the *productivity* of the sign accounts for feminist discourse itself."[17] And this is not simply to argue that feminist writing is rhetorical rather than literary.

Feminism challenges rhetoric in ways that postmodernism can theorize and endorse. Rhetoric as a tradition is patriarchal, its history constructed around the great male masters, from Aristotle to Campbell to Kenneth Burke. The rhetorical appeal to ethos or character depends upon a figure of the speaking subject which most often denies authority to women, especially if they speak in the plural, which we so often do. Feminism, like postmodernism, problematizes the speaking subject. Furthermore, modern rhetoric, perhaps since Bacon, Petrus Ramus, and the Royal Society, has been overwhelmed by the logos of science, giving up its inventive prerogatives, its contributions to the production of knowledge, and giving aid and comfort to positivism.

Feminism, reading against the grain, denaturalizes the monological discourse, making the dialogic visible. Because it arises from this kind of dialectic, feminist collaboration does not define itself in opposition to resistance. Feminism gives a local habitation and a name to the silenced Other, marking, as does Derrida, the violence of textuality. Feminism challenges the scientism which has reduced rhetoric to the study of composition skills for so many years. Feminism is postmodern—and postmodern male critics are flocking to be feminists—because our listening and our reading has uncovered the hidden male figure, and so revealed the figurativeness and rhetoricity of much that had passed for absolute doctrine. Thus feminism may be seen as a postmodern project which foregrounds a rhetoric of figure, challenges domination, and undermines the logocentric assumptions of science. Feminism gives rhetoric back to itself.

But feminism also challenges postmodernism, and from a position that overlaps with the pragmatic position of rhetoric. Oriented to persuasion and to action, feminism becomes uneasy with the reflexivity of deconstruction, which seems often in practice not to recognize the ideological component of discourse—that is, to see that all theorizing is political, and has consequences in the real world. Divided and heterogeneous, feminism itself needs nonetheless to appear as an ethos, the subject of an argument which aims to persuade, appealing to pathos, to emotions which unsettle the unsentimental stances of textual analysis. And feminism needs a rhetorical logos, the possibility of advancing knowledge or telling stories. For if we are simply content to question all knowledge, the desires of the most powerful always prevail.

Thus feminism critiques both rhetoric and postmodernism, holding itself aloof from an identification with either one. But at the same time, feminism as a discourse is mutually imbricated with both postmodern theory and rhetoric. On the other hand, feminism as a discourse also carries the mark of the gendering narratives which underwrite its history, separating male and female powers. If women's writing is productive, it is involved in the technologies of gender.

Some of Julia Kristeva's detractors allege that she makes a mistake in thinking there is a connection between what we say and what happens, between challenging the rules of language and challenging the rules of law. They criticize her interest in the revolution of poetic language as merely aesthetic, and her commitment to psychoanalysis as too involved with the individual to have political consequences. This is part of a more general argument about poststructuralism and ideology.

Kristeva relates linguistic rule and political law, but she does not associate meaning with either one. She argues that signifying practice produces meaning, and so that meaning exists only locally, in concrete, material circumstances and relationships. Certain poetic practices rupture the laws of language, producing not just transgression or subversion but an opening for what has been silenced. It is a dangerous opening as well as an opportunity because what is at risk is sanity, made vulnerable to psychosis.

Kristeva's model of social exchange could provide us with a new rhetoric, based on semiotics and psychoanalysis. She argues that the dialogue of therapist and patient—an exchange based on transference—offers the chance for both individuals to deconstruct the cultural imaginary which binds them into their positions as subjects and to produce, in the therapeutic exchange, alternative imaginary narratives which make the individuals into the agents of more desirable discourses. She calls us all "extraterrestrials suffering for want of love," but she does not advocate that we become blind believers in anything, including feminism and even psychoanalysis, to remedy our need.[18] Rather, she argues that we must avoid entering into collusion with a social order that is violent and reifying, just as we must avoid past errors of identifying with symptomatic cultures which kept order by repression. The subject, she says, is in process, on trial, in an ongoing crisis of identity.

Kristeva's notion of the subject has a number of commonalities not only with Lacan and Barthes but also with Althusser. That is, ideology produces subjectivity as a category of discourse; the individual enters into discourse as a function of imaginary relations which engage her. What are the imaginary relations which result in feminism? Kristeva suggests that the liberal imagination works in association with the ideal of the liberated woman to produce a contradiction, a failure to liberate us from the phallic mother. In "Stendhal and the Politics of the Gaze," she says: "If there is a Stendhalian feminism, it consists precisely in the worship that suggests that feminism is perhaps our last religion, that of the woman with authority. The primordial mother, absolute mistress, is not dead . . . " (364). Modernist poetics offered a shelter from the woman with authority, even if its anarchy was contained.

If the interior, private space of the psyche is like the place of the woman, a position from which one can resist patriarchy, then Kristeva's psychoanalytic approach is another kind of womanly discourse, based on the negativity of resistance. The discourse Kristeva advocates opens and so undoes the closed-off stabilities which produce figures of authority, including the liberal feminist subject. But American critics sometimes read Kristeva as if she were creating stability. Kristeva demonstrates to writing women two kinds of difficulty. The first is that danger of falling into the "last religion," or a warranted feminist discourse featuring a woman of authority as its subject. Women, writing under the sign of the banal and the deadly, writing about love, are writing under the same domesticity that governs feminism itself, more dangerous if it becomes "warranted" than in its exiled amorphousness. The second is a danger Kristeva cannot avoid herself—speaking within the contradictions of a subject in crisis, as women writers have done, she refuses either to master or to submit to the rhetorical situation, and she is vulnerable to the essentializing misreadings even of feminists whose political agenda might match her own. The anarchist is vulnerable to the organizing logics of others.

What happens to the anarchist as woman? Does anarchy make more sense for an Emma Goldman, thinking against the terms of an anti-Semitic Russian conventionality, or a Julia Kristeva, with the communist bureaucracy of Bulgaria in her past, than for the women of Western late capitalism, with its fragmenting of all discourses? Is there in a genealogical perspective the curve of a maternal return which makes sense without warrant of the rewritten past? Or are women now producing an expanding feminist discourse which, taking in the male, removes at last the woman at the pseudocenter?

Feminism separates itself from the feminine and the sentimental to prolong the illusion of political innocence, but just as woman is the effect of a cultural history which is dominated by gendered forms, feminism depends on the constituting oppression of the woman as other. Feminism and modernity are mutually defined within the history of progress which is implicated in the rise of capitalism and in colonial dominations, but which also retains a subterranean optimism: the hope for a better life.

Literature in the twentieth century has been informed by what Murray Krieger called *The Tragic Vision*, a pessimism that extends into the nihilism so often attributed to poststructuralist critics.[19] Krieger argues that literature—Kierkegaard, Dostoyevsky, Kafka—brought into question the easy humanistic positivism of the West, that the formalist "aesthetic, for all its seeming purity, can, through thematic analysis, be pushed back—perhaps where it belongs—into a metaphysic" (ix). The final question, then, is of the relationships among modernism, negativity, and women's writing, a question which I will take up by the route of *irony*.

The difference between literature and other discourses was marked in modernist aesthetics by irony; this distance between the author and the agent of intended "meaning" disrupted interpretation at the borders of narrowly defined texts. "Messages are for Western Union," Chandler Beall used to say to us, stopping us in our hot pursuit of literary morals. Irony is what enables one to avoid the sentimental mistake. What is required for modernist literature is not, Wayne Booth tells us in *The Rhetoric of Irony*, a limitless, cosmic irony but the controlled irony which accompanies the unreliability of the literal subject. But this literary irony leaves authority intact.

Henry James understood using unreliable points of view to undermine the credibility of narrative itself—thus a Nietzschean perspectivism enters the forms of fiction. It is also James who presents us with the figure of the feminized author, and James who takes up the feminist into his text, in the persons of Olive Chancellor and Verena Tarrant, and James who resists the haunting of another feminist, Margaret Fuller. Thus, as John Carlos Rowe puts it, "The association of James's will to master the supreme literary form of the novel with the woman question is not such a remote relation."[20] The negativity of literature itself, separated from the possibility of action, made the progressive feminist optimism inhabiting that assertive space into a figure of irony, perpetually frustrating the desire for consequences. The maternal return is the return of consequences to women's writing. It is an irony inscribed in the inevitable operations reproducing discourse and thus the counter to the differences of formalism.

In relationship to the revolution of poetic language inaugurated by literary modernism, feminist claims about the political significance of literature will appear as sentimental and unwarranted, just as the aspirations of Emma Goldman and Edna St. Vincent Millay appear somewhat naive. It is more credible to write as if the world will not improve, with a mature distrust of progress and the accompanying maturity to see that victims always complain and there will always be victims. I am writing, of course, under the sign of irony.

The quarrel that women's writing must have with literary modernism and its continuations into postmodernism thus involves supporting and extending the modernist irony about authority but promoting the struggle to view literature rhetorically rather than aesthetically. Feminists read literature in a rhetorical situation, as having designs upon its audience which shape it in certain ways, as having political and cultural consequences which not only are capable of being specified but also are critically interesting. This is not to deny that literature is a kind of discourse which is different from others but to imagine literary studies on a continuum with rhetorical studies, not in opposition.

As male is to female, so literature is to ordinary prose in the binaries which construct a modernism. These binaries not only conceal heterogeneity by reducing writers as various as Goldman and Bogan to a single difference, they also restrict as they privilege the female and the literary to a segregated space set apart from the public market. This has been said again and again in feminist criticism, but the struggle continues because maintaining literature as an aesthetic discourse seems to serve conservative purposes. But of course eliminating any but aesthetic attention to a text is the opposite of free speech, as the case of Emma Goldman and the modernist suppression of women writers suggests. Our responses to literature are always more than aesthetic. What do we do with writers who are fascists such as Ezra Pound and Wyndham Lewis and Louis-Ferdinand Céline? With writers who are called pornographic—and remember that this once included James Joyce's *Ulysses* and D. H. Lawrence? Shouldn't we defend our study of such texts on the grounds of open inquiry rather than ignore their political impact? To argue that we ought to study such texts just because they are aesthetically interesting is to beg the question, denying that there is a struggle over the objects of critical favor and pretending that the value is objective, in the text, instead of communal, a product of rhetorical exchange.

Poststructuralism has a moment, as voiced perhaps by Terry Eagleton, when it calls for rhetorical studies as the general category describing what we do with literature. This possibility within poststructuralism seems to me the most promising for feminist criticism, and the reason why feminist criticism should not simply turn its back on critical theory. Poststructuralism has also, in other instances, carried forward the modernist stance of irony, deconstructing the assertion of meaning in all discourses, and thus erasing the boundaries of the literary. This problematizing of all writing seems nonetheless very helpful in many ways to marginal writers, enabling a general opening up of discourses, so long as critique does not come to operate as a new fundamental.

Feminists have an uneasy relationship to the irony of poststructuralism because feminism continues to be involved in the messy still-humanistic uncritical activities of progressive politics, which cannot wholly withdraw from liberal traditions without disappearing as an agent of history. Even though we can critique the metanarratives of progress, we need to allow them back into our postcritical rhetoric. Feminism opposes a pervasive, metaphysical irony not only in the elite enclaves of the academy but also in the enclaves of living rooms everywhere where "couch potatoes" settle into the parodic space of the media. Mark Crispin Miller has argued that the chief effect of the mass media is not persuasion but disbelief; that television approaches all situations ironically and all authority is under question. The earnest outrage or hopefulness of feminists appears on the television screen as embarrassing, sentimental, and naive, just as the writing of women such as Edna St. Vincent Millay appeared under the gaze of literary modernism. To address that public audience is to contend with the power of despair and cynicism.

Books such as *The Color Purple* evoke older traditions of meaning to do battle with the ruthless innovation of mass media, asserting a persuasive purpose which contradicts the purposelessness of consumerist appeals to pleasure. The attempt to be critical may simply feed into the irony of the media, which co-opts the critical. Feminist writing, because it is situated, breaks down the distances established by irony and provokes rhetorical responsiveness—the dialectic of resistance and identification that can then lead to change. But this situating of the subject is not without problems.

To understand the position of women writing is to engage not only the way that discourses talk about women, the feminine, and the female but also the way that other discourses construct the women who would write, as women—economic, political, and social modes of understanding to be sure, but in particular the semiautonomous cluster of meanings established by the arrangement of the family and its history. This history of the family reveals the structuring of gender and age relations and the articulation of emotional life addressed by Freud. It is, in other words, hard to talk about women and writing because the histories connecting them, the liaison between the writing subject and the gendering accompanying family organization, are largely written under the monologic that authorized them. Women are also caught up in a history of "woman" that is undergoing swift and important changes, paradoxically largely unrepresented in its detail at the very moment that feminism is in the foreground, a buried but massive narrative which forms part of a "political unconscious" for all our work if we do not address it.[21]

Realistic and representational models of history by their very claims to reflect the order of the visible succeeded in repressing the historicity of woman's position, so largely defined by ideals of family life, and the revolt against it. Advocating equality or advocating difference, feminism is a position in many respects which simply continues the nineteenth-century liberal narratives of progress. Since the subject of liberal humanism is gendered, powerful, and male, this is a situation that needs to be seen as problematic. But how does one write in the structure of a double bind? This is the question which women writers have addressed in the twentieth century, and the forms of writing they have invented may provide us with a reservoir of answers.

If we assume that women have not been entirely oppressed by rhetorical history but have played some part in defining a place from which a feminine subject might exercise forms of discursive power, if not authority, it might come to seem important to recuperate some of the strategies of marginality—of influence by indirection and by narration—identified with the feminine and even with the sentimental.

In order to return to this shocking thought, I would like to suggest that we question the dogmatism of certain forms, not only realism but especially the dominance of an agonistic structure of argument, and sometimes the critical itself. Feminism has already—with poststructuralism—critiqued the ideology of phallogocentrism with its insistence on linearity and its naturalizing assumption that logical speech is transparent to its referents rather than producing the effects of meaning. We need to continue to resist the naturalizing assertion of certainty. But currently certainty comes in other guises, even in demands for an agonistic rhetoric that is "positioned," and admittedly political. These are forms which feminism is having difficulty critiquing, because they seem the very representations of engagement and commitment feminists have called for. Thus Toril Moi, in her *Sexual/Textual Politics*, attacked American feminists, including Elaine Showalter, for the positivism of their thinking and for their failure to criticize the humanistic subject of their position—for their "essentialism." But later, in an article called "Feminism, Postmodernism, and Style," Moi admits her own submission to the agonistic mode.[22]

Moi agrees, as I have tried to suggest above, that feminism is in a sense an "impossible position," because it is based on an opposition to a male domination which in turn defines it. But she herself goes on to say that feminists must "agonistically take sides: simply sitting on the fence will never demolish patriarchy" (7). She argues that making tough choices means giving up open-endedness, such as that implied by Julia Kristeva's rejection of binary logics: "Since every choice is an act of exclusion, to take up a political position means accepting the pain of loss, sacrifice, and closure, *even* if our choice entails following the free-wheeling paths of Derridean deconstruction" (7). And later, "to take up a position—to claim the truth of one's own analysis—means deliberately running the risk of being *wrong*: that is to say, we make ourselves *more*—not *less*—vulnerable by revealing our own hand in this way" (18). Moi's position is seductive because of this postmodern bluff, this tough vulnerability, but in her haste to keep the critical position of feminism for a postfeminist rhetoric, she has perhaps sacrificed too much.

Has she not acquiesced to the agonistic style of male rhetoric and thereby thrown out as useless the entire history of women's use of style in the service of subversion? Has she not, in fact, overlooked the feminized place of the whole of literature, and its relationship to the production of culture? In the very last section of her article, Moi acknowledges Gayatri Spivak's decentered style and Jane Gallop's brilliance, but she concludes only that "the risks of style are also the risks of political commitment" (22). Furthermore, she hangs on to the political commitments that her own agonistic style drags along in its wake, which include not only the ac-knowledged logocentrism of feminist critique but also the unacknowledged power relations within the profession. Setting the agenda for discussion, such an agonistic positioning circumscribes the debate, drawing a narrow circumference, Kenneth Burke might say, transfixing the conversation upon certain points of theory and its issues. In her article criticizing "The Race for Theory," Barbara Christian points out how such concentration tends to exclude discussion of race and gender.[23] For example, she wants her students to talk about the effect of powerful women's writing such as *The Color Purple* on popular culture, but she says they—and she—are pulled away from such considerations by the polemics of feminist theory itself, demanding attention.

To return, then, to the question of feminine strategies of writing. How can a feminist rhetoric account for the powerful effects of certain forms developed by women through history, even those associated with weakness and the sentimental and thus despised? Let us come back to Ann Douglas's argument: that women in the nineteenth century elevated a weak senti-mentality and contributed to the decline of thoughtful debate in public exchange. Douglas focuses in particular on the New England women who exercised a strong influence on their ministers. These women advocated, Douglas argues, a rhetoric of indirect influence, appealing to feelings of sympathy and persuading by the use of stories, images, and a style that eventually came to seem all too *genteel*. The rhetoric convinced not by direct argument but by indirection, by engaging its audience in a process of individual emotional response to images rather than a critical, thoughtful response. Furthermore, Douglas argues, this led to the degradation of rhet-oric practiced by the media, with its manipulation of emotional response through images. Art is used as an instrument of persuasion.

Toril Moi and Ann Douglas resemble one another in this respect: both idealize the seeming toughness of an agonistic rhetoric which works by confrontation and struggle, and both criticize women who engage in using other forms of persuasion as either too ineffective themselves, or else all too powerful and thus promoting weakness in the culture at large. Let me suggest, however, that in certain respects both arguments participate in what Luce Irigaray calls the "Science of Desire," the conflictive model of inquiry that since Plato has created more fragmentation and confusion in its wake:

> As for other living things—this is true at least for the males—seized by an ardent desire to gain the heights, they try to push their "heads" beyond the celestial divider, raising them and then lowering them again. But the violent agitation which urges them on, the chaos in which they pierce the barrier, means that they get only a glimpse of some of the realities that can be reached there. Powerless, as yet, to climb serenely upward, they are carried along pell-mell. Overwhelmed. Jostling, crushing each other underfoot, each trying to get ahead. And this all results in an enormous confusion, and perspiration, and extremity of effort. And also in the fact that some return from the breach lamed, that many another loses or at least damages some feathers, and that all, overcome with weariness, come down again without having been initiated into the contemplation of the real.[24]

When Jane Tompkins stresses the powerful political effectiveness of Harriet Beecher Stowe's portrayal of slavery, and its undoubted influence in arousing abolitionist emotions, she is writing against the new critical view that literature should not have rhetorical purposes, and, as I have argued, feminism has long been disrespectful about such a separation of literature from ideology. But from the point of view of literary history, this argument takes on a new look. Feminism cannot, finally, advocate that writing be limited or confined within questions of logos. Feminism raises the question of ethos—who is speaking, and how do they have the authority?—and pathos—what will move the audience? The perspective of feminism opens up a broader sense of audience, including the everyday reader. Harriet Beecher Stowe was writing for a popular audience, using a committed but undisciplined prose.

As an antidote to the parodic postmodernism of the media, we need, perhaps, not an aesthetics of literary autonomy but forms of commitment. A feminism which does not recuperate the powerful old strategies of women's writing—including fantasy, digression, stories, and the mixture of genres—is left with the weak insufficiency of the agonistic innovation. Toril Moi and Ann Douglas share a narrow vision of rhetoric which paradoxically, in the name of being strong, would weaken monstrously the effective resistance of feminism. We can see why Barbara Christian wants space for Alice Walker, with the renewals in *The Color Purple* of old sentimental forms, the epistolary, the exhortation, and her use of Black English to challenge the system of the normal installed in a hierarchy of race and gender.

Opening up the literary canon to women opens up as well the post-modern knowledge that *writing* is a way of *reading* the world. Including the gendered text within a feminist problematizing of gender can expose the relationships of gender, genre, and the politics of rhetorical forms. Thus it seems to me that feminism requires us not only to engage in the stance of agonistic critique but also to engage in the commitments of coalition and patchwork, the mixing of rhetorical and literary forms implied by voices in dialogue.

In American feminism, this hope for a coalition has found its emblem in the quilt. Alice Walker has made the quilt a figure for the kind of artistic inheritance from mothers which we might be able to put to "everyday use," and she helped the writing of *The Color Purple* along by making a quilt as she went. In her well-known story "Everyday Use," she contrasts two modes of response to our past.[25] There is the alienated attitude of a rural daughter who returns to get her mother's quilt because folk craft has become a valuable fetish among the urban arrivists, something she could hang on her wall, and there is the ordinary need of the other daughter, who would put the quilt to everyday use. The quilt as emblem of American feminist theory implies an art which will be put to use, and the turn of postmodern pastiche to coalition politics.

Elaine Showalter invoked the "strongly marked American women's tradition of piecing, patchwork, and quilting" as an emblem of feminist poetics, picking up the cue from Walker and others, including Radka Don-nell-Vogt, who "deals with piecing as jouissance, with quilting as an art expressive of the preverbal semiotic phase of mother-child bonding," and might be called "the Kristeva of quilting, the Other Bulgarian," and Rachel Blau DuPlessis, who imagined the "verbal quilt" of the feminist text as a place of "no subordination, no ranking."[26] Comparing the work of piecing to the work of writing sentimental fiction, she cites Nina Baym on women authors: "they saw themselves not as 'artists' but as professional writers with work to do' " (229).[27] The figure of quilting appears again and again in women's writing, which Showalter traces through *Uncle Tom's Cabin* and Willa Cather to a recent story by Bobbie Ann Mason which raises the question with which she must finish: "these traditions may be burdens rather than treasures of the past . . . there may be something mournful and even self-destructive in our feminist efforts to reclaim them. . . . Are we ruining our eyes finishing a female heritage that may have become a museum piece?" (245). Reminding us of the complexity of this relationship to the past, Showalter returns us to the distinction Alice Walker was trying to make.

This is perhaps related to the distinction Louise Bogan drew in her essay "Folk Art"; she thinks American folk art such as hooked rugs and pine blanket chests has been "bourgeoizified": "Only a writer thoroughly immersed in middle-class values, and soaked through and through with the sentimentality of the middle, could for a moment believe that this mummified and genteelized folk could contribute any spark of life to his purposes" (137). Writing in 1943, she does, however, approve of jazz, popular music, and the "mechanical devices" disseminating it—radio, records, juke boxes—"American folk has never been more vigorous than at this moment."[28] Disappointingly, she does not identify black contributions to this American folk specifically. The point, however, is that we continue to find it extremely hard to talk about the folk ancestry of women's art and the way it is continuously taken up and deadened by its use for other ends, not everyday but commercial use, and even Bogan, who defended women's contribution to literature through the darkest days of modernist criticism, found herself using *sentimental* as a term that would designate *both* the domestic inheritance *and* its degradation. Does it threaten the metaphor of quilting that it is now taken up by politics, specifically the coalition politics of Jesse Jackson, who tells the story of the grandmother's quilt as a way of talking about how the "Rainbow Coalition" is organized? History (whose?) will write the answer.

I set out in this section with the acknowledgment that feminism is above all multiple and contentious, and the differences have been especially so between American feminists with empiricist notions of language and French feminists, who theorize the return of the woman as the return into language of the unconscious gendered body. This ongoing challenge to the monologic discourse undertakes an *écriture féminine*, a writing committed to the *subversion* of whatever seems all too reasonable and persuasive and closed. Irigaray describes *écriture féminine* as an anarchic "disconcerting of language":

> The reproductive power of the mother, the sex of the woman, are both at stake in the proliferation of systems, those houses of ill fame for the subject, of fetish-words, sign-objects whose certified truths seek to palliate the risk that values may be recast into/by the other. But no clear univocal utterance, can in fact, pay off this mortgage since all are already trapped in the same credit structure. All can be recuperated when issued by the signifying order in place. It is still better to speak only in riddles, allusions, hints, parables. Even if asked to clarify a few points. Even if people plead that they just don't understand. After all, they never have understood. So why not double the misprision to the limits of exasperation? Until the ear tunes into another music, the voice starts to sing again, the very gaze stops squinting over the signs of auto-representation and (re)production no longer inevitably amounts to the same and returns to the same forms, with minor variations.[29]

Yet, of course, the gendered body is always already within a cultural history. Critics of Irigaray, including Julia Kristeva, have thought that the idea of *écriture féminine* depends upon the old, familiar theories of gender, since it postulates a bodied, essential feminine that lies outside language. But this is a problem at the level of theory rather than at the level of style, for women's writing as metaphor but not as practice. Inserting women's writing into the problematic history of gender paradoxically opens the possibility that the social practice of feminism might ally itself with the critical practice of poststructuralism in a feminist rhetoric. In other words, to admit that feminism is socially constructed, a product of history, does not mean that a gendered discourse cannot provide the site of effective resistance. The modernist turn against the progressive ambitions of modernity finds its remedy in the resistance of feminist discourse. Feminism as a mode of women's writing can provide a way to question certified systems, and to make the hidden gendering of rhetorical practices visible—not by substituting the figure of a female authority but by displacing the authority of this gendering.

This is to argue that women writing an "unwarranted discourse" have discovered the postmodern position from which the impossible might be asserted: that is, the utopian—and sentimental—hope that after all there might be a response to one's words, that one might be heard, that together we might work for a better life. The most terrible difficulty of the monologic is that it provides no place for reply; difference is no more than a reflection or an echo in the imaginary enclosure. In the form of an anarchic attentiveness, I have tried in this book to represent the dialogic force of the rhetorical claim advanced by women writing, and the historical, gendered, site of the revolution enacted by the poetic word of modernism: a terrain which opens to the repeated inflection of what is finally at stake in the oppositions of modernism and women's writing—the very possibility of response. At its apogee of misogyny, when John Crowe Ransom, for example, excommunicated Edna St. Vincent Millay, literary modernism threatened to isolate literature from the world altogether. Thus women's writing under postmodernism recuperates the sentimental tradition with its understanding of community, as Alice Walker exemplifies. And women's writing also recuperates from formalism what Emma Goldman understood, and Louise Bogan, Kay Boyle, and Annie Dillard exploit: the power of style.

INTRODUCTION

1. The manifesto appeared in *transition* 16–17 (June 1929) and was signed by Kay Boyle, Whit Burnett, Hart Crane, Caresse Crosby, Harry Crosby, Martha Foley, Stuart Gilbert, A. L. Gillespie, Leigh Hoffman, Eugene Jolas, Elliot Paul, Douglas Rigby, Theo Rutra, Robert Sage, Harold J. Salemson, and Laurence Vail.

2. Roland Barthes, *A Lover's Discourse*, trans. Richard Howard (New York: Hill and Wang, 1978) 175.

3. Louise Bogan, *Achievement in American Poetry* (Chicago: Henry Regnery Co., 1951) 1.

4. Nancy Armstrong, *Desire and Domestic Fiction: A Political History of the Novel* (New York: Oxford UP, 1986).

5. See Julia Kristeva, "A New Type of Intellectual: The Dissident," *The Kristeva Reader*, ed. Toril Moi (New York: Columbia UP, 1986):

> It is possible to distinguish three types of dissident today. First, there is the rebel who attacks political power. He transforms the dialectic of law-and-desire into a war waged between *Power and Resentment*. His paranoia, however, means that he still remains within the limits of the old master-slave couple. Secondly, there is the psychoanalyst, who transforms the dialectic of law-and-desire into a contest between *death and discourse*. His archetypal rival from whom he tries to distance himself is religion. . . . Thirdly, there is the writer who experiments with the limits of identity, producing texts where the law does not exist outside language. (295)

6. See Jonathan Culler, *Roland Barthes* (New York: Oxford UP, 1983). Barthes was, Culler decides, "breaking the academy's hold on nineteenth-century literature, so that it could be brought back, not as an object of knowledge or of study, but as an object of pleasure, as a source of transgressions without grandeur. . . . [making] the sentimental and unfashionable discourse of *Werther* an object of contemporary interest" (123).

7. The important presence of women was always visible at the time in the little magazines and later in the memoirs published by everyone from Hemingway to Cowley, but feminist scholarship has persuasively argued and documented the case. Sandra Gilbert and Susan Gubar have published two of their projected three-volume series on women and modernism *No Man's Land: The Place of the Woman Writer in the Twentieth Century*: vol. 1, *The War of the Words* (New Haven: Yale UP, 1988); vol. 2, *Sexchanges* (New Haven: Yale UP, 1989). Shari Benstock, *Women of the Left Bank* (Austin: U of Texas P, 1986), combines the literary and social history of a number of women writers in Paris from 1900 to 1940. William Drake, *The First Wave: Women Poets in America, 1915–1945* (New York: Macmillan, 1987), addresses a number of personal aspects of the lives of women modernist poets, without taking up

the critical relationship to modernist poetics. Other writers take up the question of women's writing and its relationship to critical issues of form and genre: Suzanne Juhasz, *Naked and Fiery Forms* (New York: Harper and Row, 1976); Alicia Suskin Ostriker, *Stealing the Language: The Emergence of Women's Poetry in America* (Boston: Beacon Press, 1986); Rachel Blau DuPlessis, *Writing beyond the Ending: Narrative Strategies of Twentieth-Century Women Writers* (Bloomington: Indiana UP, 1985); Jan Montefiore, *Feminism and Poetry: Language, Experience, Identity in Women's Writing* (London: Routledge and Kegan Paul, 1987); Kenneth Wheeler and Virginia Lee Lussier, eds., *Women, the Arts, and the 1920s in Paris and New York* (New Brunswick: Transaction Books, 1982).

For feminist theory and culture criticism, see Gayatri Chakravorty Spivak, *In Other Worlds: Essays in Cultural Politics* (New York and London: Routledge, 1988); Jane Tompkins, *Sensational Designs: The Cultural Work of American Fiction, 1790–1860* (New York: Oxford UP, 1985); Jane Gallop, *The Daughter's Seduction: Feminism and Psychoanalysis* (Ithaca: Cornell UP, 1982); Teresa de Lauretis, *Alice Doesn't: Feminism, Semiotics, Cinema* (Bloomington: Indiana UP, 1984), and *Technologies of Gender: Essays on Theory, Film, and Fiction*, (Bloomington: Indiana UP, 1987); Alice Jardine, *Gynesis: Configurations of Woman and Modernity* (Ithaca: Cornell UP, 1985); Rita Felski, *Beyond Feminist Aesthetics: Feminist Literature and Social Change* (Cambridge: Harvard UP, 1989).

8. See in particular Michel Foucault, *The History of Sexuality*, vol. 1, trans. Robert Hurley (New York: Random House, 1978).

9. The "revolution of the word" turns against the nineteenth-century revolution of literacy which brought what Cathy N. Davidson calls "the democratization of the written word," in *Revolution and the Word: The Rise of the Novel in America* (New York: Oxford UP, 1986).

10. See Peter Bürger, *Theory of the Avant-Garde*, trans. Michael Shaw, foreword by Jochen Schulte-Sasse (Minneapolis: U of Minnesota P, 1984).

11. Jean-François Lyotard in particular has contended that postmodernism is a continuation of modernism, a moment in modernism, which is characterized by its Nietzschean view of historical narrative. See *The Postmodern Condition: A Report on Knowledge*, trans. Geoff Bennington and Brian Massumi (Minneapolis: U of Minnesota P, 1984). Histories of the avant-garde include Mateo Calinescu, *Five Faces of Modernity: Modernism, Avant-Garde, Decadence, Kitsch, Postmodernism* (Durham: Duke UP, 1987); Frederick Karl, *Modern and Modernism: The Sovereignty of the Artist, 1885–1925* (New York: Atheneum, 1985); Andreas Huyssens, *After the Great Divide: Modernism, Mass Culture, Postmodernism* (Bloomington: Indiana UP, 1986). On the theory of the postmodern see also Andrew Ross, ed., *Universal Abandon? The Politics of Postmodernism* (Minneapolis: U of Minnesota P, 1988); Linda Hutcheon, *A Poetics of Postmodernism: History, Theory, Fiction* (New York: Routledge, 1988). Anglo-American history characteristically begins with, or centers around, Eliot and Pound. For example, Julian Symons, *Makers of the New* (New York: Random House, 1987); Michael H. Levenson, *A Genealogy of Modernism: A Study of English Literary Doctrine, 1908–1922* (Cambridge and New York: Cambridge UP, 1984); Hugh Kenner, *A Homemade World: The American Modernist Writers* (New York: Knopf, 1975); Andrew Ross, *The Failure of Modernism* (New York: Columbia UP, 1986).

12. A number of critics have argued the case for the sentimental. See Tompkins, *Sensational Designs*; Nina Baym, *Women's Fiction: A Guide to Novels by and about Women in America, 1820–1870* (Ithaca: Cornell UP, 1978); Davidson, *Revolution and the Word*; Janet Todd, *Feminist Literary History* (New York: Routledge, 1988); Dale Spender, *Mothers of the Novel: 100 Good Women Writers before Jane Austen* (London: Routledge and Kegan Paul, 1986); Cheryl Walker *The Nightingale's Burden: Women Poets and American Culture before 1900* (Bloomington: Indiana UP, 1982).

13. Tompkins, *Sensational Designs* xi.

14. See Jennifer Wicke, *Advertising Fictions: Literature, Advertisement, and Social Reading* (New York: Columbia UP, 1988). Wicke argues that the modernist rejection of advertising obfuscates its relationship to literature and the nature of its cultural work. For the association of women, commercialism, and art, see Rémy G. Saisselin, *The Bourgeois and the Bibelot* (New Brunswick, N.J.: Rutgers UP, 1984). For the association of women and mass culture, see Andreas Huyssens, "Mass Culture as Woman: Modernism's Other," *Studies in Entertainment: Critical Approaches to Mass Culture*, ed. Tania Modleski (Bloomington and Indianapolis: Indiana UP, 1986) 188–207.

15. Kristeva argues at length the thesis that poetic language ruptures social convention in *Revolution in Poetic Language*, trans. Margaret Waller (New York: Columbia UP, 1984), but it appears elsewhere in her work as well, notably in "The Ethics of Linguistics," *Desire in Language: A Semiotic Approach to Literature and Art*, ed. Leon S. Roudiez, trans. Alice Jardine, Thomas A. Gora, and Leon S. Roudiez (Oxford: Blackwell; New York: Columbia UP, 1980).

16. See Christine Buci-Glucksmann, "Catastrophic Utopia: The Feminine as Allegory of the Modern," *The Making of the Modern Body: Sexuality and Society in the Nineteenth Century*, ed. Catherine Gallagher and Thomas Laqueur (Berkeley: U of California P, 1987) 221.

17. As Nancy Armstrong has argued in *Desire and Domestic Fiction*, literature functioned to define and install the forms of middle-class desire.

18. See Jane Silverman Van Buren, *The Modernist Madonna: Semiotics of the Maternal Metaphor* (Bloomington: Indiana UP, 1989).

19. See Frank Lentricchia, *Ariel and the Police: Michel Foucault, William James, Wallace Stevens* (Madison: U of Wisconsin P, 1988).

20. See Nina Baym, "Melodramas of Beset Manhood: How Theories of American Fiction Exclude Women Authors," *The New Feminist Criticism*, ed. Elaine Showalter (New York: Pantheon Books, 1985) 63–80. As Teresa de Lauretis has outlined the project, what is needed is not anti-Oedipal but rather "Oedipal with a vengeance," so that the question of desire comes to appear "as precisely enigma, contradiction, difference . . . an enigma which is structurally undecidable but daily articulated in the different practices of living" (157). See her characterization of Oedipal narratives in *Alice Doesn't* and her analysis of the notion of subjectivity in *Technologies of Gender*. Of course, Giles Deleuze and Felix Guattari are responsible for raising a banner of attack on the Oedipal narrative in *Anti-Oedipus: Capitalism and Schizophrenia*, preface by Michel Foucault, trans. Robert Hurley, Mark Seem, and Helen R. Lane (Minneapolis: U of Minnesota P, 1983). The question of feminism and Oedipus is discussed in Shirley Nelson Garner, Claire Kahane, and Madelon Sprengnether, eds., *The (M)other Tongue* (Ithaca: Cornell UP, 1985), and Temma F. Berg, Anna Shannon Elfenbein, Jeanne Larsen, and Elisa Kay Sparks, *Engendering the Word* (Urbana and Chicago: U of Illinois P, 1989).

21. John Crowe Ransom, "The Poet as Woman," *Southern Review* 2 (Spring 1937): 784.

22. For a discussion of Eliot's part in reactionary modernism—and a recognition of the power of "high art"—see Cynthia Ozick, "A Critic at Large (T. S. Eliot)," *New Yorker* (November 20, 1989): 119–54. For a discussion of the political unconscious in modernism, see Fredric Jameson, *Fables of Aggression: Wyndham Lewis, the Modernist as Fascist* (Berkeley: U of California P, 1979).

23. Terry Eagleton does a good job of expressing the horror of the feminine:

Poetry had fallen foul of the Romantics, become a mawkish, womanly affair full of gush and fine feeling. Language had gone soft and lost its virility: it needed to be stiffened up again, made hard and stone-like, reconnected with the physical world. . . . Emotions were messy and suspect, part of a clapped-out epoch of high-flown liberal-individualist sentiment which must now yield to the dehumanized mechanical world of modern society.

In *Literary Theory: An Introduction* (Minneapolis: U of Minnesota P, 1983) 41. Eagleton equates this rejection of a feminine liberal humanism with a turn to fascism: Eliot's "most scandalous avant-garde techniques were deployed for the most arriere-garde ends."

24. Julia Kristeva, *Powers of Horror: An Essay on Abjection*, trans. Leon S. Roudiez (New York: Columbia UP, 1982). This theorizing of scapegoating proceeds through psychoanalysis and semiotics, but it draws on and continues the general project, which has included such critics as Mary Douglas, *Purity and Danger* (London, Boston, and Henley: Routledge and Kegan Paul, 1969), and René Girard, who address the anthropological dimension. Linda Kintz discusses the implications for post-modernism in American culture in "The Cultural Logic of Purity in a Postmodern Context," paper delivered at the Humanities Center, University of Oregon, 1989.

25. See Julia Kristeva, *Black Sun: Depression and Melancholia*, trans. Leon S. Roudiez (New York: Columbia UP, 1990).

26. This issue also has a review on Eugene O'Neill which, to my initial disappointment, does not dare to use the word *sentimental*. Instead it uses the word *anarchist*.

27. For example, Gitlin has worried about the alleged lack of political questions in our campaigns, and the concentration on personal issues, in his own television appearances on PBS.

28. "Critical Response: Andiamo!" *Critical Inquiry* 14.2 (Winter 1988): 412. This appears in the context of a response to Gilbert and Gubar in which Lentricchia avers that gender in their approach does not account for differences among women. Recently Melita Schaum has taken Lentricchia on in " 'Ariel, Save Us': Big Stick Polemics in Frank Lentricchia's *Ariel and the Police*," *Genders* 4 (Spring 1989): 122–29, where she finds him guilty of an "unexamined universalizing of the male experience" and points out that he replicates the modernist gesture for criticism: "when [theoretical relevance] implies images of rephallicizing discourse and saving criticism from its metaphorically 'feminized' 'self-trivialization' and 'inutility' it assumes the dismaying aspect of unexamined gender stereotyping" (129).

29. See Molly Hite, *The Other Side of the Story: Structures and Strategies of Contemporary Feminist Narrative* (Ithaca: Cornell UP, 1989) 2. She writes in response to a question she frames thus: "Why don't women writers produce postmodernist fiction?" (1).

30. I mean this in a sense similar to Fredric Jameson, *The Political Unconscious: Narrative as a Socially Symbolic Act* (Ithaca: Cornell UP, 1981).

31. This struggle took the form of what Judith Kegan Gardiner has called a "politics of empathy," in *Rhys, Stead, Lessing, and the Politics of Empathy* (Bloomington and Indianapolis: Indiana UP, 1989).

32. Bogan, *Achievement in American Poetry* 20.

33. See Sandra Whipple Spanier, *Kay Boyle: Artist and Activist* (Carbondale: Southern Illinois UP, 1986), Illustration #32.

1. THE SENTIMENTAL AND THE MODERN

1. Ann Radcliffe, *The Mysteries of Udolpho*, vol. 1 (New York: E. P. Dutton and Co., 1931; rpt. 1959) 43.

2. Carol McGuirk, *Robert Burns and the Sentimental Era* (Athens: U of Georgia P, 1985) xxv.

3. For definitions of the term *sentimental* and its relationship to the era, see R. F. Brissenden, *Virtue in Distress: Studies in the Novel of Sentiment from Richardson to Sade* (New York: Macmillan, 1974); Erik Erämetsa, *A Study of the Word 'Sentimental' and of Other Linguistic Characteristics of Eighteenth Century Sentimentalism in England*, Dissertations: Literature and Art, vol. 26 (Helsinki, 1951); Janet Todd, *Sensibility: An Introduction* (New York: Methuen, 1986); Fred Kaplan, *Sacred Tears: Sentimentality in Victorian Literature* (Princeton: Princeton UP, 1987); Michael Bell, *The Sentiment of Reality: Truth of Feeling in the European Novel* (London: George Allen and Unwin, 1983).

4. Dale Spender, *Mothers of the Novel: 100 Good Women Writers before Jane Austen* (London: Routledge and Kegan Paul, 1986) 14.

5. John Mullan, *Sentiment and Sociability: The Language of Feeling in the Eighteenth Century* (Oxford: Clarendon Press, 1988).

6. Todd, *Sensibility* 5.

7. *Ibid*. 49–50.

8. Jean-Jacques Rousseau, *Julie ou la nouvelle Héloïse*, ed. René Pomeau (Paris: Editions Garnier Freres, 1960).

9. See Ann Kibbey, *The Interpretation of Material Shapes in Puritanism: A Study of Rhetoric, Prejudice, and Violence* (Cambridge and New York: Cambridge UP, 1986).

10. Ann Douglas, *The Feminization of American Culture* (New York: Avon, 1977).

11. For a history of this era derived from the correspondence of Angelina Grimke and her husband, the minister Theodore Weld, see Gilbert Hobbs Barnes, *The Anti-Slavery Impulse, 1830–1844*, introd. by William McLoughlin (New York: Harcourt, Brace, and World, 1933, 1964). Although Barnes is clear about the women's rights issues involved in the rise of the antislavery movement, he is most concerned to refute the view that attributed abolitionism to a much narrower movement led in the East by Garrison. Showing how western revivalism led a much broader segment of the population to endorse social reform, Barnes also connects feminism to the broader movements. See also William Hutchison, *The Modernist Impulse in American Protestantism* (Cambridge: Harvard UP, 1976).

12. Cathy N. Davidson provides information about the book in her introduction to the Oxford UP 1986 edition, as well as in her study of American nineteenth-century fiction, *Revolution and the Word: The Rise of the Novel in America* (New York: Oxford UP, 1986). Her discussion of sentimental fiction and the "feme covert" addresses the question of ideology and genre: she argues that the novels—notably *The Coquette*—are about the conflict of women's traditional subservience and the new ideals of independence, but that the point is their entry into the debate—that they do not resolve it in favor of subservience (147).

13. George Campbell, *The Philosophy of Rhetoric* (London: William Tegg and Co., 1850).

14. Thanks to Linda Kintz for pointing this out to me.

15. Richard Chase, *The American Novel and Its Tradition* (Garden City, N.Y.: Doubleday Anchor Books, 1957) 73. Leslie Fiedler, *Love and Death in the American Novel* (New York: Criterion Books, 1960) 93.

16. Nathaniel Hawthorne, *The Scarlet Letter* (New York: C. Scribner's Sons, 1919).

17. Charles Feidelson, Jr., *Symbolism and American Literature* (Chicago: U of Chicago P, 1953), called this transformation American symbolism.

18. Samuel Monk, *The Sublime: A Study of Critical Theories in XVIII-Century England* (Ann Arbor: U of Michigan P, 1960).

19. See Marlon Ross, *The Contours of Masculine Desire: Romanticism and the Rise*

of Women's Poetry (New York: Oxford UP, 1989) 309. He argues that women writers *could not be romantics*: romanticism was the shaping of desire by an ideology of masculinity. Thus, he says, even Wordsworth's sentimentalism is masculine because "the impasse of 'solipsistic pathos' becomes itself a celebration of self-individuation."

20. See Laurence Stone, *The Family, Sex and Marriage in England, 1500–1800* (New York: Harper and Row, 1977) 238.

21. John Stuart Mill, *The Subjection of Woman* (New York: D. Appleton and Co., 1869).

22. John Stuart Mill, *On Liberty and the Subjection of Women* (New York: Henry Holt, n.d.). See especially pp. 252–53, 334–38.

23. Linda Gordon and Ellen DuBois trace the often contradictory involvement of women in contributing to this history of sexuality. See "Seeking Ecstasy on the Battlefield: Danger and Pleasure in Nineteenth-Century Feminist Sexual Thought," *Sexuality: A Reader*, Feminist Review Collective (London: Virago Press, 1987) 83.

24. See Shari Benstock, *Women of the Left Bank* (Austin: U of Texas P, 1986).

25. Ernest Hemingway, *The Sun Also Rises* (New York: Charles Scribner's Sons, 1926; rpt. 1954) 247.

26. See Robert D. Clark, "Harry Emerson Fosdick: The Growth of a Great Preacher," *Harry Emerson Fosdick's Art of Preaching: An Anthology*, ed. Lionel Crocker (Springfield, Ill.: Charles C. Thomas, 1971) 128–185, and Hutchison, *The Modernist Impulse in American Protestantism*.

27. See the preface to Sandra Gilbert and Susan Gubar, *No Man's Land: The Place of the Woman Writer in the Twentieth Century* (New Haven: Yale UP, 1988), the first volume of three in the series: "Reflecting a crucial shift in mid-nineteenth-century Anglo-American society, this sexual struggle became a key theme in late Victorian literature and ultimately a shaping element in modernist and post-modernist literature" (4).

28. My translation, from *1913*, a catalogue for an exhibition at the Bibliothèque Nationale, Paris, 1983, p. 53.

29. "The Present Function of Criticism," in Ray B. West, Jr., ed., *Essays in Modern Literary Criticism* (New York: Holt, Rinehart, 1952) 146.

30. T. E. Hulme, *Speculations* (New York: Harcourt, Brace and Co., 1924) 113–40.

31. T. S. Eliot, "Review: *Personae*," *Dial* (1928): 29. For a discussion of Eliot's part in reactionary modernism, see Cynthia Ozick, "A Critic at Large (T. S. Eliot)," *New Yorker* (November 20, 1989): 119–54.

32. For the history of this group, see Paul K. Conkin, *The Southern Agrarians* (Knoxville; U of Tennessee P, 1988). For their critical history, see Vincent B. Leitch, *American Literary Criticism: From the 30s to the 80s* (New York: Columbia UP, 1988). For their sense of their own history, see William K. Wimsatt, Jr., and Cleanth Brooks, *Literary Criticism: A Short History* (New York: Vintage Books, 1967).

33. John Crowe Ransom, *The New Criticism* (Norfolk, Conn.: New Directions, 1941).

34. See Edmund Wilson, *Axel's Castle: A Study in the Imaginative Literature of 1870–1930* (New York: Charles Scribner's Sons, 1931) 267.

35. Sharon O'Brien, "Becoming Noncanonical: The Case against Willa Cather," *Reading in America: Literature and Social History*, ed. Cathy N. Davidson (Baltimore: Johns Hopkins UP, 1989) 240–58.

36. Kenneth Burke, *Counter-Statement* (Los Altos, Calif.: Hermes Publications, 1931).

37. Dominick LaCapra, *"Madame Bovary" on Trial* (Ithaca: Cornell UP, 1982) 19–20.

38. From a 1936 letter to Rolfe Humphries, in *What the Woman Lived: Selected Letters of Louise Bogan, 1920–1970*, ed. Ruth Limmer (New York: Harcourt, Brace Jovanovich, 1973) 127.

39. Nancy Miller, *The Heroine's Text: Readings in the French and English Novel, 1722–1782* (New York: Columbia UP, 1980).

40. See Leslie W. Rabine, *Reading the Romantic Heroine: Text, History, Ideology* (Ann Arbor: U of Michigan P, 1985).

41. Terry Eagleton, *The Rape of Clarissa: Writing, Sexuality, and Class Struggle in Samuel Richardson* (Oxford: Blackwell, 1982).

42. This is one of Armstrong's points in *Desire and Domestic Fiction*, and she goes on to argue it more particularly in "The Gender Bind: Women and the Disciplines," *Genders* 3 (Fall 1988): 1–23.

43. Nancy Schnog, "Inside the Sentimental: The Psychological Work of *The Wide Wide World*," *Genders* 4 (Spring 1989): 11–25.

44. "The Heart and the Lyre," *Selected Criticism* (New York: Noonday Press, 1955) 335–42, p. 339, and see also Bogan's history of American modernism, *Achievement in American Poetry* (Chicago: Henry Regnery Co., 1951).

45. The debate has grown especially pointed since the appearance of Toril Moi's *Sexual/Textual Politics*, which uses Kristeva in particular to critique the "essentialism" of American feminists such as Elaine Showalter.

46. In Bulgaria, for example, Kristeva was not a member of what she calls the "red bourgeoisie," so that her parents did not enjoy a privileged position in the culture. Her political position comes partly from a long-standing irony about the utopian hopes of the French left, together with a long training in Marxist dialectic and in Soviet linguistics. See my interview with Kristeva in *Discourse*, forthcoming.

47. "The Bounded Text," *Desire in Language: A Semiotic Approach to Literature and Art*, ed. Leon S. Roudiez, trans. Alice Jardine, Thomas A. Gora, and Leon S. Roudiez (Oxford: Blackwell; New York: Columbia UP, 1980) 85.

48. "From One Identity to Another," *Desire in Language* 133. See also the argument in Julia Kristeva, *Revolution in Poetic Language*, trans. Margaret Waller (New York: Columbia UP, 1984).

49. See Kristeva's explanation of "sémanalyse" in *Semiotike* (Paris: Editions du Seuil, 1969). A number of critics argue that Kristeva's early, Bakhtinian focus and her argument for the political force of poetic language were modernist stances which the later Kristeva abandoned. However, it makes more sense to think in terms of the different issues she now addresses, since she has not renounced her theoretical critique of the monologic or her theory of the heterogeneity of the subject. I believe such a poststructuralist sense of the speaking subject is necessary to a reading of Kristeva's later psychoanalytic work on horror, love, and melancholy; it might help avoid misreading her as an "essentialist" of the feminine subject.

50. This stricture was codified by W. K. Wimsatt, Jr., and Monroe C. Beardsley in "The Intentional Fallacy," *The Verbal Icon* (Lexington: U of Kentucky P, 1954).

51. Wilson, *Axel's Castle* 21.

52. Anita Skokolsky, "The Resistance to Sentimentality: Yeats, de Man, and the Aesthetic Education," *Yale Journal of Criticism* 1.1 (Fall 1987): 83, says sentimentality "questions the rhetorical status of an erotics of unfulfilled and unfulfillable desire as the condition for amorous and linguistic experience."

53. Roland Barthes, "The Death of the Author," *The Rustle of Language*, trans. Richard Howard (New York: Hill and Wang, 1986) 49–56; Michel Foucault, "What

Is an Author?" *Twentieth-Century Literary Theory*, ed. Vassilis Lambropoulos and David Neal Miller (Albany: State U of New York P, 1987) 124–42.

2. ANARCHY AS A LITERARY FIGURE, ANARCHY AS A FEMALE FORM

1. Margaret C. Anderson, "Emma Goldman in Chicago," *Mother Earth* 4.10 (December 1914): 322.
2. "Editorial," *Little Review* 2.8 (November 1915): 34. The editorial is unsigned.
3. Alice Jardine, "Opaque Texts and Transparent Contexts," *The Poetics of Gender*, ed. Nancy Miller (New York: Columbia UP, 1986) 100.
4. Goldman's work contains a variety of materials, including the following:

Anthologies of Lectures and Pamphlets

Anarchism and Other Essays (New York: Mother Earth Publishing Assoc., 1911; rpt., New York: Dover, 1969).
Red Emma Speaks: Selected Writings and Speeches by Emma Goldman, ed. Alix Kates Schulman (New York: Shocken Books, 1983).
The Traffic in Women and Other Essays on Feminism, ed. Alix Kates Schulman (New York: Times Change Press 1970).
Vision on Fire: Emma Goldman on the Spanish Revolution, ed. David Potter (New Paltz, N.Y.: Commonground Press, 1983).

Books

Living My Life (New York: Alfred A. Knopf, 1931; rpt. New York: Dover, 1970).
My Disillusionment in Russia (Garden City, N.Y.: Doubleday, Page, and Co., 1923).
My Further Disillusionment in Russia (New York: Doubleday, Page, and Co., 1924).
The Social Significance of the Modern Drama (Boston: Richard C. Badger, 1914).

Journals

Mother Earth was edited by Emma Goldman; it featured a running commentary on her tours and a number of articles written by her. It was published from March 1906 to August 1917.

5. See Erica Harth, "The Virtue of Love: Lord Hardwicke's Marriage Act," *Cultural Critique* 9 (Spring 1988): 154. She says with respect to the history of sentimental love: "Only by checking the anarchy of both sex and money could the ideology of virtuous love be perpetuated."
6. Sacvan Bercovitch, *The American Jeremiad* (Madison: U of Wisconsin P, 1978).
7. See his discussion of socialism and the counterculture in Warren I. Susman, *Culture as History: The Transformation of American Society in the Twentieth Century* (New York: Pantheon, 1973, 1984) 78.
8. David De Leon, *The American as Anarchist* (Baltimore: Johns Hopkins UP, 1978).
9. Bercovitch, *The American Jeremiad* 203.
10. Lillian Browne, "Emerson the Anarchist," *Mother Earth* 4.10 (December 1909): 330.

11. William M. Van der Weyde, "Thomas Paine's Anarchism," *Mother Earth* 5.5 (July 1910): 164–67.

12. See Larry Reynolds, *European Revolutions and the American Literary Renaissance* (New Haven: Yale UP, 1988).

13. Emma Goldman, "The Hypocrisy of Puritanism," *Anarchism and Other Essays* (169).

14. "The Traffic in Women," *Anarchism* (194).

15. In Yvor Winters, "The Significance of *The Bridge* by Hart Crane, or What Are We to Think of Professor X?" *In Defense of Reason* (Denver: Alan Swallow, 1943) 47, Winters asserted the dangers of Emersonianism, which arose, he argued, from the fact that Emerson framed the anarchic and antimoral character of romanticism in the religious terms which would be persuasive to American descendants of Puritans.

16. See Emma Goldman's autobiography, *Living My Life*. See also DeLeon, *The American as Anarchist*, for a larger history of these events.

17. Anderson's first impressions of a Goldman lecture appeared in "The Challenge of Emma Goldman," in the May 1914 issue of the *Little Review*. Writing for a more elite audience than the general make-up of those who attended Goldman's lectures, Anderson took care to emphasize the connection with Nietzsche:

> She has taken her "heavy load-bearing spirit" into the wilderness, like the camel; become lord of that wilderness, captured freedom for new creating, like the lion; and then *created new values*, said her Yea to life, like the child. Somehow *Zarathustra* kept running through my mind as I listened to her that afternoon. . . .
>
> Radical changes in society, releasement from present injustices and miseries, can come about not through *reform* but through *change*; not through a patching up of the old order, but through a tearing down and a rebuilding. This process involves the repudiation of such "spooks" as Christianity, conventional morality, immortality, and all other "myths" that stand as obstacles to progress, freedom, health, truth, and beauty. One thus achieves that position beyond good and evil for which Nietzsche pleaded. (6)

18. *Living My Life* 194.

19. Emma Goldman, "Artists—Revolutionists (Anent our new cover design)," *Mother Earth* 2.9 (November 1907).

20. *Little Review* (May 1929): 37.

21. Matei Calinescu, *Five Faces of Modernity: Modernism, Avant-Garde, Decadence, Kitsch, Postmodernism* (Durham: Duke UP, 1987) 129. For his extended examination of the concept, see Calinescu's chapter, "The Idea of the Avant-Garde," which begins with rhetorical figure in the Renaissance and then goes on to trace the development of an idea of the avant-garde. Calinescu argues that the avant-garde parallels the romantic history of the idea of modernity because both rest on the same concept of *time* as linear and nonreversible. Nonetheless, he presses for a careful distinction between the more general "modernity" and the more radical turns of the avant-garde.

22. Julia Kristeva, *La Révolution du langage poétique* (Paris: Éditions du Seuil, 1974) 422.

23. *Little Review* (May 1929): 37.

24. *Anarchy* 77.

25. "Anarchism" 51.

26. Irving Howe, *The American Newness: Culture and Politics in the Age of Emerson* (Cambridge, Mass.: Harvard UP, 1986) 12.

27. See Kenneth Burke, *Permanence and Change* (Indianapolis: Bobbs-Merrill Co., 1965).

28. See Martha Solomon in "Ideology as Rhetorical Constraint: The Anarchist Agitation of 'Red Emma' Goldman," *Quarterly Journal of Speech* 74.2 (May 1988): 184–200.

29. "Preface," *Anarchism* 43–44.

30. *Living My Life*, vol. 2: 766.

31. "Anarchism," *Anarchism* 47–48.

32. "Patriotism," *Anarchism and Other Essays* 135.

33. "Anarchism" 65.

34. Jean Genet, *Un Captif Amoureux* (Paris, 1986) 119.

35. Jonathan Dollimore, "Different Desires: Subjectivity and Transgression in Wilde and Gide," *Genders* 2 (Summer 1988): 27.

36. Louise Bryant, "Emma Goldman on Trial," *Little Review* 2.6 (September 1915): 25–26.

37. "The Movement for Free Speech," *Mother Earth* 4.4 (June 1909), included statements of support for Goldman from a number of newspapers and a manifesto, "A Demand for Free Speech," signed by journalists, authors, and artists including Reedy (109).

38. "Anarchism" 58.

39. Emma Goldman and Alexander Berkman, "Mother Earth," *Mother Earth* 3.1 (March 1908): 2.

40. See Nancy Armstrong, *Desire and Domestic Fiction* (New York: Oxford UP, 1987).

41. Emma Goldman, "Woman Suffrage," *Anarchism and Other Essays* 196–97.

42. Emma Goldman, "The Tragedy of Woman's Emancipation," *Anarchism and Other Essays* 217.

43. Judith Newton, "History as Usual? Feminism and the New Historicism," *Cultural Critique* 9 (Spring 1988): 94.

44. Alan Ritter, *Anarchism: A Theoretical Analysis* (Cambridge: Cambridge UP, 1980). Ritter argues that "not freedom but community and individuality are the anarchists' chief goals," summed up as a "communal individuality" (26).

45. Emma Goldman, "Light and Shadows in the Life of an Avant-Guard," *Mother Earth* 4.12 (February 1910): 383.

46. See Candace Falk, *Love, Anarchy, and Emma Goldman* (New York: Holt, Rinehart, and Winston) 7.

47. Of all narratives, the least innocent but the most difficult to accuse may be autobiography, perhaps because an interested self as teller is represented in the text, so that innocence is denied from the beginning, though the guilt of discursive history is displaced onto the creative person of the individual writer. The other life story, biography, operates under the same conventions of authorship, ostensively omitting the productive self as storyteller in its text but not the self as object of the tale. The biographical narrative displaces writer from subject and sets up an oscillation between the two lives or the double *graph* such that writing seems to belong to the author and life to the biographical subject, at the same time that the author is represented at the moment of writing as transparently *alive* and the writing is represented as transparent to the plot, the marks left by the other's life, which often, indeed, is over.

48. In W. K. Wimsatt, *The Verbal Icon* (Lexington: U of Kentucky P, 1954) 51.

49. Emma Goldman, "The Drama," *Anarchism and Other Essays* 250.

50. Emma Goldman, "The Irish Drama: William Butler Yeats," *The Social Significance of the Drama* (Boston: Richard G. Badger, 1914) 260.

51. "Anarchism" 67.

3. *JOUISSANCE* AND THE SENTIMENTAL DAUGHTER

1. Edmund Wilson, *I Thought of Daisy* (New York: Charles Scribner's Sons, 1929) 64. This description is of Rita, Wilson's version of Millay in the novel.

2. Harriet Monroe, "Comment: Edna St. Vincent Millay," *Poetry* 24 (August 1924): 266. Monroe's uncritical endorsement suggests the power of Millay's work to generate the fantasy of becoming a poet. Later Monroe retreats in the face of criticism, still defending Millay's ability but confessing "a certain sense of frustration, of disappointment," in her review of the love sonnets in *Fatal Interview*, finding there "an emotional reservation as seductive and remote as a cloister." "Advance or Retreat," *Poetry* 38 (July 1931): 216–21.

3. Teresa de Lauretis, *Alice Doesn't: Feminism, Semiotics, Cinema* (Bloomington: Indiana UP, 1984) 131–32.

> Freud's story of femininity, as we know, is the story of the journey of the female child across the dangerous terrain of the Oedipus complex. Leaving home, she enters the phallic stage where she comes face to face with castration, engages in the uneven battle with penis envy, and remains forever scarred by the narcissistic wound, forever bleeding. But she goes on, and the worst is still to come. No longer a "little man," bereft of weapon or magical gift, the female child enters the liminal stage in which her transformation into woman will take place; but only if she successfully negotiates the crossing, haunted by the Scylla and Charybdis of object change and erotogenic zone change, into passivity. If she survives, her reward is motherhood.

4. Monique Plaza, "The Mother/The Same: Hatred of the Mother in Psychoanalysis," *Feminist Issues* (Spring 1982): 75–99.

5. References to Millay's poetry are to *Collected Poems*, ed. Norma Millay (New York: Harper and Row, 1956).

6. Sara Ruddick, "Maternal Thinking," *Feminist Studies* 6.2 (Summer 1980): 343.

7. *Alice Doesn't* 143.

8. John Crowe Ransom, "The Poet as Woman," *Southern Review* 2 (Spring 1937): 784.

9. Allen Tate, "Miss Millay's Sonnets: A Review of *Fatal Interview*," *New Republic* (May 6, 1931): 335–36.

10. Cleanth Brooks, "Edna Millay's Maturity," Book Review Section *Southwest Review* 20 (January 1935): 2.

11. William Stidger, *Flames of Faith* (New York: Abingdon Press, 1922).

12. Jane Tompkins, *Sensational Designs: The Cultural Work of American Fiction, 1790–1860* (New York: Oxford UP, 1985).

13. Charles Baudelaire, "Les Fleurs du Mal" (1861), *Oeuvres completes* (Paris: Bibliothèque de la Pléiade, 1954) 140.

14. Charles Baudelaire, *Les Fleurs du Mal*, trans. Richard Howard (Boston: David R. Godine, 1983), 70.

15. Charles Baudelaire, *Flowers of Evil*, trans. George Dillon and Edna St. Vincent Millay, preface by Edna St. Vincent Millay (New York: Harper and Brothers, 1936) 35.

16. Earl Rovit, "Our Lady-Poets of the Twenties," *Southern Review* 16 (Winter 1980): 65–85.

17. Elaine Showalter, "Critical Cross-Dressing: Male Feminists and the Woman

of the Year," *Raritan* (Fall 1983), rpt. in *Men in Feminism*, ed. Alice Jardine and Paul Smith (New York: Methuen, 1987).

18. De Lauretis writes about the danger of theory to any consideration of "woman" as opposed to the heterogeneity of women: the risk

> of elaborating a historical-materialist theory of culture which must deny the materiality and the historicity of the subject itself, or rather the *subjects* of culture. For it is not just the "speaking subject" of Kristeva's narrowly linguistic, or language-determined perspective that is at issue, but subjects who speak and listen, write and read, make and watch films, work and play, and so forth; who are, in short, concurrently and often contradictorily engaged in a plurality of heterogeneous experiences, practices, and discourses, where subjectivity and gender are constructed, anchored, or reproduced. (*Alice Doesn't* 171–72)

19. Roland Barthes, *A Lover's Discourse*, trans. Richard Howard (New York: Hill and Wang, 1978) 175.

20. Jane Gallop, *The Daughter's Seduction* (Ithaca: Cornell UP, 1982) 149.

21. Karl Shapiro, "Review: Edna St. Vincent Millay, *Collected Poems*," *Prairie Schooner* 31 (Spring 1957): 13.

22. Judith Fetterley has written about a story by Louisa May Alcott which suggests the possibility of a radicalism behind the masks of the Little Women, and the theatricality of the roles: "Impersonating 'Little Women': The Radicalism of Alcott's *Behind a Mask*," *Women's Studies* 10 (1983): 1–14.

23. Recently scholars have begun to seriously question the assumptions behind such snide judgments against the women's clubs and the "genteel codes" associated with them. Sheryl O'Donnell is responsible for persuading me that an analysis of such materials uncovers multiple, complex, and unexamined aspects of women's writing—see "Letters from Nice Girls: Genteel Codes in Women's Writings," Proceedings of GITAP, University of North Dakota, 1983; "Professing Culture: A History of North Dakota Clubwomen," *Day In, Day Out: Women's Lives in North Dakota* (Grand Forks: U of North Dakota, 1988) 31–55.

24. Susan Gubar, "Sapphistries," *Signs: Journal of Women in Culture and Society* 10.1 (Autumn 1984): 47.

25. The figure of the muse generated by female poets is as wonderful and terrible, as helpful and threatening—as ambivalent—as the figure of the mother. See, for example, Mary Kirk Deshazer's study *Inspiring Women: Re-Imagining the Muse* (New York: Pergamon, 1986).

26. R. F. Brissenden, *Virtue in Distress* (New York: Macmillan, 1974).

27. "The Poet as Woman" 797.

28. See de Lauretis re femininity:

> Desire itself, then, is in question. If desire is the question which generates both narrative and narrativity as Oedipal drama, the question is an open one, seeking a closure that is only promised, not guaranteed. For Oedipal desire requires in its object—or in its subject when female, as in Freud's little girl—an identification with the feminine position. (*Alice Doesn't* 133–34)

29. See his reflection on "God and the *Jouissance of the Woman*," *Feminine Sexuality*, ed. Juliet Mitchell and Jacqueline Rose (New York: W. W. Norton/Pantheon, 1982) 147.

30. Julia Kristeva, *Powers of Horror* (New York: Columbia UP, 1982) 5.

31. Edmund Wilson, *The Shores of Light* (New York: Vintage, 1952) 744–93.

32. In *The Letters of Edna St. Vincent Millay*, ed. Allan Ross Macdougall (New York: Grosset and Dunlap, 1952) 18.

33. Elizabeth Perlmutter, "A Doll's Heart: The Girl in the Poetry of Edna St. Vincent Millay and Louise Bogan," *Twentieth Century Literature* 23. 2 (May 1977): 157–79.

34. Later, when she had a brief but intense affair with Ficke, she wrote a sonnet which "was written both about you & about myself—we were both like that":

> I only know that every hour with you
> Is torture to me, and that I would be
> From your too poignant lovelinesses free!
> Rainbows, green flame, sharp diamonds, the fierce blue
> Of shimmering ice-bergs, and to be shot through
> With lightning or a sword incessantly—
> Such things have beauty, doubtless; but to me
> Mist, shadow, silence—these are lovely too.
> There is no shelter in you anywhere;
> Rhythmic, intolerable, your burning rays
> Trample upon me, withering my breath;
> I will be gone, and rid of you, I swear:
> To stand upon the peaks of Love always
> Proves but that part of Love whose name is Death.

Neither male nor female, Ficke nor Millay, is clearly the speaker. From Norman A. Brittin, *Edna St. Vincent Millay* (New York: Twayne Publishers, 1967) 40.

35. *Seduction* 22.

36. The omniscience that threatens Millay's speaker does not allow her separation, difference, or distance—but that does not equate it with the Kristevan "semiotic." The difference that precedes the paternal order of language is at issue. As Jane Gallop helps us see, the Lacanian and Kristevan versions of the maternal "imaginary" or "semiotic" are in conflict: "the incompatibility of Lacanian and Kristevan theories, the difficulty in thinking a relation between the 'imaginary' and the 'semiotic,' ought to be attended to as a locus of conflict between two maternals—one conservative, the other dissident—as a way of keeping the position of the mother 'both double and foreign' . . . " (125). "Renascence" seems a poem of the "imaginary" in the sense of presenting an image which resists disruption. But that's not all.

37. We would expect a description of a "soul" which is in an "imaginary" or narcissistic illusion of identification with the Other to be described as "full" or "total." Could a "flat" soul be one without desire, but also the one which does not enter into the kind of identification which we have just seen as so very traumatic? Then isn't a "flat" or even an escaped soul precisely what women want? But in this poem, the underground woman is out of touch with reality.

38. Tate, "A Review of *Fatal Interview*" 335–36.

39. See Stanley Aronowitz, *The Crisis in Historical Materialism* (South Hadley, Mass.: J. F. Bergin, 1981), and Fredric Jameson, "Reification and Utopia in Mass Culture," *Social Text* 1 (1979): 130–48.

40. Tania Modleski, *Loving with a Vengeance: Mass-Produced Fantasies for Women* (New York and London: Methuen, 1982). See also the collection edited by Modleski *Studies in Entertainment: Critical Approaches to Mass Culture* (Bloomington and Indianapolis: Indiana UP, 1986).

41. *Alice Doesn't* 140.

42. "A Doll's Heart" 162.

43. See Geoffrey Hartman, *Saving the Text* (Baltimore and London: Johns Hopkins UP, 1981).

44. This is not to say that Millay does not write about a mother figure; she most assuredly does. For example, in "The Harp Weaver" the magic gifts of the mother are used to clothe her child, and she sacrifices for him, weaving all through the frozen night. "Sonnets from an Ungrafted Tree" gives us an unyielding and grim portrayal of the woman's sacrificial part. Walter Minot ("Millay's 'Ungrafted Tree': The Problem of the Artist as Woman," *New England Quarterly* 48 [June 1975]: 260–69) argues that these sonnets demonstrate the "psychic price that she, as a woman, had to pay" and that it was "too high a penalty." Millay's domestic imagery and its part in the tradition of women's poetry are discussed by Jeanine Dobbs, "Edna St. Vincent Millay and the Tradition of Domestic Poetry," *Journal of Women's Studies in Literature* 1 (Spring 1979): 89–106.

45. *Feminine Sexuality* 144.

46. Nina Auerbach, *Woman and the Demon: The Life of a Victorian Myth* (Cambridge, Mass., and London: Harvard UP, 1982).

47. Carolyn Heilbrun, "Louisa May Alcott: The Influence of Little Women," *Women, the Arts, and the 1920's in Paris and New York*, ed. Kenneth W. Wheeler and Virginia Lee Lussier (New Brunswick and London: Transaction Books, 1982) 21.

48. *Letters* 146.

49. (June 15, 1921) "I was telling somebody yesterday that the reason I am a poet is entirely because you wanted me to be, even from the very first. You brought me up in the tradition of poetry, and everything I did you encouraged" (118).

50. Griffin Barry, "Vincent," *New Yorker* (February 12, 1927): 26.

51. "A Doll's Heart" 159.

52. See Teresa de Lauretis, *Technologies of Gender* (Bloomington: Indiana UP, 1987) 113.

4. MEDUSA AND MELANCHOLY

1. Louise Bogan, "Unofficial Feminine Laureate," *Selected Criticism* (New York: Noonday, 1955) 154. This is an essay on Edna St. Vincent Millay. Bogan's criticism also is collected in *A Poet's Alphabet: Reflections on the Literary Art and Vocation*, ed. Robert Phelps and Ruth Limmer (New York: McGraw-Hill, 1970). See also Louise Bogan, *Achievement in American Poetry, 1900–1950* (New York: Noonday Press, 1955). Quotations from her poetry in this chapter are from Louise Bogan, *The Blue Estuaries: Poems, 1923–1968* (New York: Ecco Press, 1977).

2. Hélène Cixous, "The Laugh of the Medusa," trans. Keith Cohen and Paula Cohen for *Signs* (Summer 1976). In Elaine Marks and Isabelle de Courtivron, *New French Feminisms* (Amherst: U of Massachusetts P, 1980) 245–64.

3. Jean Clair, *Méduse: Contribution à une anthropologie des arts du visuel* (Paris: Gallimard, 1989).

4. See Sigmund Freud, "Medusa's Head," *The Complete Psychological Works of Sigmund Freud: Standard Edition* (London: Hogarth Press, 1953, distributed in the U.S by the Macmillan Co.) 273–74. This particular piece was written in 1922. It is of course connected to the notion of the phallic mother.

5. "Le 'dripping' de Pollock, ce n'est autre, en fait, que le sang dégoulinant de la tête tranchée de Méduse, dessinant la figure aléatoire de notre perdition." The translation is mine. Clair, *Méduse* 237.

6. Ruth Limmer, "Circumscriptions," *Critical Essays on Louise Bogan*, ed. Martha Collins (Boston: G. K. Hall, 1984), and Louise Bogan, *Journey around My Room*, ed. Ruth Limmer (New York: Viking Press, 1980).

7. See Gloria Bowles's extremely valuable study *Louise Bogan's Aesthetic of Limitation* (Bloomington and Indianapolis: Indiana UP, 1987). I do not disagree with her carefully drawn distinctions in her examination of Bogan's connections with the symbolist aesthetic (see especially pp. 22–27), but I wish to argue a different point of view about the whole of modernism and its relationship to women's writing. Thus I will stress the continuities between Mallarmé and Bogan. It seems to me in particular that we need to see the connection between Mallarmé's *absence* and Bogan's representation of an interior experience which is disconnected from personal history. To paint the effect of the thing is precisely an aesthetic of pathos. See Bowles, *Louise Bogan's Aesthetic* 26.

8. Kay Boyle, "Writers in Metaphysical Revolt," a speech which was published in *Proceedings of the Conference of College Teachers of English of Texas* 36 (September 1971): 6–12.

9. "The Heart and the Lyre," in *Selected Criticism* 341.

10. My translation, from "Symphonie littéraire": "les jouissances d'une âme pûrement passive qui n'est que femme encore, et qui demain peut-être sera bête," in *Oeuvres* (Paris: Gallimard, 1945) 261.

11. Julia Kristeva, *Revolution in Poetic Language*, trans. Margaret Waller (New York: Columbia UP, 1984) 211–12.

12. "The Laugh of the Medusa" 248.

13. In *A Poet's Alphabet*.

14. Elizabeth Frank, *Louise Bogan: A Portrait* (New York: Alfred A. Knopf, 1985) 57.

15. *Journey around My Room* 72.

16. See the "Lettre à M. André Fontainas," *Oeuvres I* (Paris: Gallimard, 1957): "Qui saura me lire, lira une autobiographie, dans la forme. Le *fond* importe peu. Lieux communs" (1622).

17. In 1923, Alfred Thibaudet called "La Jeune Parque" "the most obscure poem in French poetry—much more obscure than 'L'Après-Midi d'une Faune' " ("le poéme le plus obscur de la poésie française, beaucoup plus obscur que *L'Après-Midi d'une Faune*"), in *Paul Valéry* (Paris: Les Chaiers Verts, 1923).

18. See Julia Kristeva, *Black Sun: Depression and Melancholy*, trans. Leon S. Roudiez (New York: Columbia UP, 1990), and "On the Melancholic Imaginary," trans. Louise Burchill, in *Discourse in Psychoanalysis and Literature*, ed. Shlomith Rimmon-Kenan (London and New York: Methuen, 1987) 104–23.

19. Frank, *Louise Bogan* 29.

20. In a presentation for the 1989 Modern Language Association.

21. See Ezra Pound, *The ABC of Reading* (New York: New Directions, 1937) 17–18.

22. But see Robert Scholes's critique of that notion, specifically with reference to Pound's story: "Is There a Fish in This Text," *Textual Power* (New Haven: Yale UP, 1985).

23. Elizabeth Frank reports Elizabeth Bishop's memory of Bogan's reaction:

I am sure Marianne never dreamed what suffering she was causing her. It seemed that Marianne took notes constantly, asked many questions, and entered into discussions with enthusiasm. But the other students were timid and often nonplussed, and so was Miss Bogan, besides feeling that she was sailing under false colors and never knowing what technical questions she might be expected to answer next" (348).

24. See Marianne Moore, "To a Snail," *Collected Poems* (New York: Macmillan, 1951) 91, and the note, p. 167.

25. *Alphabet* 428.

26. *Alphabet* 397.

27. *Alphabet* 144.

28. Frank Kermode, *Romantic Image* (London: Routledge and Kegan Paul, 1957; rpt., New York: Vintage, 1964). He says, for example: "These two beliefs—in the Image as a radiant truth out of space and time, and in the necessary isolation or estrangement of men who can perceive it—are inextricably associated . . . " (2). He also traces the figure of the dancer as motif, with Mallarmé's Hérodiade one of the Salome images. "Intellectual and physical isolation are easily represented by diseases which are the consequences of uncontrolled feeling; and when this becomes the artist's preferred subject he evolves the Hérodiade emblem, representing at once the cruelty of the idolation and the beauty (distinct from life yet vital) of its product" (70).

29. *Alphabet* 97.

30. *Letters* 282–83.

31. Hart Crane, *The Complete Poems and Selected Letters and Prose of Hart Crane*, ed. Brom Weber (New York: Anchor Books, 1966) 11.

5. REVOLUTION, THE WOMAN, AND THE WORD

1. For an account, see Sandra Whipple Spanier, *Kay Boyle: Artist and Activist* (Carbondale and Edwardsville: Southern Illinois UP, 1986) 25–26.

2. Kay Boyle, *Words That Must Somehow Be Said*, ed. Elizabeth S. Bell (San Francisco: North Point Press, 1985) 31–34.

3. For a convincing discussion of Boyle's experimental writing, her collection of stories in *Wedding Day and Other Stories*, and her contribution to the "revolution of the word," see Spanier, *Kay Boyle* 30–56.

4. These stories appear in *Wedding Day and Other Stories* (New York: Jonathan Cape and Harrison Smith, 1930). "Episode" and "Wedding Day" also appear in *Fifty Stories* (New York: Doubleday, 1980), and "On the Run" was reprinted in the special issue on Kay Boyle of *Twentieth Century Literature* (Fall 1988). References are to the most recent editions.

5. This essay, published originally in French as "Le temps des femmes" in *33/44: Cahiers de recherche des sciences des textes et documents*, no. 5 (Winter 1979), first appeared in English, translated by Alice Jardine and Harry Blake, in *Signs: Journal of Women in Culture and Society* 7 (1981), and has been reprinted a number of times. My references are to the text in *The Kristeva Reader*, ed. Toril Moi (New York: Columbia UP, 1986) 187–213.

6. Julia Kristeva, *Revolution in Poetic Language*, trans. Margaret Waller (New York: Columbia UP, 1984).

7. Catharine R. Stimpson, "Stein and the Transposition of Gender," *The Poetics of Gender*, ed. Nancy Miller (New York: Columbia UP, 1986) 2.

8. "Women's Time" 199.

9. She writes in "The Family," in *Words That Must Somehow Be Said*, that her own grandmother was a strong woman who worked in the Land Grant Division of the federal government and lived a life of independence: "I knew she ran, and

danced, and sang before the horses in the beginning of the day because she wasn't afraid of the Indians or of anything else in life" (23). Boyle does not know "where Grandma Evans had found the courage to leave Kansas and a grandfather I was never to see and to move with her two young daughters to Washington D.C." (23).

10. In the Introduction to Boyle, *Fifty Stories* 14.

11. See Atwood's introduction to Boyle's *Three Short Novels* (New York: Penguin, 1982) ix.

12. *Kay Boyle* 36.

13. See John Ruskin, "Of the Pathetic Fallacy," *Critical Theory since Plato*, ed. Hazard Adams (New York: Harcourt Brace Jovanovich, 1971).

14. "Pathetic Fallacy" 619.

15. Spanier's argument about Catherine as a heroic figure is set out in "Catherine Barkley and the Hemingway Code: Ritual and Survival in *A Farewell to Arms*," *Modern Critical Interpretations: "A Farewell to Arms*," ed. Harold Bloom (New Haven and New York: Chelsea House, 1987) 131–48. Spanier goes on in another article to situate the novel in the context of the aftermath of the Great War, and to argue that critical interpretations have often missed the significance of love and the personal to Hemingway in that novel because they have lost sight of the context: "Hemingway's Unknown Soldier: Catherine Barkley, the Critics, and the Great War," *New Essays on "A Farewell to Arms*", ed. Scott Donaldson (Cambridge: Cambridge UP, forthcoming 1990).

16. Barbara Ehrenreich and Deirdre English, *For Her Own Good: 150 Years of the Experts' Advice to Women* (Garden City: Anchor Books, 1979).

17. Sandra Gilbert, "Soldier's Heart: Literary Men, Literary Women, and the Great War," *Signs* 8.3 (Spring 1983): 422–50.

18. Paul Fussell, *The Great War and Modern Memory* (London and New York: Oxford UP, 1975).

19. *London Review of Books* (September 28, 1989): 6.

20. See the speech "Writers in Metaphysical Revolt," *Proceedings of the Conference of College Teachers of English of Texas* 36 (September 1971): 6–12.

21. Tania Modleski, *Loving with a Vengeance: Mass-Produced Fantasies for Women* (New York: Methuen, 1982).

22. Nancy Miller, *The Heroine's Text: Readings in the French and English Novel, 1722–1782* (New York: Columbia UP, 1980).

23. Alice Jardine, *Gynesis: Configurations of Woman and Modernity* (Ithaca: Cornell UP, 1985).

24. An elaboration of the subject of imprisonment appears in "A Day on Alcatraz with the Indians," "The Crime of Attica," and "Report from Lock-up," *Words That Must Somehow Be Said* 104–51.

6. THE WOMAN IN NATURE AND THE SUBJECT OF NONFICTION

1. For a history of how this repression is related to natural history, see Carolyn Merchant, *The Death of Nature: Women, Ecology, and the Scientific Revolution* (San Francisco: Harper and Row, 1980). Her study shows the mutual implication of scientific knowing and the repression of women: seeming closer to nature than men, women in the Renaissance came to be viewed as untrustworthy, incapable of mastering objective knowledge, themselves the object rather than the source of knowledge.

2. This is the more surprising because Dillard's works all have a framework of personal experience, and the observation includes her autobiography.

Books

An American Childhood (New York: Harper and Row, 1987).
Encounters with Chinese Writers (Middletown: Wesleyan UP, 1984).
Holy the Firm (New York: Harper and Row, 1977).
Living by Fiction (New York: Harper and Row, 1982).
Pilgrim at Tinker Creek (New York: Harper's Magazine Press, 1974).
Teaching a Stone to Talk (New York: Harper and Row, 1982).
The Writing Life (New York: Harper and Row, 1989).
Subsequent references are to the above editions.

3. For example, in her examination of women who made important contributions to ecology, "Women of the Progressive Conservation Movement, 1900–1916," Carolyn Merchant finds that "this enterprise ultimately rested on the self-interested preservation of their own middle-class life styles and was legitimated by the separate male/female spheres ideology of the nineteenth century aimed at conserving 'true womanhood,' the home, and the child" (57).

4. For example, William Scheick, "Narrative Fringe," *Contemporary American Women Writers: Narrative Strategies*, ed. Catherine Rainwater and William J. Scheick (Lexington: U of Kentucky P, 1985), calls attention to the liminal in Dillard but connects contradictions and marginality not with her womanhood but with the position of the artist and the mystic. Of course, the very inclusion of the essay in a book on women suggests connections, but Scheick avoids making them out loud much as Dillard's work itself does. (The woman speaks, but is not spoken?)

5. Norwood says that Dillard "frees women from safe, cultivated gardens, playing out their burden of guilt for destroying Eden" (51). Thus Dillard, Norwood argues, together with other women writers about the environment, emphasizes nature over culture: "Nature is: before culture there was nature, after culture there will continue to be nature. Their cultural drama is not one of successful challenge, nature overcome, but of full recognition, nature comprehended" (52).

6. Annie Dillard, "Is Art All There Is?" *Harper's* 261 (August 1980): 61–66, p. 63.

7. Dillard writes in "Is Art All There Is?":

> Absolutely diagnostic as a theme of contemporary modernist fiction is this: many works, granting the uncertainty of any knowledge, treat the world in a new way, as a series of imaginative possibilities. Anything may happen. . . . Writers and artists of this century may well ascribe to their work a new and real importance. If art is the creation of contexts, *and so is everything else*, how false or trivial can art be? (66)

8. For example, in "Choreographies," an interview between Derrida and Christie McDonald, *Diacritics* 12 [Summer 1982]: 66–76), he reflects on other places in his work where he has said that the woman has no place, is not implicated in the discourses of essentialism.

9. Susan Griffin, *Woman and Nature: The Roaring inside Her* (New York: Harper and Row, 1978).

10. Julia Kristeva, *Powers of Horror: An Essay on Abjection*, trans. Leon S. Roudiez (New York: Columbia UP, 1982).

11. For a thorough review of the conventions associated with the representation of nature and of pastoral topoi, see Ernst Robert Curtius, *European Literature and the Latin Middle Ages*, trans. Willard R. Trask (New York: Bollingen, 1953).

12. Rainier Maria Rilke, *Duino Elegies*, trans. C. F. MacIntyre (Berkeley: U of California P, 1968) 61.

13. See Chris Anderson, *Style as Argument: Contemporary American Nonfiction* (Carbondale: Southern Illinois UP, 1987).

14. See William Zinsser, ed., *Inventing the Truth: The Art and Craft of Memoir* (Boston: Houghton Mifflin Co., 1987).

15. See Gary McIlroy, "*Pilgrim at Tinker Creek* and the Social Legacy of *Walden*," *South Atlantic Quarterly* 85.2 (Spring 1986): 111–22.

16. The limits of otherness are more subtle. One of her earliest images of beauty is the scene of the young girl from an Irish Catholic family nearby who was skating on the icy street one night under the street lights (30). But the girl's family was forbidden. The Sheehy boy had said, "Go tell your maid she's a nigger," and Dillard had found her mother transformed, "steely," when she repeated the word. "I was never to use such words, and never to associate with people who did so long as I lived" (30). Thus class difference is mystified and the prejudice against the Catholic Sheehys rationalized by their own prejudice against race. Might gender prejudice likewise be rationalized by the gendered turn to the unuseful economy of writing taken, for example, by Annie herself? She recognizes her mother's anarchism, throws herself as restlessly as Mary Wollstonecraft against the "trivial" occupations organized for girls, and takes up baseball for herself. But she does not think of her identification with the irrational Rimbaud as a rage against gendered oppressions.

17. See Freud's discussion of the difference between a child's love of the repeated story and the adult desire for novelty in *Beyond the Pleasure Principle*, trans. James Strachey (New York: W. W. Norton, 1961) 29.

18. See Roland Barthes, *The Pleasure of the Text*, trans. Richard Miller (New York: Hill and Wang, 1975).

19. Jacques Lacan, *Ecrits: A Selection*, trans. Alan Sheridan (New York: W. W. Norton, 1977) 50.

7. THE SENTIMENTAL AND THE CRITICAL

1. Alice Walker, *The Color Purple* (New York: Harcourt, Brace, Jovanovich, 1982).

2. Alice Walker, "Saving the Life That Is Your Own," *In Search of Our Mother's Gardens* (New York: Harcourt Brace Jovanovich, 1983) 8.

3. See "A Talk: Convocation 1972," *In Search of Our Mother's Gardens* 17.

4. Definitions of *womanist* appear as a preface to *In Search of Our Mother's Gardens*.

5. Trudier Harris, "On *The Color Purple*, Stereotypes, and Silence," *Black American Literature Forum* 18.4 (Winter 1984): 155.

6. "The Black Writer and the Southern Experience," *In Search of Our Mother's Gardens* 18. This was written in 1970, so it does not reflect the debates of the seventies over separatism and assimilation. But I think it fairly stands for an enduring attitude in Walker's work, the certain lack of paranoia which (in the same essay) she attributed to her ancestors.

7. "Writing *The Color Purple*," *In Search of Our Mother's Gardens* 356.

8. Robert Towers, "Good Men Are Hard to Find," *New York Review of Books* 29.13 (August 12, 1982): 36.

9. Dinitia Smith, " 'Celie, You a Tree,' " *Nation* 235.6 (September 4, 1982): 182.

10. See the discussion in Appendix D of Kenneth Burke, *A Grammar of Motives* (New York: George Braziller, 1955) 516–17.

11. Hayden White, *Metahistory: The Historical Imagination in Nineteenth Century Europe* (Baltimore: Johns Hopkins UP, 1973).

12. Tania Modleski, *Loving with a Vengeance: Mass-Produced Fantasies for Women* (New York and London: Methuen, 1982); Leslie Rabine, *Reading the Romantic Heroine: Text, History, Ideology* (Ann Arbor: U of Michigan P, 1985); Janice Radway, *Reading the Romance: Women, Patriarchy, and Popular Culture* (Chapel Hill: U of North Carolina P, 1984).

13. Ann Douglas, *The Feminization of American Culture* (New York: Avon, 1977).

14. Madonne Miner, *Insatiable Appetites: Twentieth-Century American Women's Bestsellers* (Westport, Conn.: Greenwood Press, 1984).

15. "Writing *The Color Purple*" 359.

16. Julia Kristeva, *Tales of Love*, trans. Leon S. Roudiez (New York: Columbia UP, 1987) 364.

17. Toril Moi, *Sexual/Textual Politics* (New York: Methuen, 1985) 158.

18. In *Tales of Love*.

19. See Murray Krieger, *The Tragic Vision: Variations on a Theme in Literary Interpretation* (New York: Holt, Rinehart, and Winston, 1960).

20. John Carlos Rowe, *The Theoretical Dimensions of Henry James* (Madison: U of Wisconsin P, 1984) 87.

21. For an extended essay on this question, see Denise Riley, *"Am I That Name?": Feminism and the Category of 'Women' in History* (Minneapolis: U of Minnesota P, 1988).

22. Toril Moi, "Feminism, Postmodernism, and Style: Recent Feminist Criticism in the United States," *Cultural Critique* 9 (Spring 1988): 3–24.

23. Barbara Christian, "The Race for Theory," *Cultural Critique* 6 (Spring 1987): 51–63.

24. Luce Irigaray, *Speculum of the Other Woman*, trans. Gillian C. Gill (Ithaca: Cornell UP, 1985) 325.

25. "Everyday Use" appears in *The Norton Anthology of Literature by Women*, ed. Sandra Gilbert and Susan Gubar (New York: W. W. Norton, 1985): 2366–73. Thus it becomes a representative tale in a number of senses, canonical.

26. Elaine Showalter, "Piecing and Writing," in *The Poetics of Gender*, ed. Nancy Miller (New York: Columbia UP, 1986) 226–27. She cites Rachel Blau DuPlessis's "For the Etruscans," which appeared in Showalter's anthology *The New Feminist Criticism* (New York: Pantheon, 1985) 271–91. Feminist criticism takes on the form of piecing as well.

27. Showalter, "Piecing and Writing" 229, citing Nina Baym, *Woman's Fiction: A Guide to Novels by and about Women in America, 1820–1870* (Ithaca: Cornell UP, 1978).

28. "Folk Art," in *A Poet's Alphabet: Reflections on the Literary Art and Vocation*, ed. Robert Phelps and Ruth Limmer (New York: McGraw-Hill, 1970) 137.

29. *Speculum* 143.

Abjection: psychology of, and sentimental discourse, 10–11; Kristeva on jouissance, 82–83

Alcott, Louisa May: *Little Women*, 93

Anarchy: Goldman's politics, 42–66; feminist discourse, 193

Anderson, Chris, 167

Anderson, Margaret: revolt against stylistic convention, 34; Goldman's anarchy, 48, 50; Goldman and modernism, 51; Goldman's facial expression, 55

Angier, Natalie, 12

Apollinaire, Guillaume, 34

Armstrong, Nancy, 1, 38, 61

Aronowitz, Stanley, 89

Art: Goldman's anarchy, 49; Bogan and politics, 120–21

Atwood, Margaret, 136

Auerbach, Nina, 92

Austen, Jane, 28

Autobiography: Bogan's "The Tale," 109, 111–12; Boyle's "On the Run," 134–35; Boyle's *The Underground Woman*, 147; fiction and nonfiction, 168; biography and subject, 212n

Avant-garde: reversal against the sentimental, 1–2; Goldman's anarchy, 62–63; Dillard and feminism, 157; modernity and development, 211n

Baldwin, Roger, 58

Barney, Natalie, 30

Barry, Griffin, 94

Barthes, Roland: the sentimental, 1, 2, 203n; the body and discourse, 1–2; modernity and rebirth of the author, 41; figures of love, 76, 77; pleasure principle, 178

—*A Lovers' Discourse*, 15–16, 179

Baudelaire, Charles, 72–74

Baym, Nina, 200

Beall, Chandler, 194

Beardsley, Monroe C., 64–65

Bercovitch, Sacvan, 43, 44

Berkman, Alexander, 46, 47

Birth control: Goldman and free speech, 59

Bogan, Louise: on achievements of modernist poetry, 1; role in modernism, 14; free love, 30; on revolution, 37; modernist women writers and poetics, 38; figure of artist as criminal, 57; poetry and modernism, 99–126; on American folk art, 200–201; women's writing and power of style, 202; continuity with Mallarmé, 217n; Moore as student of, 217n–218n

—"Betrothed," 118

—*The Blue Estuaries*, 109

—"Hérodiade," 104–105

—"Medusa," 106, 113–18

—"Night," 108–109

—"The Sleeping Fury," 106–107, 123–24

—"A Tale," 106, 109–12, 113

—"Three Songs," 125–26

—"The Time of the Assassins," 108

Booth, Wayne, 194

Bowles, Gloria, 101, 102

Boyle, Kay: role in modernism, 14; free love, 30; progressive politics, 35; American modernism, 102, 120; experimental writing and modernism, 127–52; women's writing and power of style, 202; grandmother, 218n–219n

—*Death of a Man*, 145

—"Episode in the Life of an Ancestor?" 130–32

—*Generation without Farewell*, 145

—"On the Run," 134–36

—*Plagued by the Nightingale*, 140, 141–42

—*The Underground Woman*, 147–49, 152

—"Wedding Day," 132–34

—"Writers in Metaphysical Revolt," 146–47

—*Year before Last*, 140, 142–45

Brissenden, R. F., 80

Brontë, Charlotte: *Jane Eyre*, 183

Brooks, Cleanth, 10, 36, 69

Browne, Lillian, 44–45

Bryant, Louise, 59

Burke, Kenneth, 36, 53, 187

Burns, Robert, 20

Buwalda, William, 52

Calinescu, Matei, 50

Campbell, George, 25–26

Carter, Elizabeth, 27
Cather, Willa, 36
Censorship: modernist literature and sexuality, 32
Chaplin, Charlie, 125
Chase, Richard, 26
Christian, Barbara, 198, 199
Cixous, Hélène, 99–100, 107, 169
Clair, Jean, 100, 115
Class: Goldman and anarchism, 50; Millay's poetry, 69, 72; Dillard and modernism, 173, 174, 175; American folk art, 200–201
Closure: Millay's "Renascence," 90
Consumerism: Oedipal drama, 187
Crane, Hart: modernism and cultural change, 6; American literary history and modernism, 46; on Chaplin and sentimentality, 124–25; compared to Boyle, 127
Crime: Bogan's poetry, 113
Culture: feminization of and modernism, 9–10; Goldman and anarchism, 50; symbolist poetry, 105; women and theories of, 214n. *See also* Mass culture
Czolgosz, Leon, 47

Daiches, David, 135
De Leon, David, 44
Derrida, Jacques, 160
Desire: Oedipal shape and modernist criticism, 8
Detective novel: Bogan on genre, 108
Dickinson, Emily, 101, 121, 164
Difference: Millay's "Renascence," 79, 81
Dillard, Annie: popular culture and postmodern literature, 14–15; female subject and modernism, 155–81; women's writing and power of style, 202; the liminal, 220n; nature and culture, 220n
—*An American Childhood*, 156, 168, 171, 172, 174, 176
—*Encounters with Chinese Writers*, 173–74
—*Holy the Firm*, 163–64, 176
—*Living by Fiction*, 157
—*Pilgrim at Tinker Creek*, 158, 159–60, 163, 166, 168–69, 176
—*Teaching a Stone to Talk*, 164–68
—*The Writing Life*, 179
Dollimore, Jonathan, 58
Domesticity: modernist women and tradition, 29; technology and repression of, 138
Douglas, Ann: *The Feminization of America* and argument against the sentimental, 3–4, 5, 11, 15, 23, 187, 198
Du Bois, W. E. B., 185
DuPlessis, Rachel Blau, 200

Eagleton, Terry, 38, 195
Eastman, Max, 33
Education: Goldman and the maternal, 61
Ehrenreich, Barbara, 138
Eliot, T. S.: objects of desire, 31; American modernism and ahistoricism, 33; formalist criticism, 35–36; Bogan and literary tradition, 101, 102, 103; gendering and objectivity, 118–19; Boyle compared to, 140
—*The Waste Land*, 35, 118
Eluard, Paul, 122
Embarrassment: women and literature, 12
Emerson, Ralph Waldo: as anarchist, 44–45; on the masses, 52; Goldman's anarchism, 53; importance to Dillard, 173, 179; romanticism and religious terminology, 211n
England: history of sentimentalism, 22, 23
English, Deirdre, 138

Falk, Candace, 63
Family: Millay's, 93–94; industry and military, 138; Boyle's themes, 139–42; Boyle and modernism, 150–51
Feminism: modernist definition of literature, 4; discomfort with the sentimental, 15; definition of sexuality, 30; French feminism and the avant-garde, 75; Millay's poetry, 96; Kristeva and Boyle as antifeminist, 129; rhetoric and postmodernism, 190–202
Feminist criticism: women's literary tradition and the sentimental, 37–38; women writers and literature as an aesthetic discourse, 195; poststructuralism and irony, 195–96. *See also* Feminism; Literary criticism
Ficke, Arthur Davison, 84–85
Fiedler, Leslie, 26
Flaubert, Gustave, 36–37, 121
Folk art: American feminism, 200–201
Fosdick, Harry Emerson, 32
Foucault, Michel, 2–3, 32, 41
France: history of sentimentalism, 22–23; anarchism and culture, 50–51
Frank, Elizabeth, 109, 113
Free love: modernist women and sexuality, 30; Goldman's advocacy, 50, 62
Free speech: Goldman and anarchy, 43, 59–60
Freud, Sigmund: modernism and sexuality, 30–31; Goldman and sexuality, 60; Oedipal drama, 67, 68, 90, 123, 213n; Millay as poetess of love, 76; modernism and the sentimental, 137; Boyle and family, 140; association of passivity with the feminine and the religious, 161; structure of the joke, 171, 177–78; pleasure principle, 178

Fuller, Margaret, 26, 45
Fussell, Paul, 138, 139

Gallop, Jane, 77, 85
Gender: modernism and the sentimental, 2, 4–5, 6–7; women and modernism, 8; as a political unconscious and the sentimental, 11–12; discourse of reason and the sentimental, 20; romanticism and the masculine, 28; Kristeva and modernism, 39–40; Millay's poetry, 84–89, 95–96; Boyle and modernist extremism, 129; Dillard and subject, 169–70; Walker's *The Color Purple*, 183, 184; irony, 187–88; women's popular fiction and patriarchy, 188; women's writing and problematic history of, 202
Gilbert, Sandra, 32, 138
Gitlin, Todd, 11–12, 19
Goldman, Emma: modernist separation of literature from context, 6; role in modernism, 13–14, 33; free love, 30; progressive politics, 35; private experience and revolt against convention, 40; anarchy and modernist literature, 42–66; Bogan compared to, 120, 121; Boyle compared to, 147, 148, 151; Walker compared to, 190; modernist suppression of women writers, 195; women's writing and power of style, 202; Nietzsche's influence on lectures, 211n
—*Living My Life*, 65
Gothic novel: development and the sentimental, 21
Griffin, Susan, 160
Gubar, Susan, 32, 78

Hamilton, Ian, 139
Hardwick, Elizabeth, 94
Harris, Trudier, 185
Hartman, Geoffrey, 91, 166
Hawthorne, Nathaniel, 53, 60
—*The Scarlet Letter*, 26–27, 45–46
Heilbrun, Carolyn, 93
Hemingway, Ernest, 31, 138, 219n
Hicks, Granville, 36
History: Boyle's later fiction, 145; women's history as subversive, 177; Walker's *The Color Purple*, 186; models of, and feminism, 196–98
Hoffman, Eva, 12
Hoover, J. Edgar, 57–58
Howard, Richard, 72–74
Howe, Irving, 53
Hulme, T. E., 35
Humanism: women's history, 197; fascism and rejection of feminine liberal, 206n
Hutchinson, Ann, 23

Individualism: Goldman's version, 43, 58–59, 62, 64; American ideology and anarchy, 44; Walker's *The Color Purple*, 190
Intellectualism: Ransom on gender, 9; Boyle and modernism, 149–50
Irigaray, Luce, 169, 199, 201
Irony: Walker's *The Color Purple*, 182–83, 188–90; function of in twentieth-century fiction, 187; gender difference in, 187–88; in modernist literature, 194–96

Jackson, Jesse, 201
Jacobs, Harriet, 182
James, Henry, 194
Jameson, Fredric, 89
Jardine, Alice, 14, 146
Joke: Dillard's rhetoric, 170–73; Freud on structure of, 177–78
Joyce, James: novel as ideological crime, 37; Boyle compared to, 136, 137; sexuality and family relations, 139

Kant, Emmanuel, 28
Keats, John, 114, 116, 117
Kermode, Frank, 121
Klein, Melanie, 123
Krieger, Murray, 194
Kristeva, Julia: the abject, 10, 82–83; continuity between modernism and poststructuralist critique, 39–40; French culture and anarchy, 51; women and the symbolic, 86; threat of psychosis, 100; Mallarmé and avant-garde, 105; melancholy of the artist, 112; Bogan compared to, 120, 121; time in Boyle's work, 128–29, 129–30; Dillard and avant-garde, 157; association of passivity with the feminine and the religious, 161; feminine writing and gender, 169; *ideologème* of patriarchy, 188; feminist discourse and women's writing, 192–93; rejection of binary logic, 197; Irigaray and *écriture féminine*, 201–202; politics and Bulgarian origins, 209n; poststructuralism and the subject, 209n

Lacan, Jacques, 82, 91
LaCapra, Dominick, 37
Language: descriptive in Boyle, 136–37
de Lauretis, Teresa: Millay's poetry, 68, 96; female experience of power, 76; women and desire in films, 90; Oedipal narratives, 205n
Lawrence, D. H., 129, 139
Lentricchia, Frank, 12, 13
Lesbianism: modernist women and free love, 30; Walker's *The Color Purple*, 183, 184

Limmer, Ruth, 101, 102
Literary criticism: women's writing and the sentimental, 2; modernist and aesthetic antisentimentality, 5–6; reframing of modernist narrative, 8; Millay's popularity, 69; Bogan as critic, 106. *See also* Feminist criticism; New criticism
Literary history: restoration of the sentimental to modernist, 15; high modernism, 34–35; Goldman's place, 65
Literature: feminism and modernist definition, 4; modernist separation from context, 6; Dillard and subject, 156–57; horror of the feminine, 205n–206n
Logan, Ben, 12
Love: Millay as poetess of, 76–77
Lowell, Robert, 123

McCarthyism: Boyle as victim, 151
McGuirk, Carol, 20
MacLeish, Archibald, 121–22
Mallarmé, Stéphane: French culture and anarchism, 51; Bogan's poetics, 101, 103, 104–106, 217n
Marginality: Millay's poetry, 71
Mass culture: femininity and the sentimental, 3–4; modernist literary criticism, 5; Goldman's individualism, 52; Modleski on women's, 144. *See also* Culture
Maternal, the: Goldman's attitude, 60–61; Millay's poetry, 67–68; Bogan's poetry, 103; Boyle and modernism, 151–52. *See also* Mother
Maturity: modernist criticism and the sentimental, 8–9; Freud on women, 67; Millay's poetry, 91–93; Bogan's poetry, 106, 107; Bogan and psychoanalysis, 123; Dillard on Rimbaud and Freud, 172–73
Melancholy: Bogan's poetry, 112–13
Michel, Louise, 51
Mill, John Stuart, 29
Millay, Edna St. Vincent: Ransom on maturity, 9; role in modernism, 13–14; free love, 30; popularity, 34; progressive politics, 35; modernism and the sentimental, 67–96; Bogan compared to, 100; criticized by Bogan, 122; mother figure, 216n
—"Renascence," 78–92, 215n
—"Tavern," 70
Miller, Mark Crispin, 196
Miller, Nancy, 37, 145
Miner, Madonne, 187
Modleski, Tania, 89–90, 144
Moi, Toril, 191, 197–98, 198–99
Monk, Samuel H., 27
Monroe, Harriet, 78
Moore, Marianne, 107, 119–20, 217n–218n

Most, Johann, 47, 48
Mother: Millay and imagery, 85–87, 216n; Boyle and modernism, 150–51. *See also* Maternal, the
Mother Earth, 44–45, 61

Narrative: postmodern rejection, 3
Nature: Millay's "Renascence," 87–88; Dillard and subject, 159–63; scientific knowing and repression of women, 219n; Dillard and culture, 220n; family, class, and gender, 221n
New criticism: revolution of the word, 40; separation of literature from biography, 64–65
Newton, Judith, 62
Nietzsche, Friedrich Wilhelm, 48, 61–62, 211n
Nonfiction: subject and Dillard, 168–70, 178–79
Norwood, Vera, 156

Oppositions: the sentimental as a discourse, 19

Pathos: literary history, 21
Patriarchy: function of sentimental fiction, 38; women's popular fiction and gender, 188
Perlmutter, Elizabeth, 84, 90–91, 94
Personal, the: modernist criticism, 13; sentimental literature, 89; Millay's poetry, 94
Plaza, Monique, 67
Poe, Edgar Allen, 108
Politics: style and modernism, 5; modernist literature, 35–36; left and antipolitical aesthetic criticism, 37; avant-garde and twentieth century, 51; Goldman and modernist literature, 65–66; Bogan's, 120–21
Postmodernism: reversal of values against the sentimental, 3; women's writing, 14–15, 170; conflation of modernism with sentimental humanism, 19; question of banality of the subject, 41; feminism and rhetoric, 190–202; as continuation of modernism, 204n
Poststructuralism: American ideology and anarchy, 44; feminist criticism and irony, 195–96
Pound, Ezra: American modernism and ahistoricism, 33; reactionary politics, 35; antidomestic appeal to perceptual experience, 118; compared to Boyle, 140
Power: assertion of female in women's fiction, 38; women and middle-class interests, 72; Boyle and female, 132–34; of style and women writers, 202
Psychoanalysis: Bogan and the spiritual, 122–

23; Kristeva's model of social exchange, 192, 193

Puritanism: history of sentimentalism in U.S., 23; Goldman on, 45–46

Quilting: folk art and American feminism, 200–201

Rabine, Leslie, 37–38
Racism: Walker on white Southern writers, 186; Walker's *The Color Purple*, 199
Radcliffe, Anne, 21, 22
Radicalism: Millay's poetry and lifestyle, 69
Ransom, John Crowe: maturity and the sentimental, 8–9; new criticism, 36
—on Edna St. Vincent Millay: criticism of, 69, 89, 202; as poetess of love, 76; popularity of, 77–78; masculinity of, 80
Rationality: rejection of the domestic tradition, 29
Reed, John, 33
Representation: crisis and modernism, 6, 7
Revolution: Bogan on, 37; Goldman and anarchy, 43
Reynolds, Larry, 45
Rhetoric: history of women's rhetoric in U.S., 23–26
Rich, Adrienne, 107
Rilke, Rainer Maria, 165
Rimbaud, Arthur, 122, 172–73
Ritter, Alan, 62
Romanticism: history of sentimentalism, 26–28; Bogan and politics, 121; ideology of masculinity, 208n; Emersonianism, 211n
Rousseau, Jean-Jacques, 22–23
Rovit, Earl, 75
Rowe, John Carlos, 194
Rowson, Susanna, 24–25, 27

Sappho, 78
Sarton, May, 124
Schnog, Nancy, 38
Schwartz, Delmore, 78
von Senden, Marius, 161
Seward, Anna, 27
Sexuality: history of sentimentalism, 29–31; modernist literature, 31–32; Goldman, 45–46, 60; Boyle, 139–42
Shapiro, Karl, 77
Showalter, Elaine, 75–76, 200
Slavery: Walker's *The Color Purple*, 183, 184
Smith, Dinitia, 186–87
Solomon, Martha, 54, 55
Spanier, Sandra Whipple, 136, 138
Spender, Dale, 21
Spiritual, the: Bogan and poetry, 122–23
Stevens, Wallace, 7

Stidger, "Wild Bill," 69–70
Stimpson, Catharine, 129
Stowe, Harriet Beecher, 23, 199
—*Uncle Tom's Cabin*, 4, 45, 72
Subject: new criticism, 64–65; Boyle's practice, 137; Dillard and modernism, 155–81; Kristeva's notion of, 192–93
Subjectivity: Bogan's "The Medusa," 115–16
Surrealism: Bogan and politics, 122
Susman, Warren I., 43–44

Taggard, Genevieve, 10
Tate, Allen: high modernism, 35; new criticism, 36; criticism of Millay, 69, 89
Time: Kristeva on women's, 128–29, 129–30; Boyle and experimental writing, 130–32, 135, 136, 142, 152
Tompkins, Jane: importance of nineteenth-century sentimental tradition, 4; social and political reform as functions of women's fiction, 38; middle class and female power, 72; literature and rhetorical purpose, 199
Towers, Robert, 186

United States: history of sentimentalism, 23–41; history of anarchism, 43–45, 46; ideology of individualism, 64

Valéry, Paul, 7, 109
Van der Weyde, William M., 45
Violence: Goldman and anarchism, 47–48; Bogan's modernist poetics, 101–102, 108; Boyle's "Wedding Day," 134
Vogt, Radka Donnell, 200

Walker, Alice: popular culture and postmodernist literature, 14, 15; women's postmodernist writing, 182–90, 202; quilting and feminism, 200
—*The Color Purple*: popularity and "serious" literature, 13; sentimental tradition, 15; women's postmodernist writing, 182–90; traditions of meaning and purpose, 196; as challenge to racism and sexism, 199
Warren, Robert Penn, 36
White, Hayden, 187
Wilde, Oscar, 58
Williams, Linda, 114
Wilson, Edmund, 36, 40, 83
Wimsatt, W. K., 64–65
Winters, Yvor, 46
Wollstonecraft, Mary, 21, 28–29
Women: modernism and representation, 6–7; as modernist revolutionaries, 8; Goldman on equal rights, 61–62
Women writers: modernist and postmodernist history, 4, 5; gender and modernist criti-

Women writers (*Continued*)
cism, 10, 11; modernism and the sentimental, 13; history of writing, 20–21; female literary tradition before World War I, 32–33; literary modernism in 1920s, 34; modernism and suppression, 127, 195; as authors of knowing, 155–56; Kristeva's psychoanalytic approach, 193

Women's writing: modernist criticism and the sentimental, 2; popularity and literature, 12–13; postmodernism, 14–15, 170; history of sentimentalism in U.S., 23–41; tradition and the sentimental, 37; Boyle and tradition, 128; Dillard and gender, 156;

personal experience and the sentimental, 176–77; feminism, rhetoric, and postmodernism, 190–202

Woodhull, Victoria, 30

Woolf, Virginia, 163–64

Word, revolution of: poststructuralism, 6; style, 40–41; Goldman, 43

Wordsworth, William, 27

Yeats, William Butler, 102, 103

Zabel, Morton D., 10

Zinsser, William, 168